JUDGEMENTS
ON
CONSUMER CASES

PART - 1

INDEX

32	BUSHAN CHIMANLAL JAIN V/S CITY & INDUSTRIAL DEVELOPMENT CORPORATION OF MAHARASHTRA LTD & ANR.	99-109
33	PANKAJ KUMAR SHARMA V/S GHAZIABAD DEVELOPMENT AUTHORITY	10-110
34	FREIGHT SYSTEM (INDIA) PRIVATE LTD. V/S OMKAR REALTORS & DEVELOPERS PRIVATE LTD. & ANR.	110-114
35	VARUN ENGINERS V/S RSB TRANMISSION INDIA LTD.	114-116
36	SAI PRIYA ESTATES V/S VVL SUJATHA	116-118
37	MOKUL SHRIRAM EPC JV V/S EXPORT CREDIT GUARANTEE CORPORATION OF INDIA LTD.	118-124
38	GOLDEN GREEN TOWERS LTD. V/S VARUN SALWAN & ORS.	124-126
39	ORIENTAL INSURANCE CO. LTD. V/S MADHU KHANDELWAL	126-128
40	MOHAN LAL MEENA V/S UNITED INDIA INSURANCE CO. LTD. & ANR.	128-129
41	S. MANIKANNAM V/S Dr. T. PANDIARAJ & ANR.	129-131
42	MAURIA UDYOG LTD. V/S UNITED INDIA INSURANCE CO. LTD & ANR.	132-139
43	JOTINDRA STEEL & TUBES LTD. V/S UNITED INDIA INSURANCE CO. LTD. & ORS.	139-146
44	ABHISHT DEVELOPERS & BUILDERS PVT. LTD. V/S SUCHITA SINGH	146-147
45	MADHUBEN RAMESHCHANDRA SHAH V/S GUJRAT INDUSTRIAL DEVELOPMENT CORPORATION & ORS.	147-150
46	CENTRAL GOVERNMENT EMPLOYEES WELFARE HOUSING ORGANIZATION V/S SUDHIR MITTAL	152-152

<u>**CASE No. 1**</u>

CONSUMER CASE NO. 112 OF 2011

KESHAVRAO V. YADAV Complainant(s)

Versus

DR. J.V.S. VIDYASAGAR & ORS
DR. J.V.S. VIDYASAGAR –
DR. ANIL B. PATIL
DR. GUNJAL ANESTHETIST
DR. SUBHASH PATIL
DR. SANJEEV K. PATIL............Opp.Party(s)

BEFORE: HON'BLE DR. S.M. KANTIKAR,PRESIDING MEMBER
For the Complainant : For the Opp.Party :
Dated : 01 Jan 2021 ORDER -1-
Appeared at the time of arguments through Video Conferencing
For the Complainant : Mr. Kailash Pandey, Advocate Mr. Ranjeet Singh, Advocate Ms. Sushmita Mishra, Advocate
For the Opposite Parties :Mr. Basava Prabhu Patil, Advocate Mr. Shailesh Madiyal, Advocate Mr. T. C. Mopagi, Advocate Mr. Kartik Anand, Advocate
Pronounced on: 1 January 2021

ORDER

The Facts:

1. The Complainant Keshavrao V. Yadav is father of Dr. Sunil K. Yadav (since deceased, hereinafter referred to as the "patient"). The patient himself was an Orthopaedic Surgeon and Professor & HOD of Orthopaedics in Bhartiya Vidyapeeth University Medical College & Hospital at Sangli (Maharashtra). Dr. Sunil was to attend the Continuation of medical Education (hereinafter referred to as 'CME' or Conference) arranged by Karnataka Orthopaedic Association, on 07.06.2009 at Yash Hospital, Belgaum, Karnataka. He informed his father that during the CME he was to get operated his left knee by the hands of Orthopaedic surgeons expert in Arthroscopy doctors at Yash Hospital having all the facilities available. On 06.06.2009 after breakfast, he drove himself with his colleague Dr. Gautam Tarlekar and reached Belgaum at 2.30pm. It was alleged that Dr. Anil B. Patil (hereinafter referred to as the Opposite Party No. 2) arranged the CME and forced the patient to get operated by the hands of Dr. Vidyasagar, from Hyderabad the expert in Arthroscopy (hereinafter referred to as the "Opposite Party No. 1"). The Complainant's second son Dr. Rajshekhar (alias Shekhar), a practising Gynaecologist at Belapur also joined the patient on 07.06.2009 at 8.00 am during proposed operation. At around 11.30 am, Dr. Shekhar telephoned his father and informed that Dr. Sunil's health became in danger and asked him to come immediately to Belgaum with mother. However, the Complainant's wife and -2- niece Pintu Shitole went to Belgaum and the Complainant stayed at home. At about 6.00pm by ambulance the patient's dead body was brought to the Complainant's house at Miraj and in the same night, cremation was completed at their native place

Ganeshwardi in Kolhapur District. Thereafter, on 08.06.2009 the Complainant inquired with his son Dr. Shekhar about the details of Dr. Sunil's death and he told that on 07.06.2009 at around 10.00am, the patient was taken inside the Operation Theatre (hereinafter referred to as 'OT') for the left knee operation. Dr. Anil was not available there and not contactable. The doctors did not allow Dr. Shekhar to enter the OT but asked him to remain at the conference hall and watch the live demo of the said operation. Accordingly, he went to conference hall but the live demo was not started even after 15-20 minutes. Therefore, immediately Dr. Shekhar approached the OT but he was not allowed to enter there as the patient was serious. On enquiry, the doctor informed that the heart of Dr. Sunil had suddenly stopped and at that time the necessary lifesaving equipment and the presence of Cardiologist was not there, therefore the patient was to be shifted to KLE Hospital. There was no ambulance facility; therefore ill equipped ordinary ambulance was called by Dr. Anil Patil. In the ambulance, the doctors were pressing the patient's chest. However by the time ambulance reached KLE Hospital, the patient was declared dead.

2. The Complainant further averred that 09.06.2009, the news came out in the newspaper that Dr. Sunil Keshavrao Yadav died during the operation and the Anaesthetist Dr. Vivek Sawant had committed suicide. Then the Complainant was doubly sure that the death of his son was not natural but it was caused due to the negligence of the doctors at the CME. After gathering all the information, the Complainant filed an FIR with the Police at Sangli in Marathi language. The Complainant wrote several letters to the Managing Director of Yash Hospital to furnish the entire Medical Record of his deceased son. The Complainant further alleged that his son died on 07.09.2009 whereas the Medical Record was issued on 27.10.2009 without death certificate with wrongly mentioned time and place of death. It was further alleged that after the death of Dr. Sunil, the documents were created and intentionally mentioned that Dr. Sunil chose his Anesthetist. Even otherwise, it was the duty of the hospital and the surgeon to verify whether the Anesthetist was qualified to give a proper dose. Therefore, ample time was there to fabricate the Medical Record which speaks volume against the Opposite Parties about the concocted record. The Opposite Parties did not conduct mandatory post-mortem in the said case.

3. The Complainant set out the following points of alleged negligence caused by the Opposite Parties during surgical procedure and caused the death of his son: (i) Pre anaesthesia fitness of Sunil was not obtained from any doctor; leave aside qualified cardiologist. (ii) Dr. Anil Patil had not conducted any tests on Sunil at Belgaum; (iii) Doctors from Yash Hospital or doctors managing the CME, had not taken any pains to discuss with relatives present in the hospital even though there was danger to give general anaesthesia to Sunil; (iv) Verification was not taken by the doctors of Yash Hospital as to whether the anaesthetist who gave anaesthesia to Sunil, is having recognized post graduate qualification and registration from Karnataka State and whether that doctor was permitted to work as anesthetist in Karnataka State; -3- (v) Dr. Gunjal who is working as anaesthetist in Yash Hospital was sitting outside while the patient was on the operation table. Did he administer anaesthesia to Sunil? Is this not negligence or deliberately causing his death; (vi) The operation theatre was neither well equipped nor had sufficient number of specialist doctors; (vii) The doctors who were supposed to be present at the time of emergency were not even in the Operation theatre; (viii) No advice was taken from any other doctor regarding General anaesthesia though it was initially decided to give spinal anaesthesia. (ix) The owner and Managing Director of Yash Hospital is Homeopath, but he falsely prints his title as M.D. Only when the complainant asked letters/copies of case papers, he has written "Hom" in "ink" after his title MD. Even his resident staff is either Ayurvedic or Homeopathic, to the best of knowledge & belief of the

complainant. The nursing staff at Yash Hospital is not qualified or registered nurses to the best of knowledge & belief of the complainant; (x) No Post-Mortem was done mostly to hide their mistakes and the real cause of death which is highly suggestive of their guilty mind; (xi) It is not clear whether the surgeon to perform operation had permission to operate in Belgaum as he is registered in Andhra. No proof whether he was present in the operation theatre; (xii) The Anaesthetist – Dr. Vivek Sawant who gave spinal anaesthesia committed suicide. Even he was registered with Maharashtra Medical Council and not in Karnataka State;

4. The Complainant is a senior citizen aged 76 years, lost his young son Dr. Sunil due to alleged medical negligence of the Opposite Parties and his entire family suffered irreparable loss and mental agony. Being aggrieved the Complainant filed the Consumer Complaint before this Commission under Section 21(a) (i) of the Consumer Protection Act 1986 (for short, the Act, 1986) and prayed for Rs. 3 Crore as compensation.

5. The Opposite Parties Nos. 2 & 3 jointly filed written version and denied the allegations. The Opposite Parties Nos. 1, 4 and 5 have adopted the same written version. The preliminary objection that the present case was not maintainable under the Act, 1986 as it was not a 'service' under section 2(o) the Act, 1986. The surgery / procedure were a part live demonstration during the CME Workshop and completely free wherein even the consumables were not charged. The opposite parties further submitted that the owner of the hospital is the Opposite Party No. 5 who provided facility for the CME workshop. The Yash Hospital is well quipped and having all facilities including specialized surgery and ICU etc. the Opposite Parties Nos. 1 and 2 are Orthopedic surgeons, the Opposite Party No. 3 is an Anesthesiologist and the Opposite Party No. 4 Dr. Subhash Patil were working under the Opposite Party No. 1. The operating procedure on the patient was not started by any of these Opposite Parties. Though the Opposite Party No. 3 an Anesthesiologist was present in the hospital, he did not administer anesthesia to the patient but it was administered by Dr. Vivek Sawant. The sudden death of Dr. Sunil due to massive cardiac arrest after administration of anesthesia was an unexpected unfortunate incident. It was not due to no negligence from the Opposite Parties.

6. Both the sides have filed their respective affidavits of evidence.

7. Heard the arguments from both sides. The parties have filed their written arguments. The learned Counsel for Complainant vehemently argued that the Opposite Party No. 5 Dr. Sanjeev K. Patil who claims to be Managing Director of Yash Hospital is an MD Homeopath, but he deliberately omits to write it and he does not have requisite qualifications to run a Hospital & that too a critical care center with the help of Ayurvedic & Homeopathic resident doctors. Therefore he mislead several patients and playing with their lives on account of his false degree mentioned in the hospital board and letter head. The Complainant placed on record the copy of the visiting card of Dr. Sanjeev K. Patil, showing his degree and also facilities available in Yash Hospital. The Hospital does not have qualified nursing staff as per the medical standards therefore the details of the nursing staff and other staff had purposefully been not given.

8. The learned Counsel further argued that Dr. Vivek Sawant was stated to have committed suicide on 07.06.2009 and in said connection a Complaint was filed with police on 05.07.2009 against the Opposite Parties and Dr. Vivek Savant for the offence punishable under section 304 A, 209 and 34 of IPC. The Belgaum police while investigating the Complaint and after recording the statements of Dr. Rajashekhar Yadav (Dr. Shekhar) and Dr. Gautum Tarlekar did not find any case made out against the opposite parties and no Charge sheet has been filed and came to the conclusion that the Complaint as against Dr. Vivek Sawant got abated in view of his death. The learned Counsel relied upon the following decisions: Rajat Jain &

Anr. vs. D. R. Nursing Home & Ors., (IV) 2012 (CPJ) 123 (NC); D. Uma Devi vs. M/s Yashoda Hospital & Ors., First Appeal No. 1169/2014 (NCDRC); Dr. Pinnamaneni Narasimha Rao vs. Gundavarapu Jayaprakasu&Ors., AIR 1990 AP 207; Dr. U.K. Kini & Anr. vs. K. Vasudeva Pai & Ors., 2001 ACJ 2141 ; Smt. Bhanupal vs. Dr. Prakash Padode & Ors., (II) 2000 CPJ 384; Arunaben D. Kothari & Ors. vs. Navdeep Clinic & Ors., (III) 1996 CPJ 605

9. The learned Senior Counsel for the Opposite Parties vehemently argued that Dr. Anil Patil, the Opposite Party No. 2 is a qualified Orthopedic Surgeon and having expertise in the surgical work. The CME workshop was arranged under the aegis of Karnataka Orthopedics Association at Yash Hospital, Belgaum. The patient Dr. Sunil Yadav had knee problem and was desirous and volunteered to undergo surgery during the workshop, which was free of cost. Even on the face of the Complaint, the case of negligence or deficiency in service against the Opposite Parties is not made. Even before the surgery commenced, the patient Dr. Sunil Yadav expired due to Cardiac Arrest after the administration of Anesthesia by Dr. Vivek Sawant. Therefore, negligence cannot be attributed to the Opposite Parties Nos. 1, 2 and 4, who are the Orthopedic Surgeons and had no role to play in the administration of Anesthesia. So far as the Opposite Party No. 3 Dr. Gunjal, the senior anesthetist, Yash Hospital, is concerned, he was neither involved in any manner with the proposed surgery nor he administered Anesthesia to the deceased. Therefore, the instant Complaint is not maintainable against the Opposite Parties Nos. 1 to 4. He further argued that the -5- 1. 2. Opposite Party No. 5 is Managing Director of Yash Hospital at Belgaum and the patient was not under treatment of Yash Hospital but it was the venue for CME wherein the patient was to be operated. The Yash Hospital had provided only the premises and the facilities for the said CME. Therefore, the Complaint is not maintainable against the Opposite Party No. 5. The Hospital is well-equipped and recognized by the Government of Karnataka under Government Employees Medical Reimbursement Scheme. It is also recognized for National Health Insurance Scheme, Bharat Sanchar Nigam Ltd., Yashaswini Co-operative Farmers Health Care Scheme (Yashaswini Scheme) introduced by the Government of Karnataka.

10. Dr. Sunil (the patient) who himself was an Orthopedic Surgeon and Professor at Bharatiya Vidyapeeth University Medical College and Hospital at Sangali, Maharashtra had history of injury to the left knee. He suffered Haemarthrosis and previously had been treated conservatively. However, it was affecting his routine activities. In order to avail the opportunity to get operated by the experts, he volunteered to undergo Arthroscopic knee operation and its live demonstration during the CME at Belgaum. The entire procedure including the cost of consumables was free. Dr. Sunil on 06.06.2009 from Sangli at about 9.30 am telephonically called to Dr. Anil Patil (the Opposite Party No. 2) and told that he would be reaching Belgaum for the surgery. The Opposite Party No. 2 recommended Dr. Sunil to bring an attendant for surgery along with him. Accordingly, the hospital staff was directed to prepare an In-patient Medical Record in the name of Dr. Sunil Yadav and to book a private room for him which was done at about 12.00 pm. The entire medical record of the patient is in the form of a Booklet (Annexure R-7).

11. On 06.06.2009, Dr. Sunil Yadav reached the Yash Hospital at Belgaum between 1.00 pm and 2.00 pm with his colleague Dr. Gautam Taralekar as a patient's attendant, who also was an Orthopedic Surgeon having worked with him in Medical College. Dr. Sunil brought his reports of MRI Scan of left knee joint, Electro cardiogram (ECG) and other blood tests which he underwent at Bharatiya Vidyapeeth Medical College and Hospital on 05.06.2009 i.e. a day prior his admission to the CME. The reports were examined by the anesthetist and the patient

was found fit for surgery. After admission at Yash Hospital, Dr. Sunil was clinically examined by the Opposite Party No. 1 and the Opposite Party No. 2, and recorded the clinical findings as : CVS-NAD i.e., Cardio Vascular System- No abnormality detected; No history of IHD (Ischemic Heart Diseases)

12. It was further argued that the patient who himself was an Orthopedic Surgeon, insisted that his anesthesiologist friend one Dr. Vivek Sawant the Anesthesiologist associated with him, would administer the anesthesia for the proposed surgery. Though it was not a normal practice, but considering the factual position, the request was conceded and the same was recorded in the consent form for the surgery. Dr. Vivek Sawant, verified the arrangements in the OT and the equipments, being satisfied commenced the process of administering Spinal aneasthesia to the patient. The OT was fitted with multipara monitor which shows real time ECG, SPO and NIBP, 2 Anaesthetist work station having oxygen and Nitrousoxide cylinders fixed, syringe pump and central line catheter for emergency cardiac medication/resuscitation, cardiac defibrillator and all emergency medicines.

13. On the day of procedure 07.06.2009, the Opposite Parties Nos. 1 and 4 were present in the OT who were about to scrub/paint the left lower limb of the patient. The anesthetist Dr. Vivek Sawant immediately after administration of spinal anesthesia noticed respiratory problem to the -6- patient and immediately asked the doctors to stop the procedure. He intubated the patient with Endotracheal tube (ETT) and started ventilating with 100% oxygen. Dr. Gunjal was also called to assist. For resuscitation, Dr. Vivek Sawant injected Atropine and Adrenaline, the external cardiac massage was continued. The Physician was also called immediately who after examination, advised medicines and to continue external cardiac massage, also the Cardiologist Dr. Sanjay Porwal reached OT within 10-15 minutes. In the meantime other doctors including the Opposite Party No. 2 came to the OT.

14. At that juncture as insisted by the patient's brother Dr. Rajashekhar it was decided to shift the patient to KLE Society's Dr. P.K. Hospital and the ambulance from the said Hospital was called for immediately. The patient was taken to KLE Hospital in the ambulance equipped with all emergency medicines and equipment, including Oxygen Cylinders and CPR Kit accompanied with Dr. Gautam Taralekar, Dr. Vivek Sawant and Dr. Rajeshkhar Yadav and Dr. Zobin. However, despite all resuscitative measures the patient expired due to cardiac arrest at KLE Dr. P.K. Hospital Belgaum.

15. The Opposite Parties file few judgments of Hon'ble Apex Court viz: i. Indian Medical Association vs. V.P. Shantha, (1995) 6 SCC 651; ii. Kishore Lal vs. Chairman ESI Corpn. (2007) 4 SCC 579 , iii.Iswar Bhai C. Patel alias Bachu Bhai Patel vs. Harihar Behera & Anr(1999) 3 SCC 457

Observations & Discussion:

16. I have perused the entire material on record inter-alia details of facilities available at Yash Hospital and the Medical Record of the patient (Annexure 'C' colly).

17. Admittedly the Belgaum Knee Orthoscopy CME was organized at Yash Hospital Critical Care Centre at Belgaum. The Yash Hospital provided an equipped OT facility, the Conference Hall and basement for catering at free of cost. Dr. Anil Patil and Dr. Gunjal were visiting consultants at Yash Hospital. The patient's medical record revealed Dr. Sunil was given IPD No. 2019 and was provided a private room. It was free for CME. So far as the hospital facilities are concerned, the information sheet revealed all facilities were available including ICU, Lab, Radiology Department and Operation Theatres for Neurosurgery, laparoscopic surgery and plastic surgery. I have perused patient's relevant laboratory reports like Hemogram, Biochemical and ECG done on 05.06.2009 at Bharatiya Vidyapeeth Medical College and Hospital. Those reports were necessary for pre anesthetic check-up and fitness. The reports were within normal limit. The Admission record revealed that

the patient was admitted at 12' noon on 06.06.2009 under the CME Arthroscopy. The names of the patient's brother Dr. Rajshekhar Yadav and a friend Dr. Gautam Tarlekar were mentioned as the patient's attendants. The referring doctor was the patient himself and the mode of payment mentioned was stated as " free" . The clinical history recorded was the pain in knee on long standing and walking, pain aggravates on activity and partial relief on taking rest, instability of knee not allowing him to do routine activity. The examination findings are as below: -7- "On examination: Afibrile R.R.- 16/min Vitals – Pulse – 60/min BP – 130 / 80 mm of Hg Left knee - Tenderness present over medial joint line - Anterior Drwyer Test positive, 3+, complete ACL tear - Lacthman's test positive, 3+ - Mcmarry's test positive for medial meniscus tear CVS – NAD, CNS – NAD, DA-NAD, R.S.- NAD The provisional diagnosis was 'ACL Tear of left knee'. At the caption of operative procedure mentioned as " NOT DONE ". The name of Anesthetist mentioned as Dr. Vivek Sawant and also mentioned about patient suffered Cardiac arrest while anesthesia was given. The Consent form shows the name of the Anesthetist as Dr. Vivek Sawant and mentioned as "the patient's own Anesthetist " and the operating surgeon was Dr. J.V.S. Vidyasagar. The Consent was signed by his brother Dr. Rajshekhar Yadav. The patient had no history of DM/HTN/TB/IHD. The investigations Hemogram, Blood Sugar, Urea were within normal limits. As stated by Dr. Sunil Yadav, he has consulted his family Physician who declared him fit for anesthesia and same had been discussed with his anesthetist Dr. Vivek Sawant, who actually was to give anesthesia during CME.

18. 18. After the clinical examination, Dr. J.V.S. Vidyasagar recorded findings as below: "6/06/09 c/s Dr. J.V.S. Vidyasagar And advised Case to be posted for LA knee Arthroscopy under spinal /GA on 7/06/09 at around 9.00 am Pre-operative orders: -- NBM from 10.00 pm -- Take informed consent -- Prepare parts -- Inform anaesthetist For evaluation Dr. Sawant -- I V Cannula to be put before shifting pt to O.T. -- shift pt to O.T. at 9.00 am" -8- His family physician who investigated and Dr. Gautam confirmed the same during discussion. sign 7.6.09 -- pt examined XXXXX by Dr. Savant Vivek -- Cannula put by him to rt hand -- Patient taken to O.T. sign

19. The treatment chart as on 07.06.2009 mentioned the drugs used were Inj. Atropine 1) amp IV, Inj. Xylocaine 2% 1cc, Inj. Sensorcaine IV, Inj. Nervovac3amp, Inj Pantothane 4,1%, Inj Adrenaline, Inj Sodabiocarbonate, Inj Corts-S 1 vial, IV DNS, IV RL, IV NS. These medicines are necessary during resuscitation of cardiac arrest.

20. Dr. M. K. Gunjal, the visiting Anesthesiologist of Yash Hospital during enquiry submitted the events happened in the OT. The enquiry note is reproduced as below: At about 9.30 am today, I was in OT for preparation of next case arrangement. xxxxx Dr. Yadav (patient) came with Dr. Sawant, anesthesiologist into OT, Dr. Sawant verified arrangements in OT and started giving spinal anaesthesia to the pt. I asked whether any assistance is required? He said "No I will manage". I went to changing room. After sometime, I was called again in OT when I entered the OT, Dr. Sawant had intubated the pt with ET tube and was ventilating the pt. Dr. Sawant told me the condition of the pt is critical and requested me to ventilate the pt. At his request, I started ventilating the pt. In the mean time, Dr. Sawant asked to stop the painting (the part) and asked the sister to load Inj Atropine and adrenaline and he started giving ext. cardiac massage. I xxxx continued to ventilate the patient with 100% O2. The physician came, examined the pt and started giving ext cardiac massage and instructed Dr. Sawant to administer the drugs. Meanwhile other doctors came, shifted the pt to KLE Hopsital with ambubag. Dr. Sawant accompanied the Pt.

21. The events happened during surgery are mentioned in "The operation record". It is reproduced as below: "L lower limb was scrubbed Electronic pneumatic tourniquet

applied but was not inflated Dr. JVS Vidyasagar & myself were about to paint the L lower limb Dr. Sawant asked us to stop Dr. Sawant started giving ext cardic massage to pt. Dr. Gunjal was giving mechanical ventilation Signature -9- xxxxxxxxxx

22. It is more relevant to peruse the statement of Dr. Gautam Tarlekar, the relevant paragraph is reproduced as below: "On 07/06/2009 at about 6.00 A.M. Dr. Rajshekar Yadav, elder brother of Dr. Sunil was come from Bombay to the Yash Hospital. He has signed all the pre operation Documents after Signing at about 10 'O clock Dr. Sunil shifted to operation theatre of Yash Hospital, at that time Dr. Vidyasagar, Dr. Anil Patil, Dr. Vivek Sawant, Dr. Gunjal, Dr. Basavaraj, Dr. Naveen Malagi, Dr. Subhash Patil and Hospital staff were present in the operation theatre. Dr. Sunil told that his friend Dr. Vivek has to give bull to him, hence Dr. Vivek was administered bull (Anastasia); at that time immediately after administering the bull Dr. Sunil received heart pain, with the help of emergency medical treatment equipments he was treated and who were present at that time were shocked and started pressing the chest immediately ambulance was brought and shifted to KLE Hospital, after examination the Doctors told that Dr. Sunil has dead. Knowing this fact with a fear Dr. Vivek Sawant has committed suicide." ... xxxxx.... "Now I seen the complaint shown to me, this is the complaint given by Shri. Keshavrao Venkatrao Yadav the father of deceased Dr. Sunil Yadav. As the Dr. Rajshekar do not want to conduct the post mortem on the dead body of his brother Dr. Sunil, the dead body was handed over for funeral by taking in writing. Dr. Rajshekar and his elder sister Sangeeta Komalrao Rani took the dead body and they have conducted the funeral as per their custom."

23. I have perused the affidavit of the staff nurse Ms. Shivaleela, working at Yash Hospital who was on OT duty on 07.06.2009. She submitted that Dr. Vivek Sawant came to the hospital at around 8am and after examination of the patient, put IV canula in the right hand, and instructed her to shift the patient to OT around 10 am and at that time Dr. Rajshekar Yadav (patient's brother) and Dr. Tarlekar were also present. After verifying the arrangements in the OT prior to administration of anesthesia, Dr. Vivek Sawant administered anesthesia. At the same time, Dr. Gunjal a senior visiting consultant anesthetist was present to attend another surgery in Yash Hospital. She further submitted the events happened in the OT.

24. In the instant case the allegation was that the deceased Dr. Sunil's autopsy was not done. It is pertinent to note that the cause of death was known without existence of any suspicious circumstances and as desired by Dr. Rajashekhar, no post-mortem was conducted. Dr. Rajashekhar expressed difficulty in transporting the dead boy from Belgaum (Karnataka) to his native place in Miraj, Maharashtra. The Yash Hospital issued a Death Certificate (Annexure 10) certifying that the patient expired due to massive cardiac arrest. In the Progress Note (page 143 of the paperbook), Dr. Rajashekhar had signed a note and denied the autopsy/Post Mortem. It is reproduced as below: "07/06/2009 I, the undersigned Dr. Shekhar K Yadav, elder Brother of Dr. Sunil K Yadav have understood the complications that caused the death of my younger brother (Dr. Sunil K. Yadav). And further declare that I do not wish to carry out an autopsy (Post-mortem) for the cause of the death. Kindly issue me the death certificate. -10- (Dr. Shekhar K. Yadav)"

25. Unfortunately, Dr. Vivek Sawant the Anesthesiologist committed suicide at his home town on 07.06.2009. On perusal of the Complaint given by Sh. Laxman Sawant, the father of Dr. Vivek Sawant, at Police Station Belgaum who categorically stated as below: "My son was anesthetist and he got mentally heart due to the death of his friend Dr. Yadav and committed suicide by injecting the injection of poison to himself. We do not suspect on anybody, and my son Vivek age 35 years, r/o Ichalkaranji is expired due to heart fail or due to getting the injection of

poision, and we have got doubt about it. So the further action may be taken and his dead-body may be handed over to us. Humble request to you. Date: 08/06/2009 Belgaum Yours faithfully Sd/ (Laxman Pandurang Sawant)

Conclusion:

26. The Knee Arthroscopy CME was organized under the aegis of Karnataka Orthopedic Centre at Yash Hospital, Belgaum. The Yash Hospital is owned by the Opposite party No. 5 Dr. Sanjeev Patil, a Homoeopathist, who had no active role in the CME either in procedure or surgery. The hospital information brochure is mentioned about facilities and names of Consultants. It is a well-equipped hospital having Radiology, Laboratory, ICU and OTs with Consultants of different specialties and super-specialities. Dr. Anil Patil - the Opposite Party No. 2 is one of visiting Consultant Orthopedic Surgeon, having experience and trained in Arthroscopy in India and USA. The hospital is empaneled under various government schemes and National Health Insurance schemes like BSNL and Yashaswini Scheme. (Govt. of Karnataka). Therefore allegations of Complainant (para 7 supra) against the hospital facilities and the qualification of Dr.Sanjeev Patil (the owner of the hospital) are not sustainable. Moreover, for the CME he provided the hospital facilities and venue for free of cost.

27. It is evident from the medical record, that the necessary pre-operative investigations viz laboratory reports and ECG were done by Dr. Sunil (the patient) on 05.06.2009 (a day prior) at his working place Bhartiya Vidyapeeth University, Medical College, Sangli. All the reports were within normal limits and fitness for the operation was obtained from his Physician and same was mentioned in the clinical notes by Dr. Vidyasagar. Those reports were again checked by the Anesthesiologist Dr. Vivek Sawant, on 07.06.2009 before the Arthroscopic procedure.

28. Admittedly Dr. Vivek Sawant, a patient's colleague from Ichalkaranji, who was called by the patient himself to administer anesthesia during the procedure. Dr. Vivek Sawant, administrated Spinal anesthesia to the patient and suddenly the patient developed respiratory problem and Cardiac arrest. Therefore, he instructed to the doctors to stop the scrubbing and painting procedure. Immediately, Dr. Vivek Sawant started Cardiac resuscitation, the patient was intubated and administered Atropine and Adrenaline. The ventilation with 100% oxygen started. -11- The physician was called. Dr. Gunjal and other doctors in the OT were assisting during resuscitation of the patient. In my view the doctors present in the OT were competent and have performed cardiac resuscitation as per standard protocol. The unexpected cardiac arrest during spinal anesthesia is rarely seen. I would like to refer one medical article "Unexpected cardiac arrest in spinal anesthesia" -Acta Anaesth. Belg., 2006, 57, 365-370, noted that: "The common mechanisms of cardiac arrest during spinal anaesthesia seems to involve still poorly understood relations among vasodilatation, reduced venous return, reduced cardiac output and brady-cardia mediated by direct and/or vagal cardiac reflexes." In my view the Anesthesiologist is the most appropriate person to decide on the fitness for surgery and use proper drugs for the cardiac resuscitation. [Ref: standard book "Physiologic and Pharmacologic Bases of Anesthesia by Vincent J. Collings, M.D., SC.D].

29. Thus it is apparent that after the administration of anesthesia patient suffered massive cardiac arrest; it was before the commencement of the surgical procedure. Therefore in my view the team of Orthopedic Surgeons (Opposite parties) cannot be attributed with negligence as their role did not commence at all. In this context, I do not find any deviation from standard of practice from the doctors in the OT who immediately initiated cardiac resuscitation and despite all efforts patient could not survive. Moreover, it is sad to note that subsequently the Anesthesiologist Dr. Vivek Sawant who administered anesthesia to the deceased Dr. Sunil had committed suicide under depression at his home town.

30. The four ' D s ' of medical negligence are duty, dereliction (breach), direct cause (causa causens) and damages. Each of these four elements must be proved to have been present, based on a preponderance of the evidence, for negligence to be found. Nevertheless, a simple lack of care, an error of judgment or an accident is not a proof of negligence on the part of doctor. So long as the doctors follows a practice acceptable to the profession on that day he can't be held liable for negligence merely because a better alternative course of treatment was available or a more skilled doctor would not have chosen to follow or resort to that practice which the accused followed.

31. The Hon'ble Supreme Court through various judgments laid down the vital legal principles for determining the fundamental aspect of medical negligence on part of a skilled medical practitioner. In the case Dr. Laxman Balkrishna Joshi v. Dr. Trimbak Bapu Godbole and Anr AIR 1969 SC 128, the Hon'ble Supreme Court elaborated the duties which a doctor owes to his patients came up for consideration. The Court held that a person who holds himself out ready to give medical advice and treatment impliedly undertakes that he is possessed of skill and knowledge for that purpose. Such a person when consulted by a patient owes him certain duties, viz a duty of care in deciding whether to undertake the case, a duty of care in deciding what treatment to be given or a duty of care in the administration of that treatment. A breach of any of those duties gives a right of action for negligence to the patient. The practitioner must bring to his task a reasonable degree of skill and knowledge and must exercise a reasonable degree of care. Neither the very highest nor a very low degree of care and competence judged in the light of the particular circumstances of each case is what the law requires.

32. In the present case, it was an unfortunate and unexpected death of Dr. Sunil (Patient) even before the surgeons putting a knife for surgery. For me the 'causation' of medical negligence is not visible. In my view the general test for causation is that which requires the Complainant to show that the injury would not have occurred " but for " the negligence of the doctors – the -12- Opposite parties. It is important that the Complainant has to establish on a balance of probabilities that the defendant's tortious act was a necessary cause of alleged injuries. I do not find any failure of duty of care from the doctors or there was any evidence to indicate any unexplained deviation from the standard protocol in the Operation Theatre. Further, I would like to rely upon the recent judgment of Hon'ble Supreme Court in the matter Vinod Jain Vs. Santokba Durlabhji Memorial Hospital and Ors., JT 2019 (3) SC 9, which has upheld the Order passed by this Commission exonerating the opposite parties i.e. the hospital and treating doctor from any medical negligence.

33. To conclude, there is not much one can do to prevent a disgruntled Complainant/ Patient from approaching a Court or redressal Forum. In the instant case, I do agree the agony of the Complainant, but then, that by itself cannot be a cause for awarding damages for the passing away of his son. Though my sympathy is for the Complainant, but it cannot translate into a legal remedy. 34. In obtaining the facts and the evidence adduced, in the instant case it is not feasible to determine medical negligence or deficiency in service on the part of doctors and hospital. Resultantly the Consumer Complaint fails. It is dismissed. There shall be no order as to costs. .... DR. S.M. KANTIKAR PRESIDING MEMBER

<u>**CASE No. 2**</u>
FIRST APPEAL NO. 727 OF 2015

(Against the Order dated 03/08/2015 in Complaint No. 05/2014 of the State Commission Maharashtra)

M/S. ARIHANT INDUSTRIES THROUGH ITS PARTNER, JITENDRA SHANTILA JAIN UNITED INDIA INSURANCE COMPANY LTD.,...........Appellant(s)

Versus

UNITED INDIA INSURANCE CO. LTD............Respondent(s)

BEFORE: HON'BLE MR. C. VISWANATH,PRESIDING MEMBER

For the Appellant : Mr. S.M. Tripathi, Advocate

For the Respondent : Ms. Nanita Sharma, Advocate

Dated : 04 Jan 2021

ORDER

1. The present Appeal, under Section 19 of the Consumer Protection Act, 1986 has been filed by the Appellant against the order dated 03.08.2015 of the Maharashtra State Consumer Disputes Redressal Commission, Circuit Bench at Aurangabad (hereinafter referred to as "the State Commission) in CC/05/2014.

2. The Complainant/Appellant obtained "Standard Fire and Special Perils" Insurance Policies for stocks of cotton etc. and plant and machinery. Complainant's factory met with a fire incident on 29.03.2009 at about 9.30 am. Huge stock of the cotton was damaged in the accident. The accident was reported to the Police and an FIR No.3/2009 was registered. The Complainant stated that he informed the Opposite Party/Insurance Company regarding the loss and thereafter submitted all the relevant documents as sought for by the Surveyor, Mr. J.C. Bhansali. The Surveyor assessed the loss at Rs.32,92,525/- only, though the total loss suffered was to the tune of Rs.99,45,286/-. The Opposite Party also appointed M/s Charter House Detective Services to ascertain the actual loss, who submitted their investigation report. Police after investigation found that the fire was accidental. The Opposite Party, on 22.03.2012, offered the Complainant a -1- settlement of Rs.39,72,829. As a part of the settlement, the Complainant was made to execute an indemnity bond in favour of the Opposite Party. As per the Complainant, he was facing financial difficulties and therefore accepted the settlement offered by the Opposite Party and accordingly executed an Indemnity bond and a Discharge Voucher in the name of the Opposite Party. The Complainant stated that he had accepted the settlement under protest. Alleging deficiency in service by the Opposite Party, he filed Complaint before the State Commission with the following prayer: - "1. It is prayed that, the respondent be directed to pay the complainant an amount of Rs.59,72,457/- being the amount due towards respondent of claim. 2. It is prayed that, the complainant is entitled to claim interest at the rtate of 15% from the date of the fire/incident i.e. 29.03.2009. 3. It is prayed that, the complainant is entitled to compensation of Rs. 10.00 Lac or such other higher amount as may found fit and proper towards harassment and mental agony. 4. The cost of the complaint may kindly be awarded to the complainant."

3. The Complaint was contested by the Respondent/Opposite Party. Though the Surveyor could not ascertain the cause of fire, assessment was carried out without prejudice and subject to findings of CID inquiry/police investigations. The District Collector, Aurangabad appointed a Committee to go into the cause of fire and initiated investigation. Since it was taking a long time, it was decided to settle the claim as per the assessment made by the Surveyor, subject to the Complainant executing an indemnity bond in favour of the Opposite Party. The Complainant was paid an amount of Rs.39,72,829 towards full and final settlement of the claim on 22.03.2012, after signing the Discharge Voucher and executing an Indemnity Bond. The Opposite Party stated that the Complainant having accepted the full and final settlement was barred from raising a dispute. The Consumer Complaint was not maintainable as it was falsely filed after a lapse of more than 2 years.

4. The State Commission after hearing both the Parties and perusing the record, directed as follows: - "1. Consumer complaint No.05/14 is dismissed. 2.

13

Considering peculiar facts of the case we direct the parties to bear their own cost

3. Copies of the judgment be supplied to both the parties"

5. Aggrieved by the State Commission's order dated 03.08.2015, the Appellant/Complainant preferred the present Appeal before this Commission. -2-

6. Heard the Learned Counsels for the Parties and carefully perused the record. It is an admitted fact that the Appellant obtained "Standard Fire and Special Perils" Insurance Policies from the Respondent/Insurance company and on 29.03.2009, the Appellant's factory met with a fire incident , which was reported to the Police and the Insurance Company. Stock of cotton and other material was damaged and the Appellant filed a claim with the Respondent for the loss. The Appellant thereafter submitted documents to the Surveyor, who assessed the loss at Rs.32,92,525/-. As per the Appellant, the total loss suffered by him was to the tune of Rs.99,45,286/-, though in the Complaint he prayed for Rs.59,72,457/-. Since investigation regarding the cause of fire was pending, the Respondent offered the Appellant a settlement of Rs.39,72,829/-. As a part of the settlement, the Appellant was made to execute an indemnity bond in favour of the Respondent. The Appellant also signed Discharge Vouchers in favour of the Insurance Company. Thereafter, the Appellant filed a Complaint before the State Commission and alleged deficiency in service by the Opposite Party. The Complaint was filed on 28.02.2014 after receiving amount of Rs.39,72,829/- on 22.03.2012. The State Commission therefore held that the Complaint was not barred by limitation. The main issue involved was whether the Complainant received Rs.39,72,829/- towards full and final settlement or under protest pending investigation.

7. Learned Counsel for the Appellant stated that the Appellant was told by the Respondent that the settlement money would not be given unless the Discharge Voucher was signed. As per the Counsel for the Appellant, the Discharge Voucher, therefore, was obtained by the Respondent through means of coercion and undue influence. He further stated that the Appellant had executed an Indemnity bond in favour of the Respondent, thereby agreeing to indemnify the Respondent in case of an adverse finding against the Appellant. According to him, this itself showed that the Settlement was not full and final but was subject to the final result of the Insurance Company's investigation into the cause of the fire.

8. Learned Counsel for the Respondent submitted that the State Commission had rightly dismissed the Complaint filed by the Appellant. He stated that the amount paid to the Complainants was towards full and final settlement of his claim and, therefore, the Complainant is estopped by law from filing the present Complaint. He specifically denied the Complainant's allegation that the Discharge Voucher signed by him was through coercion or undue influence.

9. Both the Counsels have cited several judgments of the Hon'ble Supreme Court as well as this Commission in support of their arguments. In several insurance claim cases arising under the Consumer Protection Act, 1986, it has held that if a Complainant satisfies the Consumer Forum that Discharge Vouchers were obtained by fraud, coercion, undue influence etc., they should be ignored, but if they were found to be voluntary, the Complainant will be bound by it resulting in rejection of the Complaint.

10. It is settled law that mere signing of Discharge Voucher will not bar the Complainant/Claimant from raising a dispute before this Commission. The only question to be decided is whether the Discharge Voucher was signed under undue influence or coercion. The burden of proof, however, is on the Complainant to satisfy this Commission that the Discharge Voucher was signed under undue influence or coercion.

11. Learned Counsel for the Respondent stated that it was made clear to the Complainant that unless the Discharge Voucher was signed, payment would not be released and therefore, the Discharge Voucher was signed under coercion. The Complainant, however, was unable to furnish any evidence to substantiate this plea. The conduct of the insured becomes relevant on the facts of each case to ascertain whether the discharge voucher in full and final settlement was given -3- voluntarily or there was coercion or under influence on the Complainant. The only evidence provided were the letters of protest sent after signing the Discharge Voucher, which do not prove undue influence or coercion on the Appellant. Moreover the Complaint was filed few days short of two years after receiving the settlement amount, but not any earlier. No evidence has been filed to show coercion or undue influence on the Complainant to enter into a settlement. Despite pendency of Investigation into the cause of fire, as it was taking some time, the Opposite Party offered settlement based on the assessment report of the Surveyor. Even though the Complaint was deemed as not barred by limitation, the conduct of the Appellant showed that the plea of coercion was taken as an afterthought. If at all the Complainant had an objection to the nature of the settlement, he should have recorded the same while signing the settlement. Regarding the contention of undue influence and coercion, the State Commission held that "in the absence of any specific contention and evidence that it was under any undue pressure, coercion or fraud such bare contention of the complainant cannot be accepted."

12. In view of foregoing discussion, I find no infirmity in the impugned order of the State Commission. The present Appeal is dismissed. .... C. VISWANATH PRESIDING MEMBER

CASE No. 3
REVISION PETITION NO. 1041 OF 2014

(Against the Order dated 08/10/2013 in Appeal No. 156/2012 of the State Commission Rajasthan)
NAGARPALIKA, JAISALMER & ANR. THROUGH COMMISSIONER, JAISALMER RAJASTHAN
THE CHAIRMAN, NAGAR PALIKA , JAISALMER, (NOW MUNICIPAL COUNCIL) JAISALMER JAISALMER RAJASTHAN ....Petitioner(s)

Versus

UPENDRA SINGH & 3 ORS. S/O LATE SH.ROHTASH SINGH,

SMT. ICHRAJ, D/O. LATE SH.ROHITASH SINGH, W/O SH. RAGHUNATH SINGH,

MANGAT SINGH, S/O. LATE SH. ROHITASH SINGHH

SMT. VIMLESH, D/O. LATE SH. ROHITASH SINGH, W/O. SH. TEJ SINGH, ...Respondent(s)

BEFORE: HON'BLE MR. C. VISWANATH,PRESIDING MEMBER

For the Petitioner : Mr. Madhurima Tatia, Advocate
For the Respondent : Mr. H.S. Bhati, Advocate -1-
Dated : 04 Jan 2021

ORDER

1. The present Revision Petition, under Section 21 (b) of the Consumer Protection Act, 1986 (for short "the Act") has been filed by the Petitioner against order dated 08.10.2013 of the Rajasthan State Consumer Disputes Redressal Commission, Circuit Bench, Jodhpur (for short "State Commission") in First Appeal No.156/2012 wherein the Appeal filed by the Petitioner was dismissed.

2. Case of the Respondents/Complainants was that the mother of the Complainants, late Smt. Omwati had applied for allotment of a 35 x 70 ft plot under the Laxmi Chand Sawal Residential Scheme which was floated by the Opposite Parties. Along with the Application Form, she submitted Rs.7,000/- as well as her widow card. In the Application Form at Serial No. 10, she had stated that she was the widow of a 'Freedom Fighter, Indian Army'. The Opposite Parties accepted the application but it was placed under General Quota and not Defence Quota. When the Complainants sought a copy of all the applications submitted under the scheme, via RTI, they found that their mother's application was not listed under the Defence Quota. They also found that under Defence Quota, there were a total of 28 plots available out of which only 25 plots were allotted and therefore the Opposite Parties could have allotted a plot under Defence Quota. Aggrieved by the actions of the Opposite Parties, the Complainants filed a Complaint before the District Forum :- "1. That due to not placing the application of mother of the complainant in the proper category by the non-applicant – Department, the mother of the complainant was deprived from the plot allotment and therefore, on the above application, by lottery, order of allotment of plot size of 35 x 70 ft., out of the remaining 3 plots of the defence quota, may kindly be passed and an order be passed for handing over the possession of the same after executing the perpetual lease deed and registering the same after taking balance amount as per the price on the relevant day 2. Mental, financial and physical harassment is caused to the complainant while visiting non-Applicant again and again shock was caused to the complainant due to the said reason and he remained under treatment under medical observation for approximately 12 months, wherein, approximately, Rs.1,00,000/- have been spent and unnatural death of mother due to above mental shock and due to which the complainant suffered financial, mental loss and towards that the complainants are entitled to get amount of Rs.80,000/. 3. The no-applicant be directed to pay the litigation expenses of Rs.15,000/- to the complainants. 4. Any other relief, which is in the interest of justice, may kindly be allowed to be given to the complainants from the non-Applicant." -2-

3. The case was contested by the Petitioner/Opposite Parties before the District Forum who stated that the Complainant had not annexed the certificate of widow of defence personnel who died in war, as required by the Application Form. They further stated that there was no quota for allotment of land to the widow of a 'freedom' fighter. It was further stated that freedom fighters do not fall in the category of defence personnel and no evidence was placed on record that Late Smt. Omwati's deceased husband was a defence personnel. On the basis of information submitted by late Smt. Omwati, her application was not placed under the defence quota.

4. The District Forum having heard the Learned Counsels for the Parties and also considering the evidence and material placed on record, dismissed the complaint as under: - "Consequently, while rejecting the complaint of the complainants, same is hereby dismissed."

5. Aggrieved by the order of the District Forum, the Complainant filed an Appeal before the State Commission. After hearing Learned Counsels for the Parties and perusing the record, the State Commission allowed the Appeal with the following order: - "Consequently, while setting aside the order dated 30.05.2012 passed by the District Forum, Jaisalmer I Complaint No. 98/2011, the appeal and complaint of the appellants are hereby allowed. The Respondents are hereby directed to allot the plot of 35 x 70 ft to the complainants within a period of three months and hand over the possession and the respondents will also make a payment of lump sum amount of Rs.25,000/ to the complainants being compensation for mental harassment and litigation expenses."

6. Aggrieved by the order of the State Commission, the Opposite Parties preferred the present Revision Petition before this Commission.

7. Heard Learned Counsels for the Parties and have carefully gone through the record. Brief facts of the case are that the Complainants are the legal heirs of late Smt. Omwati, who had applied for allotment of a plot admeasuring 35 x 70 ft under the quota of widow of defence personnel in the Laxmichand Sanwal Residential Scheme, which was floated by the Opposite Parties. On 12.02.2008, the Complainants' mother submitted her widow card and a demand draft of Rs.7,000/- towards the application fee. The Opposite Parties accepted the application, though it was not listed under the Defence Quota. The Complainants filed an RTI and found that out of 28 plots under the Defence Quota, only 25 were allotted.

8. Learned Counsel for the Petitioner contended that the Complaint was filed after more than 3 years since the cause of action arose and the State Commission had wrongly condoned the delay and allowed the complaint which was barred by limitation. He further contended that the Complainants' mother stated in the application form that she was the widow of a 'freedom fighter' and therefore, she wasn't considered under the defence personnel quota. The -3- Complainants' mother, moreover, had not annexed any certificate or any other document to show that she was the widow of a defence personnel and hence the State Commission had erred in directing the Opposite Parties to allot a plot to the Complainants.

9. The Learned Counsel for the Respondents contended that the Complainants had learnt, that her case was not considered under the defence quota, through an RTI only in 2011. Out of a total 28 plots under Defence Quota, only 25 were allotted. The cause of action, therefore, arose in 2011. They further contended that by not placing their late mother's application under the Defence Quota, the Petitioner committed deficiency in service. They stated that if the application had been placed under the Defence Quota, one of the 28 plots would have been allotted.

10. The District Forum accepted the contention of the Opposite Parties and dismissed the Complaint on the ground of it being barred by limitation. It was only through RTI that the Complainants became aware that the application was not placed under the Defence Quota. Information under RTI was sought in November 2011 and the Complaint was filed immediately thereafter. Furthermore, the District Forum itself had accepted the Condonation of Delay application filed by the Complainants. The State Commission therefore rightly condoned the delay in filing the Complaint.

11. The State Commission also observed that "if the certificate would not have enclosed with application or they were not enclosed, then, it was the responsibility of the respondents that they would have at least informed the applicant in this regard, or would have given one opportunity to produce the certificate, but this was not done by Respondents."

12. As regards the claim under defence quota, the District Forum held "in our opinion, Indian Army alongwith freedom fighter is written in the Application Ext.5 and the certificate of Ex-Serviceman or his widow is enclosed at serial No.6 of the certificate enclosed at its back, is written. So, this contention of non-applicants that Smt. Omwati had not produced any document regarding her husband being military personnel, is not valid."

13. It is clear from a perusal of the record that the husband of the Complainants' mother was an ex-serviceman. In the Application Form, the Complainant's mother had mentioned that she was the widow of a "Freedom Fighter, Indian Army." She was a widow of a soldier who died in harness is also underlined in the application form. The contention that there was no document to prove that her husband was an ex-serviceman is, therefore, untenable. It is also an admitted fact that out of 28 plots available under the Defence Quota and only 25 were allotted. I, therefore agree with the State Commission that the Respondents, while not considering the

application of Smt. Omwati, mother of the Complainants for allotment of plot, had committed gross negligence and there is deficiency in service on their part.

14. In view of the above, there is no infirmity or illegality in the impugned order, warranting interference under Section 21 (b) of the Consumer Protection Act, 1986. Revision Petition is therefore dismissed. .... C. VISWANATH PRESIDING MEMBER

CASE NO. 4

REVISION PETITION NO. 1093 OF 2020

(Against the Order dated 31/08/2020 in Appeal No. 127/2019 of the State Commission Orissa)

RELIANCE NIPPON LIFE INSURANCE COMPANY LTD.............Petitioner(s)

Versus

PUNI DAS...Respondent(s)

BEFORE: HON'BLE MRS. JUSTICE DEEPA SHARMA,PRESIDING MEMBER For the Petitioner : Mr. B. S. Banthia, Advocate

For the Respondent :

Dated : 04 Jan 2021

ORDER

JUSTICE DEEPA SHARMA (ORAL) THROUGH VIDEO CONFERENCING

1. The present Revision Petition, under Section 58(1)(b) of the Consumer Protection Act, 2019 (for short "the Act") has been filed against the three orders dated 17.12.2019, 28.08.2020 and 31.08.2020 of the State Consumer Disputes Redressal Commission, Odissa (for short "the State Commission") in Appeal No.127 of 2019 alleging that these orders are arbitrary, illegal and without jurisdiction. -2-

2. The brief facts of the case are that a Complaint had been filed by the Respondent before the District Forum. The District Forum vide its order dated 03.09.2018 allowed the Complaint ex parte against the Petitioner holding that the Petitioner had failed to appear before it despite service of notice of the Complaint. -1-

3. The Petitioner filed Appeal No.127 of 2019 before the State Commission wherein they had challenged the order of the District Forum on several grounds. The Appeal was delayed. An application for condonation of delay in filling the Appeal was filed. One of the arguments for condonation of delay was that they had not been properly served with the notice of the Complaint and that they had come to know of the filing of the Complaint only after receipt of the notice in the execution petition. The State Commission considered the arguments of the Petitioner. The Appeal was apparently filed with a delay of 236 days and this delay in filing of the Appeal was condoned by the State Commission vide its order dated 17.12.2019. While condoning this delay, cost of 1 Lakh was imposed.

4. It is argued by learned Counsel for the Petitioner that the State Commission had imposed an exorbitant cost and that is why an application for recalling of the said cost had been filed before -3- the State Commission. Vide order dated 28.08.2020, this application was dismissed and the Petitioner was given an opportunity to deposit the cost during the course of the day and the matter was adjourned for 31.08.2020. Finally on 31.08.2020, the Appeal was dismissed on account of non-compliance of the order dated 17.12.2019 and 28.08.2020. Learned Counsel for the Appellant has challenged this order on the ground that the direction in the order dated 28.08.2020 that the cost is to be deposited during the course of the day is harsh and could not have been complied with because an Advocate is not expected to pay the cost out of his pocket and therefore, this order is arbitrary and is liable to be set aside. It is also argued that the subsequent order dated 31.08.2020 is,

therefore, liable to be set aside. 5. I have given thoughtful consideration to the arguments of learned Counsel and have perused the file.

5. Admittedly, the Petitioner had filed an Appeal before the State Commission with a delay of 236 days and sought condonation of such delay on the ground that it was not served with the notice of the Complaint and came to know of the order under challenge when a notice of execution petition was served upon it. The condonation of delay in filing of the Appeal was -4- sought on this ground. It is, therefore, apparent that the State Commission in its order dated 17.12.2019 has not considered the issue on merit regarding service of notice of Complaint upon the Petitioner/Appellant but prima facie considering the arguments of learned Counsel for the Appellant to this effect condoned the delay in filing the Appeal and adjourned the matter for arguments on admission and listed the matter for admission of Appeal for 24.01.2020. The order dated 17.12.2019 is reproduced as under: "This is an application for condonatian of delay of 236 days in filing FA No. 127 of 2019. Heard. -2- Ex parte order impugned in this appeal was passed on 3.9.2018. The appeal has been field on 31.5.2019. The sole contention raised by the learned counsel for the appellant is that no notice was received by the appellant from the District Forum regarding the complaint case. The appellant could know about the complaint only after receipt of notice in the execution proceeding. Written objection has been filed by the respondent/complainant against the limitation petition. It was contended by the learned counsel for the respondent that notice was duly sent by the District Forum on 19.1.2017 which is evident from the order sheet in CC No. 482 of 2016. Therefore, the assertions made by the appellant that they had not received the notice from the District Forum is not acceptable. We have perused the District Forum record from which it appears that in compliance of order dated 9.1.2017, notice was issued on 17.1.2017. Therefore, it is presumed that the appellant received the notice within 30 days from the despatch of the notice. Hence, the appellant is found not made any acceptable and reasonable ground for condonation of delay. -5- However, in order to afford the appellant an opportunity to contest the appeal on merit, we are inclined to condone the delay subject to payment of reasonable cost keeping in view that the consumer complaint was filed in the year 2016. Accordingly, the delay in filing the appeal is condoned subject to payment of cost of Rs.1.00 lac (Rupees one lac) by the appellant to the respondent/complainant within a period of four weeks from today. Put up on 24.1.2020 for payment of cost and hearing on admission."

6. From the perusal of this order, it is apparent that the State Commission had neither heard the learned Counsel on the merits of the Appeal nor had admitted the Appeal since the order itself reflects so. It has only dealt with the prayer for condonation of delay in filing of the Appeal. The State Commission had also clearly held that they did not find any reasonable ground for condoning the delay, yet they condoned the delay in the interest of justice so that the Appeal could be heard on merit. This clearly shows that the issue whether the Petitioner/Appellant was duly served with the notice of the Complaint or not before the District Forum was kept open and the cost only relates to the condonation of delay in filing the Appeal. The argument of learned Counsel, therefore, that without going through the record of the proper service upon the Petitioner/Appellant the impugned order had been passed, has no merit. It is an order which relates only to the -6- issue whether the delay in filing the Appeal be condoned or not. There is no finding in the impugned order to the effect that the ex parte order passed by the District Forum was right -3- or wrong. Also, the State Commission had been considerate enough towards the Petitioner/Appellant that despite its holding that there was no ground for condoning the delay on merit, it had yet condoned the delay in the interest of justice with imposition of costs. If the Appellant found the cost to be on higher side, nothing

had stopped it from challenging the said order before the appropriate Forum within stipulated period of limitation. The Petitioner/Appellant instead of taking that recourse, filed an application before the State Commission for recall of the said order knowing very well (since ignorance of law is not an excuse and the Petitioner was duly represented by Counsel) that the Consumer Protection Act, 1986 did not confer any jurisdiction upon the State Commission to recall/review/set aside its own order. From the act of filing an application for recall of the order, it is apparent that the Petitioner was simply buying time.

7. The next argument of learned Counsel is that the State Commission had acted arbitrarily on 28.08.2020 while dismissing its application for recall of the order dated 17.12.2019, and giving -7- time to the Petitioner to deposit the cost imposed vide order dated 17.12.2019 during the course of the day. The detailed argument of learned Counsel has already been recorded. I found no illegality in the order dated 28.08.2020. The State Commission did not have authority, under the old Consumer Protection Act, 1986 to either recall, review or modify its order. The State Commission on the other hand had been considerate enough to give one more opportunity to the Petitioner to deposit the cost. In case, the Petitioner had difficulty in depositing the said cost during the course of the day, nothing had stopped the Petitioner from filing an appropriate application seeking more time for deposit of the cost. Further, on 28.08.2020, the State Commission had adjourned the matter for 31.08.2020 and even within that period of three to four days, the Petitioner made no efforts to deposit the said cost.

8. The order dated 28.08.2020 of the State Commission is reproduced as under: Heard. Mr U.N.Sahoo, learned counsel appearing for the appellant submits that he has filed the Misc. Case to recall the order whereunder the appellant has been directed to pay cost to the respondent for condoning the delay. -8- 2. Mr Sahoo, learned counsel submits that the appellant is unable to comply the order dated 17.12.2019 passed by this Commission in Misc. Case No. 385 of 2019. -4- 3. Mrs.Pragyan Mohanty, learned counsel appearing for the respondent submits that the appellant has taken eight adjournments to pay the cost to the respondent but finally has filed the present Misc. Case to harass the respondent. So, she submits to dismiss the Misc. Case. 4. Considered the submission of learned counsel for both the parties and perused the order sheets. 5. It appears from the order dated 17.12.2019 that this Commission has condoned the delay subject to payment of cost of Rs.1.00 lac by the appellant to the respondent within a period of four weeks. Since then the matter has been adjourned form time to time. On the last occasion i.e., on 14.8.2020 for the larger interest of justice time was granted as last chance. This Misc. Case has been filed to recall the order dated 17.12.2019 passed in Misc. Case No. 385 of 2019. 6. On perusal of petition, it appears, it is designed to harass the respondent and defect the purpose of order dated 17.12.2019. Hence, we do not find any merit in the Misc. Case as such, the Misc. Case stands dismissed. The appellant is directed to deposit the cost of Rs.1.00 lac before this Commission in course of the day failing which put up the matter on 31.8.2020 for further orders.

9. From the above orders, it is apparent that the State Commission had acted within its jurisdiction while dismissing the application for recall of the order dated 17.12.2019 and has acted fairly while giving one more opportunity to deposit the cost during the course of the day. There is no explanation given by the Petitioner as to why it could not deposit the cost from 17.12.2019 till the date it filed the application for recall of the order. No -9- explanation has also been given as to why the order dated 17.12.2019 was not properly challenged before the appropriate Forum. Hence, the order was binding and needed to be complied with. However, on account of non-compliance of the order dated 17.12.2019 by which the delay in filing the Appeal was condoned on payment of cost and subsequently on account of

non-compliance of order dated 28.08.2020, the State Commission has rightly dismissed the Complaint for failure on the part of the Petitioner to comply with the directions. I found no illegality in any of the orders of the State Commission. The present Revision Petition has no merit and the same is dismissed. ....J DEEPA SHARMA PRESIDING MEMBER

CASE NO. 5
REVISION PETITION NO. 240 OF 2012

(Against the Order dated 21/09/2011 in Appeal No. 1401/2006 of the State Commission Maharashtra)

ORIENTAL INSURANCE CO. LTD. ....Petitioner(s)

Versus

VIJAY KUMAR J. MEHTA R/o ....Respondent(s)

BEFORE: HON'BLE MR. ANUP K THAKUR,PRESIDING MEMBER

For the Petitioner : For the Petitioner : Mr. Abhishek Kumar, Advocate

For the Respondent : For the Respondent : Nemo

Dated : 04 Jan 2021

ORDER
ANUP K. THAKUR

1. Under challenge in this Revision Petition No. 240 of 2012 is the impugned order of the State Consumer Disputes Redressal Commission, Maharashtra, Circuit Bench Nagpur (State Commission, hereafter), in F.A. No.A/06/1401 dated 21.09.2011 . Vide this order, the State Commission had partly allowed the appeal. The impugned order reads as below: "1. Appeal is partly allowed.

2. Impugned order is modified as under:- i. The claim of the complainant is partly allowed to the extent of Rs.5.00 lacs. -1- ii. Since, admittedly the complainant has already received the amount of Rs.2,52,700/- from the appellant/O.P., appellant/o.p. is directed to pay the balance amount of Rs.2,47,300/- to the respondent with interest @ 9% p.a. w.e.f. 17.03.2001 till realization of entire amount. 3. No order as to cost. 4. Copy of this order be supplied to the parties." 2. This revision petition was heard on 23.12.2020. It was decided to proceed in the absence of any representation by a counsel or in person, on behalf of the respondent/complainant (complainant hereafter) as it was noted from the record that after 29.8.2019 , no one had appeared for the complainant. On that date, a last and final opportunity had been given to the complainant to submit written synopsis of arguments. This also however was not submitted as per report of the Registry. In such circumstances, it was decided to go ahead with the disposal of this revision petition.

3. Very briefly, the facts are that the complainant has a business of processing of all kinds of dal(s), in the name and style of M/s Ashok Dal & Oil Mill, M.I.D.C. Amravati. Two insurance policies, one for stock of all kinds of pulses, channi, bhusa and processed dal and the other for machineries and accessories, both valid from 19.5.2000 to 18.5.2001, had been purchased by the complainant from the petitioner/Opposite Party- Oriental Insurance Co. Ltd. (OP hereafter). On 17.12.2000 , at about 8.40 p.m., a fire occurred in the factory premises. The fire brigade was immediately informed; they rushed and put out the fire; as this process involved throwing of water to extinguish the fire, the stocks suffered damage. The OP was also intimated on the same day. A report was also filed on 18.12.2000 with the local police station who prepared a spot panchnama on the same date. A report was issued by the fire brigade department on 1.6.2001 which, apart from noting loss of toor dal etc., also estimated the probable loss to be Rs. 4 lakh. The police spot panchnama dated 18.12.2000 mentioned that pulses and processing machine were completely damaged, and that in all 220 bags i.e. 220 quintal toor dal was completely burnt etc. and estimated the loss at Rs.5.5 Lakh. An insurance claim was lodged with the OP who, vide letter dated 29.12.2000 , requested the complainant to submit all relevant documents. Delay in submission of these documents was acknowledged by the

complainant and these were produced only by 22.3.2001 . Thereafter, the surveyor, vide letter dated 22.3.2001, asked the complainant to submit remaining documents and these were submitted immediately with the request to settle the claim before 31.3.2001 . On 20.7.2001 , the complainant was informed that the surveyor had settled his claim for Rs.2,52,700/-. Copy of surveyor's report however was not given to the complainant. With this letter dated 20.7.2001 , OP had also sent a discharge voucher of Rs.2,52,700/-. Per the complaint, this discharge voucher was initially not accepted; however, OP was subsequently intimated vide letter of 23.7.2001 that the complainant would accept the amount due to it's financial crisis. On 10.08.2001 , the complainant received a registered letter from the OP with a cheque of Rs.2,52,700/-, and with a letter stating that the complainant had signed the discharge -2- voucher on 20.7.2001 and the cheque was being released in full and final settlement in favour of the complainant. The complainant immediately issued a registered letter to the OP intimating that the amount was being accepted under protest. Per the complaint, the total loss sustained was Rs.7,70,000/-. The complainant had received only Rs.2,52,700/- on 10.8.2001 . As such, per the complaint he was entitled to Rs.5,27,300/-, this being the balance. However, this claim was restricted to Rs.5,00,000/- (Rs. 5 Lakh) in order that it came within the jurisdiction of the District Forum.

4.   The complaint was resisted through a written reply by the OP. Preliminary objection challenging the locus standi of the complainant, Mr. Vijay J. Mehta, was raised on the ground that it was partnership firm and therefore, Mr. Mehta in his individual capacity could not have filed the claim. It was further submitted that Shri L.D. Gupta, surveyor, was appointed, without any delay, on 18.12.2000 . He visited the spot on the same date, requested for relevant documents, sent a reminder letter dated 29.12.2000 ; however, requirements of the surveyor were met only by 22.3.2001; as such, the assessment of loss on the basis of stock statement etc. could be carried out by the surveyor only from 24.3.2001 . Surveyor completed his report in the last week of June 2001 and submitted its report on 2.7.2001 . He assessed the loss of stock due to fire at Rs.2,39,925/-, and loss to machinery at Rs.13,089/-, making the total assessed loss Rs.2,53,014/-. On this basis, OP immediately wrote to the complainant that the claim had been approved for Rs.2,52,700/-, sending the discharge voucher for joint signatures of the complainant and the financer, Central Bank of India, towards full and final settlement of the claim. The said voucher was duly signed and discharged on 26.7.2001 . It is claimed by the OP that a copy of surveyor's report was made available to the partner of the complainant firm and it was only after their satisfaction that they issued a receipt for Rs.2,52,700/- towards full and final settlement dated 26.7.2001 . It is the case of the OP that, in these facts and circumstances, the complainant firm was estopped from any further pursuit of the present complaint; that the OP had not committed any act of deficiency as the claim had been processed and settled as per the surveyor's report and as such, the complaint deserved to be dismissed with cost.

5.   District Forum, Amravati, vide order dated 6.6.2006 , allowed the claim of Rs.5 lakh, making it clear that it was over and above the amount of Rs.2,52,700/- which had already been paid to the complainant. This amount of Rs.5 lakh was to carry interest at 9% p.a. from 17.3.2001 till the date of District Forum's order. Cost of Rs.2,000/- was also to be paid by the OP to the complainant. All these payments were to be made within 30 days from the date of receipt of the District Forum's order failing which OP would be liable to pay 10% interest p.a. till final payment.

6.   The State Commission disposed off the appeal against this order vide its order dated 21.9.2011 (supra). Hence, this revision petition.

7.   As already noted earlier, there was no appearance on behalf of the complainant. Learned counsel for the petitioner/OP therefore presented his arguments in the revision petition which were heard on 23.12.2020 . The learned counsel submitted his arguments. **First** , the report of the surveyor was made on 02.07.2001 ; complainant was informed vide

letter dated 20.7.2001 about the amount approved at Rs.2,52,700/-, along with discharge voucher for being discharged jointly by the complainant and Central Bank of India and the same was duly discharged on 26.7.2001 . -3- **Second** , it was only after around 15-20 days that the complainant, vide letter dated 10.8.2001 , registering it's protest that the complainant had accepted only due to financial crises and illegal tactics of OP to send a cheque of Rs.2,52,700/- by Registered A.D.. He emphasized that a plain reading of this letter would show that the complainant was merely stating that he had accepted the amount because of financial crisis etc., but had nowhere alleged that there was any fraudulent design or any pressure by the OP in this regard. He argued that if a protest had to be made, it ought to have been made immediately or soon after, certainly not after 15-20 days. **Third** , he argued, referring to the order of the District Forum, that the only substantive reasoning adopted by the complainant was that the three reports of fire brigade, police and it's own representation of loss seemed to have been ignored by the surveyor. He argued that the surveyor was a professional and that such a view of the surveyor's report was untenable and unacceptable. He further argued that it should be obvious that the reports of the fire brigade (assessing the loss at Rs.4 lakh) and the police panchnama (assessing the loss at Rs.5 lakh) were at the complainant's instance. Complainant's own assessment was for Rs.7.2 lakh. As such, there were three estimates of loss in the complaint. The surveyor, after investigation, with proper reasoning and logic, had arrived at the figure of loss at Rs.2,52,700/-. He drew attention to the complaint itself and submitted that upon a plain reading of paras 8 to 12, it would be clear that the complainant had offered no reasoning for the loss of Rs. 7.20 lakh claimed, other than describing the communication that took place with the OP, followed by the prayer to allow the complaint. In fact, while the complaint has mentioned that the total loss sustained was Rs.7,70,000/- and he had received Rs.2,52,700/- on 10.8.2001 , and therefore, was entitled to recover the balance, he was restricting the claim to Rs.5 lakh only in order to come within the pecuniary jurisdiction of the District Forum. Learned counsel argued that this itself would show that the complainant had come to the District forum without any clarity of purpose. There was no discussion in the consumer complaint on the surveyor report as to why it was wrong and in what way. **Fourth** , he referred to the impugned order of the State Commission. Drawing attention to paras 15,16,17 and 19 thereof, learned counsel argued that no reasoning as such was to be found in the impugned order. He argued that the State Commission had allowed the complaint only to the extent of Rs.5 lakh as this was the amount demanded by the complainant in the original complaint, implying thereby that the amount already received be deducted and only the balance amount of Rs.2,47,300/- to the complainant be paid, with interest @ 9% p.a. with effect from 17.3.2001 till realization. His simple argument was that there was no basis argued or stated in the impugned order which would justify the view ultimately taken by the State Commission.

8. After hearing arguments and carefully perusing the record, it has to be said that the fora below have apparently erred in not giving due importance to the report of the surveyor, without any reasons to explain why they did so.

9. Admittedly, the complainant had two valid insurance policies on the date the fire took place. It is also an admitted fact that there was some delay by the complainant in supplying the documents asked for by the surveyor. The surveyor submitted it's report on 2.7.2001 and the OP, within a few days, made an offer of settlement of the claim vide letter dated 20.7.2001 . With this letter, the discharge voucher was sent; the same was duly signed by the complainant and the Central Bank of India, after which, payment vide cheque was sent to the complainant. The letter of protest against this payment of Rs.2,52,700/-, was sent 15-20 days after signing of the discharge voucher. This delay has not been explained at all by the complainant. This clearly shows that it was in the nature of an afterthought. As pointed out by the learned counsel, in the -4- letter dated 10.8.2001 , vide which the complainant informed the OP that it had accepted discharge

voucher under protest, because of its own financial crisis, no allegation as such was made against the OP. Clearly, the delay had therefore to do with the complainant itself. The sequence of dates vis. fire on 17.12.2000 , production of documents to the surveyor on 22.3.2001 by the complainant i.e. after almost three months, the surveyor's report ready on 2.7.2001 , offer of settlement on 20.7.2001 and discharge of settlement cheque sent thereafter, does not reveal any deficiency in service on the part of the OP.

10. A perusal of the surveyor report shows that it has been prepared with due diligence based on reasoning and logic. If the complainant had any issue with the surveyor report, it would have been expected that it would present some cogent and reasoned arguments. As discussed earlier, no reasoning to support the claim presented of over Rs. 7 lakh or to counter the surveyor report has been offered, even in the consumer complaint itself. This point has been eloquently made by the counsel for the OP during the arguments. I entirely agree.

11. In view of the discussion above, this revision petition is allowed. The order of the State Commission, as also of the District Forum, is set aside. No order as to costs.
.... ANUP K THAKUR PRESIDING MEMBER

CASE NO. 6
REVISION PETITION NO. 664 OF 2020

(Against the Order dated 27/02/2013 in Appeal No. 109/2011 of the State Commission Rajasthan)
NAGAR NIGAM KOTA ....Petitioner(s)

Versus

MOHAMMAD USMAN ....Respondent(s)
BEFORE: HON'BLE MR. C. VISWANATH,PRESIDING MEMBER
For the Petitioner : Mr. B. S. Sharma, Advocate
For the Respondent :
Dated : 04 Jan 2021

1. The present Revision Petition has been filed by the Petitioner/Opposite Party against the order dated 27.02.2013 of Rajasthan State Consumer Disputes Redressal Commission, Circuit Bench at Kota (for short "the State Commission") in First Appeal No.109/2011, whereby the Appeal filed by the Petitioner was dismissed.

2. Alongwith the Revision Petition, IA/7358/2020, an application for condonation of delay of has also been filed by the Petitioner. The Petitioner, however, does not mention the delay in filing this Revision Petition. According to the Registry, there is a delay of 2621 days.

3. I have heard the Learned Counsel for the Petitioner on IA/7358/2020, application for condonation of delay and also carefully perused the record.

4. Learned Counsel for the Petitioner submitted that substantial delay in filing the Revision Petition occurred due to missing of the file and this fact came to their knowledge on 06.07.2016. After more than one year, 28.08.2017 legal advice was taken from Shri Sanjeev Vijay, Advocate on filing of the Revision Petition. He advised that the matter being time barred, there was no jurisdiction to initiate proceedings before the NCDRC. On 05.01.2018 Legal Adviser again advised not to file Appeal before the NCDRC, as it was likely to be dismissed with heavy costs, being barred by limitation. However, it was decided to file Appeal before the NCDRC. On 05.06.2020 approval was obtained for filing the Revision Petitioner and after necessary formalities, the Revision Petition was filed on 31.07.2020. It was further submitted that the Respondent/Complainant played fraud on the Court and supressed material facts in drafting the Complaint and obtained orders in his favour. In support of his arguments, Learned Counsel for the Petitioner has relied on the judgment of Hon'ble Supreme Court in A.V. Papayya Sastry & Ors. Vs. Government of Andhra Pradesh & Ors., Civil Appeal No.5097- 5059 of 2004.

5. Impugned order was passed by the State Commission on 27.02.2013. From 27.02.2013 till 05.07.2016, for delay of more than 3 years, there is no explanation, except that the case file was missing. Moreover, from 06.07.2016 till the filing of the Revision Petition i.e. 31.08.2020, Petitioner took more than four years in filing the Revision Petition and the delay has been explained in terms of the process adopted by the Petitioner in filing the Revision Petition. Except administrative procedures and delay, no other reasonable explanation has been offered for the inordinate delay in filing the Revision Petition. At every stage their Counsels had pointed out that the case was badly barred by limitation.

6. Learned Counsel for the Petitioner also pleaded that the Complainant/Respondent played fraud on the Court and obtained the order in his favour to get wrongful gain and relied on Hon'ble Supreme Court order in A.V. Papayya Sastry & Ors. Vs. Government of Andhra Pradesh & Ors., Civil Appeal No.5097- 5059 of 2004 . Facts in the present are distinguishable. In the Application for condonation of delay, the Petitioner has not mentioned as to what fraud had been played by the Respondent/Complainant. In the District Forum it was stated that the file was missing and there was no deficiency in service by not registering the land strip in favour of the Complainant. The size of the land was more than what had been mentioned by the Complainant/Respondent, it being only an issue of fact and not fraud. As sufficient explanation for delay could not be adduced, the Petitioner took the shelter of alleged 'fraud' merely to escape limitation.

7. Hon'ble Supreme Court inre : Cognizance for extension of limitation in Suo Motu Writ Petition (Civil) No(s).3/2020 on 23.03.2020 held that to obviate the difficulties and to ensure that lawyers/litigants do not have to come physically to file such proceedings in respective Courts/Tribunals across the country including this Court, ordered that a period of limitation in all such proceedings, irrespective of the limitation prescribed under the general law or Special Laws whether condonable or not shall stand extended w.e.f. 15 March, 2020 till further th order/s to be passed by this Court in present proceedings. Excluding the period from 15 March, 2020, then also this Revision Petition has been filed with an inordinate delay of more than 6 years. th -1-

8. Hon'ble Supreme Court has held that party who has not acted diligently or remain inactive is not entitled for condonation of delay. The Hon'ble Supreme Court in the case of "R. B. Ramlingam vs. R. B. Bhavaneshwari, I (2009) CLT 188 (SC)" has also described the test for determining whether the petitioner has acted with due diligence or not. The Hon'ble Supreme Court has held as under:- "We hold that in each and every case the Court has to examine whether delay in filing the special appeal leave petitions stands properly explained. This is the basic test which needs to be applied. The true guide is whether the petitioner has acted with reasonable diligence in the prosecution of his appeal/petition."

9. Condonation of delay is not a matter of right and the applicant has to set out the case showing sufficient reasons which prevented them to come to the Court/Commission within the stipulated period of limitation. The Hon'ble Supreme Court in the matter of Ram Lal and Ors. Vs. Rewa Coalfields Limited, AIR 1962 Supreme Court 361 has held as under: "It is, however, necessary to emphasise that even after sufficient cause has been shown a party is not entitled to the condonation of delay in question as a matter of right. The proof of a sufficient cause is a condition precedent for the exercise of the discretionary jurisdiction vested in the Court by Section 5. If sufficient cause is not proved nothing further has to be done; the application for condoning delay has to be dismissed on that ground alone. If sufficient cause is shown then the Court has to enquire whether in its discretion it should condone the delay. This aspect of the matter naturally introduces the consideration of all relevant facts and it is at this stage that diligence of the party or its bona fides may fall for consideration; but the scope of the enquiry while exercising the discretionary power after sufficient cause is shown would naturally be limited only to such facts as the Court may regard as relevant."

10. The burden is on the applicant to show that there was sufficient cause for the delay. The expression 'sufficient cause' has been discussed and defined by the Hon'ble Supreme Court in the case of Basawaraj&Anr. Vs. The Spl. Land Acquisition Officer, 2013 AIR SCW 6510, as under: "Sufficient cause is the cause for which defendant could not be blamed for his absence. The meaning of the word "sufficient" is "adequate" or "enough", inasmuch as may be necessary to answer the purpose intended. Therefore, the word "sufficient" embraces no more than that which provides a platitude, which when the act done suffices to accomplish the purpose intended in the facts and circumstances existing in a case, duly examined from the view point of a reasonable standard of a cautious man. In this context, "sufficient cause" means that the party should not have acted in a negligent manner or there was a want of bonafide on its part in view of the facts and circumstances of a case or it cannot be alleged that the party has "not acted diligently" or "remained inactive". However, the facts and circumstances of each case must afford sufficient ground to enable the Court concerned to exercise discretion for the reason that whenever he court exercises discretion, it has to be exercised judiciously. The applicant must satisfy the Court that he was prevented by any "sufficient cause" from prosecuting his case, and unless a satisfactory explanation is furnished, the Court should not allow the application for condonation of delay. The court has to examine whether the mistake is bonafide or was merely a device to cover an ulterior purpose. (See: Manindra Land and Building Corporation Ltd. V. Bhootnath Banerjee &Ors, AIR 1964 SC 1336; LalaMatadin V. A.Narayanan, AIR 1970 SC 1953; Parimal V. Veena alias Bharti AIR 2011 SC 1150 L2011 AIR SEW 1233); and ManibenDevraj Shah V. Municipal Corporation of Brihan Mumbai, AIR 2012 SC 1629: (2012 AIR SCW 2412). …………… It is a settle legal proposition that law of limitation may harshly affect a particular party but it has to be applied with all its rigour when the statute so prescribes. The Court has no power to extend the period of limitation on equitable grounds. " A result flowing from a statutory provision is never an evil. A Court has no power to ignore that provision to relieve what it considers a distress resulting from its operation ." The statutory provision may cause hardship or inconvenience to a particular party but the Court has no choice but to enforce it giving full effect to the same. The legal maxim "dura lexsedlex" which means "the law is hard but it is the law", stands attracted in such a situation. It has consistently been held that, "inconvenience is not" a decisive factor to be considered while interpreting a statute. ………… The law on the issue can be summarized to the effect that where a case has been presented in the court beyond limitation, the applicant has to explain the court as to what was the " sufficient cause" which means an adequate and enough reason which prevented him to approach the court within limitation . In case a party is found to be negligent, or for want of bona fide on his part in the facts and circumstances of the case, or found to have not acted diligently or remained inactive, there cannot be a justified ground to condone the delay. No court could be justified in condoning such an inordinate delay by imposing any condition whatsoever. The application is to be decided only within the parameters laid down by this court in regard to the condonation of delay. In case there was no sufficient cause to prevent a litigant to approach the court on time condoning the delay without any justification, putting any condition whatsoever, amounts to passing an order in violation of the statutory provisions and it tantamounts to showing utter disregard to the legislature". -2-

11. Also in the case of " Anshul Aggarwal Vs. New Okhla Industrial Development Authority (2011) 14 SCC 578, the Hon'ble Supreme Court has warned the Commissions to keep in mind while dealing with such applications the special nature of the Consumer Protection Act. The Hon'ble Supreme Court has held as under: "It is also apposite to observe that while deciding an application filed in such cases for condonation of delay, the Court has to keep in mind that the special period of limitation has been prescribed under the Consumer Protection Act, 1986 for filing appeals and revisions in consumer

matters and the object of expeditious adjudication of the consumer disputes will get defeated if this court was to entertain highly belated petitions filed against the orders of the consumer foras."

12. In a recent judgment the Hon'ble Supreme court observed that condonation of delay would depend on the background of each and every case; and routine explanation would not be enough. The Hon'ble Supreme Court in University of Delhi vs. Union of India & Ors. in Civil Appeal Nos.9488-9489 of 2019 (Arising out of SLP (Civil) Nos.5581-5582 of 2019) decided on 17.12.2019 has held as under: - "The consideration for condonation of delay would not depend on the status of the party namely the Government or the public bodies so as to apply a different yardstick but the ultimate consideration should be to render even- handed justice to the parties. Even in such case the condonation of long delay should not be automatic since the accrued right or the adverse consequence to the opposite party is also to be kept in perspective. In that background while considering condonation of delay, the routine explanation Page 24 of 34would not be enough but it should be in the nature of indicating "sufficient cause" to justify the delay which will depend on the backdrop of each case and will have to be weighed carefully by the Courts based on the fact situation ……. That apart when there is such a long delay and there is no proper explanation, laches would also come into play while noticing as to the manner in which a party has proceeded before filing an appeal. "

13. Hon'ble Supreme Court in Post Master General and others vs. Living Media India Ltd. and another (2012) 3 Supreme Court Cases 563 held that the departments are not absolved from observing the period of limitation prescribed by the statute. Hon'ble Supreme Court has held as under: - "27. It is not in dispute that the person(s) concerned were well aware or conversant with the issues involved including the prescribed period of limitation for taking up the matter by way of filing a special leave petition in this Court. They cannot claim that they have a separate period of limitation when the Department was possessed with competent persons familiar with court proceedings. In the absence of plausible and acceptable explanation, we are posing a question why the delay is to be condoned mechanically merely because the Government or a wing of the Government is a party before us. 28. Though we are conscious of the fact that in a matter of condonation of delay when there was no gross negligence or deliberate inaction or lack of bonafide, a liberal concession has to be adopted to advance substantial justice, we are of the view that in the facts and circumstances, the Department cannot take advantage of various earlier decisions. The claim on account of impersonal machinery and inherited bureaucratic methodology of making several notes cannot be accepted in view of the modern technologies being used and available. The law of limitation undoubtedly binds everybody including the Government. 29. In our view, it is the right time to inform all the government bodies, their agencies and instrumentalities that unless they have reasonable and acceptable explanation for the delay and there was bonafide effort, there is no need to accept the usual explanation that the file was kept pending for several months/years due to considerable degree ofprocedural red-tape in the process. The government departments are under a special obligation to ensure that they perform their duties with diligence and commitment. Condonation of delay is an exception and should not be used as an anticipated benefit for government departments. The law shelters everyone under the same light and should not be swirled for the benefit of a few. 30. Considering the fact that there was no proper explanation offered by the Department for the delay except mentioning of various dates, according to us, the Department has miserably failed to give any acceptable and cogent reasons sufficient to condone such a huge delay." -3-

14. In view of the above, I find no sufficient ground to condone the inordinate delay of 2621 days. The application for condonation of delay is accordingly dismissed. Present Revision Petition is nothing but an abuse of process of law. Accordingly Revision

Petition is dismissed being barred by limitation. .... C. VISWANATH
PRESIDING MEMBER

CASE NO. 7

FIRST APPEAL NO. 545 OF 2020

(Against the Order dated 18/03/2020 in Complaint No. 127/2019 of the State Commission
Punjab)

NATIONAL INSURANCE COMPANY LIMITED, ...Appellant(s)

Versus

JATINDER SINGH & ANR. S/O. LATE SH. ARJINDER SINGH,.

HERITAGE HEALTH TPA PVT. LTD., ...Respondent(s)

BEFORE: HON'BLE MR. C. VISWANATH,PRESIDING MEMBER

For the Appellant : Mr. Niraj Singh, Advocate

For the Respondent : For Respondent No.1 : Mr. Abhimanyu Tewari, Advocate

For Respondent No.2 : NONE

Dated : 05 Jan 2021

ORDER

1. The present Appeal is filed by the Appellant against Order passed by the Punjab State
   Consumer Disputes Redressal Commission, Chandigarh (hereinafter referred to as the
   "State Commission") in MA/1857/2019 in/and CC/127/2019 dated 18.03.2020.

2. Father of Respondent No.1/Complainant obtained Medical Insurance Policy
   No.404000501810000094 from the Opposite Party/Insurance Company, which was
   valid from 05.05.2018 to 31.10.2018. The Policy covered medical expenses of USD
   2,50,000/- for Illness, USD 2,50,000/- for accident, USD 25,000/-, for Personal
   Accident, USD 1,000/- for loss of checked in Baggage, USD 100/- for delay of checked
   in Baggage, USD 250/- for Loss of Passport and USD 2,00,000/- for Personal Liability.
   At the time of taking the Policy, the insured had -1- disclosed that he was suffering from
   hypertension and diabetes. Opposite Parties got the insured medically examined and
   thereafter issued the Medical Insurance Policy.

3. On 05.05.2018, the Insured went to Birmingham alongwith his family. On the night of
   30.08.2018, he suffered heart attack and was taken to the hospital. On 01.09.2018,
   Angiography was done and claim for reimbursement was filed on 03.09.2018. The
   Complainant's father expired on 14.09.2018. Opposite Parties repudiated the claim on
   the ground that the deceased father of the Complainant was having pre-existing disease.
   Claiming deficiency in service on the part of the Opposite Parties, the Complainant filed
   a Complaint before the State Commission with the following prayer: - i. Pay the medical
   expenditure to the tune of Sterling Pounds 39549.63, Sterling Pounds 3645 for
   Repatriation services of late father of the complainant total amounting to Rs.36,30,656/-
   and Rs.3,34,611, as per the prevalent exchange rate total amounting to Rs.39,65,267/- ii.
   Pay compensation to the tune of Rs.10,00,000/- on account of pain, mental agony and
   harassment suffered by the complainant. iii. To pay litigation cost of Rs.1,00,000/-

4. Opposite Parties contested the Complaint and took preliminary objection that the
   Complaint was not maintainable, as the deceased father of the Complainant obtained the
   Medical Insurance Policy concealing the facts regarding pre-existing disease. On merits,
   the Opposite Parties admitted that the father of the Complainant had taken the Policy
   which was valid from 05.05.2018 to 31.10.2018. Insured father of the Complainant died
   during the currency of the Policy on 14.09.2018. Opposite Parties repudiated the claim
   on the ground that the insured had supressed the material fact of pre-existing disease at
   the time of taking the Policy.

5. The State Commission after going through the evidence and documents on record and
   hearing the arguments of both the Parties directed as follows:- "i) To pay £39,549 minus
   100 USD It is made clear that the exchange rate in rupees shall be prevailing as on the

28

date of repudiation of claim i.e. 14.11.2018. The amount so calculated shall be paid along with interest at the rate of 9% per annum from the date of repudiation of the claim i.e. 14.11.2018 till realization. ii) To pay Rs.50,000/- as compensation on account of mental agony and harassment." -2-

6. Aggrieved by the order of the State Commission, the Appellant/Insurance Company filed the present Appeal. Heard the learned Counsel for the Parties and carefully perused the record.

7. Learned Counsel for the Appellant submitted that the State Commission passed the impugned order without properly appreciating the terms and conditions of the Insurance Policy and the extent of indemnification. It was submitted that the proposal form was to be completed by the proposer and the competent Doctor was to certify that the proposer is fit to travel abroad. In the proposal form the proposer had wrongly answered the question at A2 "Have you ever suffered from any illness or disease upto the date of making this proposal" as "NO." It was further submitted that the deceased insured had also given wrong answer to the question "Have you ever been admitted to any hospital/nursing home/clinic for treatment or observation" as "NO", though in the proposal form itself proposer had disclosed that he had undergone CABG in 1998. It was submitted that the father of the Complainant died due to heart attack and the factors leading to heart attack were Ischemic Heart Disease, Hypertension and Diabetes. Learned Counsel for the Appellant/Opposite Party submitted that exclusion clause of the Policy excludes "Pre-existing and related complications" and the father of the Complainant was having pre-existing disease and he supressed this material information from the Appellant/Insurance Company.

8. Learned Counsel for the Respondent/Complainant submitted that the insured had clearly declared in the proposal form that he was suffering from Hypertension and Diabetes and there was no question of suppression of any material fact. It was also submitted that the Insurance Company got his father medically examined before issuance of Policy. Therefore, repudiation of insurance claim by the Appellant was not justified and the State Commission rightly allowed the Complaint filed by the Respondent/Complainant.

9. It is an admitted case that the Complainant obtained Medical Insurance Policy No.404000501810000094 from the Opposite Parties, which was valid from 05.05.2018 to 31.10.2018. In the proposal form the proposer disclosed that he was suffering from hypertension and diabetes. He was also got medically examined by the doctor of the Opposite Parties before issuance of the Policy. On the night of 30.08.2018, the insured suffered heart attack and he was taken to the hospital and on 01.09.2018, Angiography was done. On 03.09.2018, claim for reimbursement of the medical expenses was filed. On 14.09.2018, father of the Complainant expired. Opposite Parties repudiated the claim on the ground that deceased father of the Complainant was having pre-existing disease.

10. Main issue in this case relates to disclosure of pre-existing disease of the insured. Learned Counsel for the Appellant, Insurance Company submitted that the insured did not disclose in the proposal form that he was having history of Hypertension and Diabetes. On the other hand, Opposite Parties admit in their reply that "father of the complainant had disclosed that the father of the complainant was suffering from hypertension and diabetes." Appellant/Insurance Company also admitted that " on second page at II B (1) History, it is clearly written CABG in 1998. CABG cannot be done without hospitalization. Before taking the Insurance Policy, the insured was suffering from Hypertension and Diabetes, which he had clearly disclosed in the proposal form. The fact that he had undergone CABG in 1998 was also disclosed and known to the Doctor as well as the Appellant. Moreover, the Insurance Company itself got the insured medically examined by a Doctor and it was after medical examination that the Policy was issued. Now, at the time of reimbursement of claim, the Appellant cannot take the plea that the proposer had -3- supressed material fact. Being fully aware

of his health status and after due Medical examination, the Appellant cannot feign ignorance of the Insured's health and deny the claim.

11. In view of the above discussion, the impugned order passed by the State Commission is justified. Appellant failed to point any illegality or irregularity in the order passed by the State Commission, warranting interference in exercise of Appellate jurisdiction Appeal is accordingly dismissed with no order as to cost. .... C. VISWANATH PRESIDING MEMBER

CASE NO. 8
FIRST APPEAL NO. 850 OF 2020

(Against the Order dated 07/10/2020 in Complaint No. CC/38/2018 of the State Commission Delhi)

HYUNDAI MOTOR INDIA LIMITED ....Appellant(s)

Versus

SHAILENDER BHATNAGAR ....Respondent(s)

BEFORE: HON'BLE MR. C. VISWANATH,PRESIDING MEMBER

For the Appellant : Mr. Rajeev Kumar Yadav, Advocate Mr. Divjot Singh Bhatia, Advocate

For the Respondent : In Person

Dated : 05 Jan 2021

ORDER

1. The present Appeal is filed by the Appellant/Opposite Party against Order passed by Delhi State Consumer Disputes Redressal Commission (hereinafter referred to as the "State Commission") in CC/38/2018 dated 07.10.2020.

2. Alongwith the Appeal, IA/7429/2020, application for condonation of delay of 33 days has also been filed by the Appellant. However, according to the Registry, there is no delay in filing the Appeal. Accordingly, IA/7429/2020 is allowed.

3. Case of the Complainant is that on 21.08.2015 Complainant/Respondent purchased a vehicle, Creta 1.6 VTVT SX+ bearing Engine No.95120, Chasis No.MALC381CLFM018320 from the Appellant/Opposite Party. In the car, there was facility of two front airbags. On 16.11.2017, when the Complainant was travelling with his family, the car met with an accident on -1- Delhi-Panipat Highway, resulting in major damage to RH front pillar, RH front roof, side body panels front RH door panels and LH front wheel suspension. In the accident, front airbags of the car did not open, due to which the Complainant and his family members were severely injured. On 16.11.2017, Complainant lodged police report at Police Station G.T. Road, Ghanaur, District Sonepat. On 23.11.2017, Complainant sent a legal notice to the Appellant/Opposite Party demanding Rs.50 Lakhs for the loss and physical and mental trauma suffered by the Complainant and his family. Opposite Party got the accidental inspected car and admitted that the airbags did not open but did not make payment of the amount demanded by the Complainant. Complainant filed Complaint before the State Commission with the following prayer: - "a. Direct the Respondent to compensate the amount of Rs.2,00,000/- including the medical expenses and professional loss borne by the complainant for him and his family also. b. Direct the Respondent to pay a sum of Rs.20,00,000/- (Twenty Lakhs only) on account of harassment and mental agony faced by the Complainant. c. Pay Rs.1,60,000/- (One lakh sixty thousand) towards litigation expenses. d. Pass any other order as this Hon'ble Court deems fit in the interest of justice."

4. Opposite Party contested the Complaint by filing reply. It was stated that the allegations made in the Complaint were false and frivolous. Complainant failed to make out a case against the Opposite Party and failed to prove that the Opposite Party had promised or assured any service which was not provided to the Complainant. It was also stated that the Complaint was barred by limitation as the limitation shall be reckoned from the date of purchase of the vehicle i.e. 21.08.2015. Complaint was also not maintainable on the

ground of mis-joinder of party, as the Dealer from whom the car was purchased, was not made a party in the Complaint. Opposite Party also stated that as there was no manufacturing defect in the car, it was not liable as its liability was only limited to the performance of the car. Once the car was damaged in the accident, the same is not covered under warranty/extended warranty and the repair was carried out on chargeable basis.

5. State Commission after going through the evidence and documents placed on record and hearing the arguments of both the parties directed as follows:- "Keeping in view the facts and circumstances of the present consumer complaint, we direct the opposite party to: a. Compensate the complainant an amount of Rs.2,00,000/- for medical expenses and loss of income. -2- b. Compensate the complainant an amount of Rs.50,000/- for mental agony. c. Pay to the complainant an amount of Rs.50,000/- as cost of litigation."

6. Aggrieved by the order of the State Commission, the Appellant/Opposite Party filed the present Appeal. Heard the learned Counsel for the Appellant and the Respondent in person and carefully perused the material on record.

7. Learned Counsel for the Appellant submitted that the State Commission passed the impugned order without properly appreciating the facts of the case. He submitted that the Complaint itself was not maintainable before the State Commission for non-joinder of necessary party, because the Dealer from whom the Complainant had purchased the car was not made a party in the Complaint. It was submitted that the Dealer purchases the car from the Opposite Party and the purchased cars are sold to the customers. There is no privity of contract between the Complainant and the Opposite Party. The State Commission failed to appreciate this legal aspect of the matter. Learned Counsel for the Appellant relied on the judgment of this Commission in Maruti Udyog Limited vs. Nagender Prasad Sinha II (2009) CPJ 295 (NC) . He also submitted that the Complaint was barred by limitation as the cause of action for filing the Complaint accrued to the Complainant on 21.08.2015, when the car was purchased. Learned Counsel for the Appellant relied on the judgment of this Commission in Ishwarlal Amarnai vs. Hero Puch & Anr. [III (2011) CPJ 132 NC] . On merits, it was submitted that the liability of the Opposite Party was limited to the performance of the car and there was no complaint regarding performance of the car, hence the claim against the Opposite Party did not sustain. It was submitted that the airbags deploy only when there is severe impact of force and airbags may not deploy if the vehicle collides with the objects like poles and trees, when full force of the impact is not delivered to the sensors.

8. Respondent/Complainant submitted that the Complaint was within limitation period since the cause of action arose on the date of accident i.e. 16.11.2017 and not from the date of purchase i.e. 21.08.2015. He also submitted that the dealer was only a formal party and not necessary party and the deficiency was only on the part of the Opposite Party. The Complaint was, therefore, maintainable. On merits, the Respondent/Complainant submitted that the accident occurred with a high impact of force and resulted in damage to RH front pillar, RH front roof, side body panels front RH door panels and LH front wheel suspension. He submitted that due to defective airbags, the Complainant and his family members sustained major injuries and the State Commission, therefore, rightly held the Opposite Party liable to pay compensation.

9. State Commission observed that the major impact of collision of the vehicle was on the right hand front pillar, right hand front roof and the left hand front wheel suspension, all three of -3- which lie on the front side of the vehicle. It was also observed that the airbags in the vehicle purchased by the Complainant was defective as the same did not work when the vehicle collided with the truck.

10. On 21.08.2015, Complainant purchased a vehicle, Creta 1.6 VTVT SX+ bearing Engine No.95120, chasis No.MALC381CLFM018320 from the Appellant/Opposite Party. On 16.11.2017, car met with an accident, resulting in major damage to RH front pillar, RH front roof, side body panels front RH door panels and LH front wheel suspension.

Airbags of the car did not deploy, due to which the Complainant and his family members sustained severe injuries. On 16.11.2017, Complaint was also lodged with Police Station G.T. Road, Ghanaur, District Sonepat, On 23.11.2017, Complainant sent a legal notice to the Appellant/Opposite Party demanding Rs.50 Lakhs for the loss and physical and mental trauma suffered by the Complainant and his family. Opposite Party got the vehicle inspected and admitted that the airbags did not deploy but did not make payment of the amount demanded by the Complainant.

11. Learned Counsel for the Opposite Party submitted that the limitation will start from the date of purchase i.e. 21.08.2015. In this case, however, cause of action arose on the date of accident i.e. 16.11.2017, when the defect relating to non-deployment of airbags came to the notice of the Complainant. Judgment relied by Learned Counsel for the Opposite Party in Ishwarlal Amarnai (supra) is distinguishable in the facts. In that case, Complainant purchased Hero Puch EZ, which started giving trouble including overflow of fuel, high consumption of petrol and trouble with the steering, from the very beginning. In the present case, the defect was noticed only on the date of accident i.e. 16.11.2017. The argument of the Opposite Party that the Complaint was time barred, therefore, does not sustain.

12. Regarding privity of contract, Learned Counsel for the Appellant/Opposite Party submitted that there was no privity of contract between the Complainant and the Opposite Party and therefore the Opposite Party was not liable to pay any damages to the Complainant. Judgment relied by Learned Counsel for the Appellant in Maruti Udyog Limited vs. Nagender Prasad Sinha (supra) is not applicable in the facts of the case. In that case, this Commission held that principal is not liable for the act done by its agent. In the present case, there is no issue regarding act of the agent and liability of the principal. In the case on hand, the issue relates to a manufacturing defect and the manufacturer is the Appellant/Opposite Party. Learned Counsel for the Appellant/Opposite Party submitted that the airbags deploy only when there is severe impact of force and airbags may not deploy if the vehicle collides with objects like poles and trees, when full force of the impact is not delivered to the sensors. Learned Counsel for the Appellant argued that the SRS Investigation report dated 01.12.2017 clearly stated that the impact of the accident was such that the minimum threshold force required for the deployment of the airbags was not delivered to the front sensors installed in the engine compartment and hence, the airbags did not deploy. No expert evidence was produced by the Respondent to substantiate any manufacturing defect. The Complainant contended that he purchased the car for its safety features highlighted by the Manufacturer, but the airbags did not function when required, due to which he sustained serious injuries as can be seen from the medical prescriptions and bills furnished by the Complainant. The impact/force required for triggering the front airbags was not made known to the Complainant. Nowhere has the minimum threshold force been quantified and this defence can never be refuted. Highlighting safety features including airbags while selling the car and not elaborating and disclosing the threshold limits for their opening is by itself an unfair trade practice. Complainant, however, had filed photographs of the accidental car. Major damage to RH front pillar, RH front roof, side body panels front RH door panels and LH front wheel suspension is seen in the photographs of the car. Without forceful impact, the car would not have -4- been so badly damaged. The accident was a major accident in which the entire deriver side of the car, the side part and even the front mirror of the car got smashed and broken. The impact of the accident was so intense that the front bumper grill, dash board and the radiator got totally damaged. The State Commission rightly observed "that expert evidence need not be relied upon where the facts speak for themselves. This is a case of Res Ipsa Loquitur where the photographs of the damaged vehicle placed on record clearly show the impact of the accident on the vehicle."

13. In view of the above discussion, the impugned order passed by the State Commission is justified. Appellant failed to point any illegality or irregularity in the order passed by the State Commission, warranting interference in exercise of Appellate jurisdiction Appeal is accordingly dismissed with no order as to cost. .... C. VISWANATH PRESIDING MEMBER

CASE NO. 9

REVISION PETITION NO. 1101 OF 2020

(Against the Order dated 29/08/2020 in Appeal No. 2187/2012 of the State Commission Madhya Pradesh)

KOTAK MAHINDRA BANK LTD..........Petitioner(s)

Versus

DHEERAJ SINGH BELDAR S/O SH. MADU SINGH R...........Respondent(s)

BEFORE: HON'BLE MR. C. VISWANATH,PRESIDING MEMBER

For the Petitioner : Mr. R.K. Ranjan, Advocate

For the Respondent :

Dated : 05 Jan 2021

ORDER

C. VISWANATH

1. The present Revision Petition has been filed by the Petitioners against the order dated 29.08.2020 of Madhya Pradesh State Consumer Disputes Redressal Commission, Bhopal (for short "the State Commission") in First Appeal No.2187/2012 whereby the Appeal was partly allowed.

2. Complainant/Respondent purchased a Farmtech 35 Champion Tractor, bearing Registration No.M.P.-42-A-0908 and took a loan of Rs.3,23,255/- from the Appellant/Opposite Party. The loan was to be repaid in 14 half yearly instalments of Rs.39,250/-. According to the Appellant, Complainant paid six instalments. Seventh instalment which was due in May, 2010 was not paid by the Complainant on time. Opposite Party issued recalling notice on 28.07.2010, whereby the Complainant was given seven days time to deposit the payment. Thereafter, on 13.08.2020, the Appellant seized the tractor. In order to realise the loan amount, the Petitioners/Opposite Parties - 1- auctioned the tractor on 01.10.2020. Alleging deficiency in service and unfair trade practice on the part of the Opposite Party, the Complainant filed a Complaint before the District Forum with the following prayer: - " Therefore, it is requested that the complaint be allowed and the amount of Rs.42,000/- along with interest to be recovered from the opposite party pertaining to damage occurred due to lack in service, compensation for mental agony and expenses of present case and the tractor of the applicant be released. The opposite party to be further directed to produce the loan account details. Any other relief which deems fit and proper to this Hon'ble Forum may pass in favour of applicant."

3. The Complaint was contested by the Respondent/Opposite Party. It was stated that since the Complainant neither replied to the notice, nor deposit the loan amount within the stipulated time, the tractor was seized by the Petitioners and the loan amount was adjusted by selling the same.

4. The District Forum after hearing both the Parties and perusing the record, directed as follows: - "Therefore, the complaint filed on behalf of complainant is disposed off in such a way that the opposite party has to pay the deposited amount Rs.2,46,678/- along with the interest of 9% per annum from the date of payment last instalment to the date of payment within 2 months to the complainant. The opposite party should pay the amount of Rs.5,000/- against financial and mental agony to the complainant. The demand notices were sent by the opposite party to the complainant in respect of recovery of the loan is also set aside in view of their act of illegally possessing and

33

selling the tractor of complainant. The complaint expense of Rs.1,000/- is decided which shall be paid by the opposite party.

5. Aggrieved by the order of the District Forum, Petitioners/Opposite Parties preferred an appeal before the State Commission. State Commission observed as follows: - "Therefore, the appeal is partly allowed while amending in clause 12 of order of the Forum that the amount compensated by the Forum to the respondent is reduced to Rs.1,30,423/- in place of Rs.2,46,678/-. The appellant should pay the above said amount to the respondent along with 9% interest per annum from the date of payment of last instalment to the date of payment. The order in respect of mental agony amount of Rs.5,000/- and case expense amount of Rs.1,000/- passed by the Forum is upheld. The parties shall bear expenses of this appeal in its own."

6. Aggrieved by the order of the State Commission, Petitioners/Opposite Parties preferred the present Revision Petition. Heard the Learned Counsels for the Petitioners and carefully perused the record. -2-

7. Learned Counsel for the Petitioners submitted that the tractor of the Complainant was seized as the Respondent/Complainant failed to deposit the amount within the stipulated period. It was also submitted that the Petitioners sent several reminders before auction of the tractor. He also submitted that the tractor was auctioned, since there was an apprehension that the Respondent will become a defaulter in future.

8. Admitted facts of the case are that Complainant/Respondent purchased a Farmtech 35 Champion Tractor, bearing Registration No.M.P.-42-A-0908 and took a loan of Rs.3,23,255/- from the Petitioners/Opposite Parties. According to the Petitioners, the Complainant paid six instalments in time. Seventh instalment which was due in May, 2010 was not paid by the Complainant on time. Petitioners issued recall notice on 28.07.2010, whereby Complainant was given seven days time to deposit the payment. Thereafter, on 13.08.2020, the Petitioners seized the tractor. In order to realise the loan amount, the Petitioners/Opposite Parties auctioned the tractor on 01.10.2020.

9. Learned Counsel for the Petitioners contention was that the tractor was seized, as the Complainant did not pay the instalment amount in time nor he replied to their notice. Petitioners themselves admitted that the Complainant had paid six instalments in time. Recall notice was issued on 28.07.2010 and the tractor was seized on 13.08.2010. Learned Counsel for the Petitioners admitted that the auction notice was also given on 13.08.2010 itself, after seizure of the tractor. As per the Petitioners, the Respondent was issued many reminders to deposit the amount. However, notices were issued by the Petitioners to deposit the entire amount, beyond the means of the Respondent. The Respondent sought to deposit the demanded amount, after the crop season, which is expected of a farmer. If the Respondent was to deposit the entire amount and not in instalments, there was no purpose of taking a loan. It defeats the very scheme of scheduling repayment of loans. In a tiring hurry, the tractor was seized, causing great hardship to the Respondent. Merely based on an apprehension that the Respondent would become a defaulter in future, the Learned Counsel for the Petitioners stated that action was taken to seize and auction the vehicle to realise the dues. Apprehension of the Petitioners that the Respondent/Complainant would become defaulter in future, cannot be a valid ground for seizure and auction of the tractor. Hurried seizure of the tractor and auctioning the same on the basis of assumptions and surmises, certainly amounts to unfair trade practice on the part of the Petitioners.

10. In view of foregoing discussion, I find no infirmity in the impugned order of the State Commission. Revision Petition is dismissed. .... C. VISWANATH PRESIDING MEMBER

<u>CASE NO.10</u>
FIRST APPEAL NO. 1222 OF 2014

(Against the Order dated 16/09/2014 in Complaint No. 6/2014 of the State Commission Chhattisgarh)

ANITA SHARMA W/O. LATE SHRI YOGENDRA SHARMA, R..........Appellant(s)

Versus

IFFCO TOKIO GENERAL INSURANCE CO. LTD. & ANR.

PUNJAB NATIONAL BANK HOUSING FINANCE LIMITED, ...Respondent(s)

BEFORE: HON'BLE MR. C. VISWANATH,PRESIDING MEMBER

For the Appellant : Mr. Anis Ur Rehman, Advocate

For the Respondent : For the Respondent No. 1 : Mr. D Varadarajan, Advocate

For the Respondent No. 2 : Mr. Satish Kumar, Advocate

Dated : 06 Jan 2021

ORDER

1. The present Appeal has been filed by the Appellant against the order dated 16.09.2014 of the Chhattisgarh State Consumer Disputes Redressal Commission, Pandri, Raipur (hereinafter referred to as "the State Commission) in CC No.14/2006. -1-

2. Case of the Complainant is that the Complainant had taken a housing loan from OP No. 2, with her husband as the co-borrower. Complainant took an Insurance Policy from OP No. 1 for personal accident benefit of Rs. 34,00,000/- and the Policy was valid upto 12.06.2028. The Policy also insured the aforesaid loan in case of death of the insured. The Complainant's husband, who was also the co-borrower died due to Naxalite attack on 25.05.2013. The matter was reported to the Police Station. As per the Complainant, in case of death of the Complainant or her husband, the insured amount was to be adjusted against the loan obtained by the Complainant from Op No. 2 Bank. The claim of the Complainant was repudiated on the ground that it fell under the Exclusion Clause of the Policy. Since the claim of the Complainant was repudiated, a Complaint was filed in the State Commission with the following prayer:- "A. That the OP No. 1 may be directed to pay the amount of Rs. 34,00,000/- alongwith interest to the complainant. B. That the OP No. 2 may be directed to discharge the complainant from paying the home loan and for which the OP No. 2 will be liable,. C. That on the claim amount of Rs.34,00,000/- the interest @ 18% may be awarded from date of filing of the complaint till the payment. D. That the complainant from 11-06-2013 and after that on various dates has paid the installment of home loan of Rs.3,41,275/- from the Ops. The Ops may be direct to pay the said amount jointly or severally. E. Any other relief which the Hon'ble Commission deems fit may also be granted against OPs"

3. The Complaint was contested by the OPs. OP No. 1/Insurance Company stated that the Complainant's husband died due to naxalite attack and by virtue of the Insurance Policy's Exclusion Clause, the Complainant was not entitled to get the insured amount from OP No. 1 and therefore, the claim was rightly repudiated. OP No. 2/Bank stated that since the claim of the Complainant was repudiated by OP No. 1, the Complainant is liable to deposit the loan amount with the OP No. 2. The dispute was between the Complainant and the Insurance Company, and was not related to OP No. 2 and therefore, Complaint against OP No. 2 was liable to be dismissed.

4. The State Commission after hearing both the parties and perusing the record of the case, passed the following directions: - "Therefore, the complaint filed by the complainant against the Ops, is liable to be dismissed, hence the same is dismissed. Parties shall bear their own cost."

5. Aggrieved by the order of the State Commission, the Complainant preferred the present Appeal. -2-

6. Heard the Learned Counsels for the Parties and carefully perused the record. Brief facts of the Case are that the Complainant purchased a Plot bearing No. 14 situated at Avani Pride, Daldalseoni Road, Mowa, Raipur by obtaining a loan from OP No. 2 for an amount of Rs.25,00,000/-. The husband of the Complainant was the co-borrower. The Complainant insured the loan by obtaining an Insurance Policy which was valid upto

12.06.2028. The husband of the Complainant, who was also the co-borrower, died on 25.05.2013 at Jhiram Ghati due to Naxalite attack. The matter was reported to the Police Station, Darbha, Jagdalpur. The Complainant made a claim before OP No 1. The claim, however, was repudiated on the ground that the said incident and death of Complainant's husband was not payable as per the terms and conditions of the Insurance Policy. The Learned Counsel for the Complainant/Appellant contended that the State Commission erred in holding that the claim of the Complainant fell under the Exclusion Clause of the Insurance Policy. As the death of Complainant's husband was accidental, the amount insured was liable to be paid as per the terms and conditions of the Insurance Policy. Counsel for Respondent No. 1 contended that the Complainant's husband died due to Naxalite attack and such a situation falls in the Exclusion clause of the Insurance Policy and therefore, the claim of the Complainant was not liable to be paid. Counsel for Respondent No. 2 contended that the dispute was between the Complainant and the Insurance Company, and was not related to Respondent No. 2 and therefore, Complaint against Respondent No. 2 was liable to be dismissed.

7. As per the General Exclusion clause of the Insurance Policy, the Insurance Company was not liable to pay compensation in respect of death, injury or disablement of the insured as consequence of "war, invasion, act of foreign enemy hostilities or war like operations (whether war be declared or not), civil war, mutiny, civil commotion assuming the proportions of or amounting to a popular rising, military rising, rebellion, revolution, insurrection or military or usurped power and any act of terrorism." It is admitted that the complainant's husband died due to Naxalite attack, which squarely falls within the ambit of the aforementioned Exclusion Clause of the Policy. The State Commission has rightly observed that "In the instant case also the deceased Yogendra Sharma died due to Naxalite attack, therefore, General Exclusion Clause of the insurance policy is applicable in this case. On the basis of General Exclusion Clause of the insurance policy, the OP No. 1 (Insurance Company) is not liable to indemnify the complainant."

8. Based on the foregoing discussion, I find no infirmity in the impugned order of the State Commission. The present Appeal is dismissed. .... C. VISWANATH PRESIDING MEMBER

<u>CASE NO. 11</u>
FIRST APPEAL NO. 807 OF 2020

(Against the Order dated 07/11/2016 in Complaint No. 131/2013 of the State Commission Karnataka)

M/S. CITI GREEN FARMS (P) LTD. & ANR. REPRESENTED BY ITS CMD

 B.RADHARAMANA, CMD OF M/S CITI GREEN FARMS(P)LTD,...........Appellant(s)

Versus

RISHIKESH BORKOTOKY REPRESENTED BY HIS GPA HOLDER D.C. BORKOTOKY S/O D.C. BORKOTOKY ....Respondent(s)

BEFORE: HON'BLE MRS. JUSTICE DEEPA SHARMA,PRESIDING MEMBER

For the Appellant : Mr. Suyodhan Byrapaneni, Advocate

For the Respondent :

Dated : 06 Jan 2021

ORDER

JUSTICE DEEPA SHARMA (ORAL) THROUGH VIDEO CONFERENCING

1. The present Appeal, under Section ---51(1) of the Consumer Protection Act, 2019 (for short "the Act") has been filed by the Appellant against the order dated 07.11.2016 of the State Consumer Disputes Redressal Commission, Bangalore, Karnataka (for short "the State -1- Commission") in Complaint No.131 of 2013 whereby the Complaint of the Respondent was allowed

2. Since the present Appeal has been filed with a delay of about four years, an application IA No.7246 of 2020 has also been filed. Arguments on this application for condonation of delay are heard. IA 7246 of 2020 (condonation of delay)

3. Vide this application, the Appellant has sought condonation of delay of four years in filing the present Appeal. It is contended that the Appellant had no knowledge of the passing of the impugned order since during the pendency of the Complaint before the State Commission it had changed the address and therefore, copy of final order was not received by it. Secondly, the Counsel for the Appellant did not inform it that the matter had been reserved for order on 13.07.2016 and the order was pronounced on 07.11.2016, copy of which was not received by it. It learnt of the passing of the impugned order only as its property was attached in the execution proceedings. On these grounds, the condonation of delay in filing the present Appeal has been sought.

4. Admittedly, the Appellant had been served with the notice of the Complaint and had participated in the trial. When the case was fixed for final arguments, repeated adjournments were sought on behalf of the Appellant. Finally, the State Commission after giving final opportunity to the Appellant to argue the matter reserved the matter for order on 13.07.2016. Thereafter, the final order was pronounced on 07.11.2016. The argument is that during the pendency of the Complaint before the State Commission, the Appellant/Opposite Party had changed its address and therefore, they never received copy of the impugned order. On enquiry, learned Counsel for the Appellant admits that the change of address was not brought to the notice of the State Commission or to the Complainant. Neither any application for bringing on record the changed address of the Opposite Party/Appellant was ever filed nor any oral submission to this effect was made before the State Commission. It is the bounded duty of the parties to bring to the notice of the Commission the correct facts and inform them of the changes in its status which occurs during the pendency of the Complaint. Therefore, when the Appellant had changed its address during the pendency of the Complaint, it was its boundened duty to bring on record the changed address. By not doing so, it is the Appellant who had acted negligently and carelessly and now he cannot be permitted to take advantage of its own wrong by arguing that it had never received copy of the impugned order. The Commission in discharge of its statutory duty is required to send free copies of the order to the parties at the address on record. The Appellant, therefore, cannot be allowed to take advantage of its own wrong at this stage for seeking condonation of delay on this ground.

5. Another argument of learned Counsel for the Appellant is that the Appellant was never informed by its Counsel that the matter had been reserved for order and that he had not argued the matter before the State Commission. It is expected from all the clients/parties in a case to act diligently and take reasonable care of their case. Where the parties are sleeping over their rights or on performance of their duties, they cannot be permitted to take advantage of their sloppy attitude during the trial. -2-

6. The Hon'ble Supreme Court in the case of " Ram Lal and Ors. vs. Rewa Coalfields Limited, AIR 1962 Supreme Court 361" has held that the condonation of delay is not a matter of right and the courts can exercise its discretion to condone the delay only where sufficient reasons are shown. The Apex Court has held as under: "12. It is, however, necessary to emphasize that even after sufficient cause has been shown a party is not entitled to the condonation of delay in question as a matter of right. The proof of a sufficient cause is a discretionary jurisdiction vested in the Court by S.5. If sufficient

cause is not proved nothing further has to be done; the application for condonation has to be dismissed on that ground alone. If sufficient cause is shown then the Court has to enquire whether in its discretion it should condone the delay. This aspect of the matter naturally introduces the consideration of all relevant facts and it is at this stage that diligence of the party or its bona fides may fall for consideration; but the scope of the enquiry while exercising the discretionary power after sufficient cause is shown would naturally be limited only to such facts as the Court may regard as relevant."

7. It is also a settled preposition of law that delay of each and every day has to be explained. If a person acts in lethargic manner and continues sitting over the file and takes long time for preparing the file or in getting translations done, or delay in collecting documents, such delay cannot be said to be sufficient and reasonable as are not the reasons which could not have been avoided. The basic test to determine whether the delay is reasonable or whether the party has been acting with due diligence, has been laid down by the Hon'ble Supreme Court in the case of "R. B. Ramlingam vs. R. B. Bhavaneshwari, I (2009) (2) CLJ (SC) 24". The Hon'ble Court has held as under: "5. We hold that in each and every case the Court has to examine whether delay in filing the special appeal leave petitions stands properly explained. This is the basic test which needs to be applied. The true guide is whether the petitioner has acted with reasonable diligence in the prosecution of his appeal/petition."

8. The Hon'ble Supreme Court has also warned this Commission to keep in mind the special nature of the Consumer Protection Act, 1986 while dealing with the applications for condonation of delay. In the case of "Anshul Aggarwal vs. New Okhla Industrial Development Authority, (2011) 14 SCC 578," the Hon'ble Supreme Court has held as under: "5. It is also apposite to observe that while deciding an application filed in such cases for condonation of delay, the Court has to keep in mind that the special period of limitation has been prescribed under the Consumer Protection Act, 1986 for filing appeals and revisions in consumer matters and the object of expeditious adjudication of the consumer disputes will get defeated if this court was to entertain highly belated petitions filed against the orders of the consumer Fora." -3-

9. From the above, it is apparent that the Appellant had neither acted diligently nor took reasonable care of its case. Even if the Counsel had not informed the Appellant about the fact that the matter had been reserved for final order on 13.07.2016, it was the bounded duty of the Appellant to enquire from its Counsel or do inspection of the court file to know as to what was happening in its case. The Appellant apparently has come before this Commission when its property has been attached in the execution proceeding.

10. From the above, it is apparent that the Appellant has not made out any ground for condonation of delay of four years in filing the present Appeal. The Application stands dismissed. Appeal 11. Since the Appeal is delayed by four years and the application seeking condonation of delay stands dismissed, the present Appeal is also dismissed being barred by limitation. ....J
DEEPA SHARMA PRESIDING MEMBER

CASE NO. 12
FIRST APPEAL NO. 53 OF 2010

(Against the Order dated 09/12/2009 in Complaint No. 57/2001 of the State Commission Orissa)

SHYAM SUNDER DASH Preseently Working in IMFA,Thuribali Rayagada Orissa
...........Appellant(s)

Versus

TATA MEMORIAL HOSPITAL & ORS. Tata Memorial Hospital,Dr.E. Borges
Marg,Parel, Mumbai

The Medical Superintendent Tata Memorial Hospital,Dr.E.Borges Marg, Parel, Mumbai

Dr.Rajesh Badhwar C/o Tata Memorial Hospital,Dr.E.Borges Marg, Parel, Mumbai

M/s Howmedica Duchem Laboratories Ltd. Pfizer Hospital Products Group,

M/s. Christian Hospital

M/s.IMFA Hospital

Consumer Assistance & Rural Empowerment (CARE)...........Respondent(s)

FIRST APPEAL NO. 115 OF 2010

(Against the Order dated 09/12/2009 in Complaint No. 57/2001 of the State Commission
Orissa)

TATA MEMORIAL HOSPITAL & ANR...........Appellant(s)

Versus

CONSUMER ASSISTANCE & RURAL EMPOWERMANT (CARE) & ANR

Shyam Sunder Dash S/o.Late Jadumani Dash,...........Respondent(s)

BEFORE: HON'BLE DR. S.M. KANTIKAR,PRESIDING MEMBER

For the Appellant :

For the Respondent :

Dated : 08 Jan 2021

ORDER

Appeared at the time of arguments For Tata Memorial Hospital : Mr. Sandeep Narain,
Advocate

For Shri Shyam Sunder Dash : Mr. Shibashish Misra, Advocate

Pronounced on: 8 January 2021 th -2-

ORDER

1. Both the Appeals have been filed against the Final Judgement / Order dated 09.12.2009
   passed by the State Consumer Disputes Redressal Commission, Odisha, Cuttack
   (hereinafter referred to as the "State Commission") in Consumer Complaint No. 57 of
   2001 wherein the State Commission did not hold the Opposite Parties liable for medical
   negligence and dismissed the complaint. However it held the Tata Memorial Hospital
   for functional irregularities and ordered the Opposite Parties Nos. 1 & 2 to compensate
   the Complainant No. 2 by making a payment of Rs. 1 lakh plus Rs. 10,000/- towards the
   cost of litigation.

2. For the convenience, the facts are drawn from First Appeal No. 53 of 2010. The
   Appellants were complainants and the Respondents were the Opposite Parties in the
   complaint and they are accordingly referred in this Order.

3. Brief facts: The Complainant No. 1 is voluntary Consumer Association and the
   Complainant No. 2 (Shyam Sundar Dash) is the employee of IMFA Ltd. at Therubali
   (Odisha). His daughter Shrutilekha Dash, about 16 years of age, (since deceased,
   hereinafter referred to as the "patient") was taken to IMFA Hopsital, Therubali in the
   month of December 1998 for pain in left leg / knee. She was further referred to the
   Orthopedic Surgeon, Dr. Rama Chandra Rao at District Hospital, Raigad, wherein
   Biopsy of left knee joint was performed and it was diagnosed as Osteosarcoma of left
   knee. Thereafter, the IMFA Hospital referred the patient to Tata Memorial Hospital
   (hereinafter referred to as "TMH") at Mumbai. On 26.02.1999, the Complainant No. 2
   admitted his daughter to TMH. On 29.06.1999, Dr. Rajesh Badhwar (hereinafter
   referred to as the "Opposite party No. 3") Surgeon, Bone & Soft Tissue Service at TMH
   examined her and confirmed the diagnosis of Osteosarcoma. She was advised for few
   cycles of Chemotherapy followed by knee replacement with artificial limb at a later
   stage. The patient underwent Chemotherapy for more than five weeks and on

29.04.1999 was advised by the attending surgeon for Total Knee Replacement (TKR) with KOTZ Modular Implant. A total estimate of Rs. 3 lakh was intimated to the Complainant. It was alleged that the order for prosthesis (implant) from M/s Howmedica - the Opposite Party No. 4 was delayed because of the faulty internal administration of TMH. The supplier did not supply the required Prosthesis within the stipulated time because TMH did not clear previous dues of the supplier. The prosthesis having different measurement was requisitioned. Though the Prosthesis was available at discounted price with the help of Cancer Patient Aid, but TMH refused to accept it. It was further alleged that the patient was admitted in February, 1999 but the surgery was delayed to 15.09.1999, which caused additional expenditure due to increased higher price for prosthesis and the patient had undergone one more dose of Chemotherapy which was harmful for the patient. The Complainant further alleged that both the operative teams i.e. Cancer Surgeon and Plastic Surgeon were not present during the surgery which has a norm in such surgical process. The Plastic Surgeon too came to the Operation Theatre after two hours of the knee replacement surgery only on getting an emergency call. He expressed his dissatisfaction for such delay and told that it may cause infection to the operative wound. The plastic surgeon also expressed displeasure that there was no water available in the Operation Theatre for hand scrubbing; therefore he had to go to another Operation Theatre. It was further alleged that the Prosthesis was not implanted properly which caused damage to the blood vessels and profuse bleeding. It was the carelessness and deficiency in service of treating doctors due to which the patient developed infection at operated site. Thereafter, the doctors at TMH again advised to replace the Prosthesis with free fibula grafting with additional dose of Chemotherapy. It was alleged that though, the Surgeons at TMH were aware that further treatment would not yield any positive result, yet, they asked the Complainant No. 2 to deposit additional Rs. 1.5 lakh for Surgery and Rs. 2 lakh for post-surgery -3- Chemotherapy. However, the patient's father did not agree and he returned to Therubali. On 08.03.2000, the patient got admitted in nearby Christian Hospital, Bischam at Cuttack. The infected Prosthesis was removed on 15.04.2000, however the severe wound infection persisted. It was alleged that after removal of the Prosthesis, it came to light that different size of prosthesis was used during surgery at TMH. It was bigger in size, did not fit in to the patient, which caused damage to the vessels and caused further delay in reconstructive Plastic Surgery. The Prosthesis bears different numbers, and nowhere the name of the manufacturer or the place of its manufacture was mentioned , thus it gave the suspicion that the Prosthesis used was of an inferior quality. As a life saving measure, the Doctors at Christian Hospital, Cuttack (Opposite Party No. 5) carried out amputation of the leg. She stayed in the Hospital from 08.03.2000 to 20.06.2000 but could not recover from infection and expired on 08.12.2000. Being aggrieved by alleged deficiency of service and medical negligence of the treating doctors, a Consumer Complaint No. 57 of 2001 was filed against the Opposite Parties Nos. 1 to 4 before the State Commission, claiming compensation of Rs. 19, 90,400/- with interest at the rate of 18% p.a. jointly and severally.

4. The Opposite Parties Nos. 1 and 2 jointly filed their Written Version through the Medical Superintendent of TMH and they denied any negligence or deficiency in the treatment of the patient. The Opposite Party No. 4 M/s Howmedica Duchem Laboratories Ltd. filed a separate written version stating that it cannot be held liable as the business of the company had already been transferred. The Opposite Party No. 3, Dr. Rajesh Badhwar had expired and accordingly the claim as against him was abated. The Opposite Parties Nos. 5 & 6 are formal parties, against whom no relief had been claimed. The Opposite Parties Nos. 1 & 2 raised preliminary objections that the State Commission neither had the (i) pecuniary jurisdiction, nor the (ii) territorial jurisdiction, to entertain and try the present Complaint under the Consumer Protection Act, 1986, as the Complainant prayed for the compensation and costs of Rs. 19,90,400/- along with

interest @ 18% p.a. i.e. from 15.09.1999 till the date of realization of the amounts; which after calculation exceeds Rs. 20 lakhs which is beyond the pecuniary jurisdiction of the State Commission. The Opposite Parties further submitted that the State Commission did not have the territorial jurisdiction to entertain the Complaint because both the Opposite Parties are located at Mumbai and do not have any branch or other office in Odisha and/or do not carry on their activities in any other city other than Mumbai.

5. It was submitted that, the patient was referred from IMFA Hospital to the TMH on 26.02.1999. The patient was admitted at TMH under the care and supervision of Senior Consultant, Dr. Rajesh Badhwar (hereinafter referred to as the "Opposite Party No. 3"). After investigations, the diagnosis of a highly aggressive bone tumour - Osteosarcoma of left leg was confirmed. The patient was advised for Chemotherapy sessions, and thereafter, resection of the cancer affected bones i.e. Total Knee Replacement (TKR) Surgery and implant of an Artificial Prosthesis in lieu of the amputated limb. The Chemotherapy in four cycles was completed between March to June, 1999 and on 28.06.1999, Dr. Badhwar examined the patient and suggested that to undergo TKR Surgery within short span of time with Prosthesis of 9 mm diameter would require to be implanted. As the patient was running fever, therefore for short period she left the Hospital and again came back to TMH in August, 1999. As the patient was immuno-compromised and highly prone to the infections, therefore the 5 session of Chemotherapy for September, 1999. th Accordingly, an Indent Order was placed by TMH on 27.08.1999 to the Opposite Party No. 4 for obtaining Howmedica Modular Prosthesis. The Prosthesis was received by TMH on 31.08.1999.

6. On 15.09.1999, Dr. Rajesh Badhwar and his Orthopaedic team performed TKR- i.e. resected the bones afflicted with cancer and implanted the Prosthesis (Howmedica Modular Resection System / KOTZ Modular Femur & Tibia Reconstruction System) while the Plastic Surgery team of TMH successfully carried out the reconstruction of the limb. The patient then attended the OPD of TMH, after three months on 16.12.1999, and complained of pain for which she was taken to Dr. Ajay Puri at TMH, who after examination advised immediate admission and removal of Prosthesis at the earliest. However, the patient's -4- father refused for admission and removal of Prosthesis at TMH. He took the patient to his native Village at Therubali. Thereafter the patient for on 18.03.2000 got admitted to Christian Hospital at Bisam, Cuttack on 18.03.2000 wherein the Prosthesis was removed on 15.04.2000. Therefore, the patient's father himself was negligent who did not follow the advice of Dr. Ajay Puri and the removal of Prosthesis was done after four months delay.

7. It was submitted by the Opposite Parties Nos. 1 & 2 that the Prosthesis being a foreign body, sometimes it may not suit every patient and may cause infection, therefore its removal was recommended. It is a known complication that about 15% of cases show infection on implantation of Prosthesis. After the removal of the Prosthesis at Christian Hospital, Cuttack, the Complainant wrote two letters to TMH on 07.06.2000 and 24.07.2000 by which he thanked TMH for the co-operation and treatment of his daughter. He expressed his desire to return the removed Prosthesis to the Hospital and requested to refund the cost of Prosthesis. However, in reply the Medical Superintendent of TMH pointed out by letter dated 04.08.2000 that the Prosthesis was custom built and once implanted, same cannot be re-used on any other patient. The patient eventually died on 08.12.2000 due to the aggressive nature of Osteosarcoma as a consequence of lung metastasis. There was no deformity.

8. Being aggrieved by the Order passed by the State Commission, the Complainant No. 2 filed First Appeal No. 53 of 2010 for enhancement of compensation, whereas the TMH Hospital filed First Appeal No. 115 of 2010. The First Appeal No. 53 of 2010 filed by Complainant for enhancement of compensation, whereas the Opposite Parties Nos. 1 &

2 filed First Appeal No. 115 of 2010 for the dismissal of the complaint and to set aside the observations of alleged irregularities State Commission.

9. I have heard the learned counsel for both the sides.

10. The learned Counsel for the Complainant reiterated the facts and their affidavit of evidence. The learned Counsel for the Complainant submitted that vide Order dated 29.08.2017 of this Commission, the Opposite Parties Nos. 5 to 7 are formal parties against whom no relief is sought, therefore, the notice was not issued. He further submitted that since the Opposite Party No. 3 had expired, no cause of action survived qua the Opposite Party No. 3. The name of the Opposite Party No. 3 was deleted vide Order dated 17.07.2015.

11. The learned Counsel for the Opposite Parties Nos. 1 & 2 vehemently argued and reiterated the submissions made in affidavit of evidence. On the preliminary objection the learned counsel argued that the State Commission did not have Pecuniary Jurisdiction in view of the judgment of Ambrish Kumar Shukla Vs Ferrous Infrastructure (P) Ltd., 2016 SCC Online NCDRC 1117 and Anil Textorium (P) Ltd. Vs Rajiv Niranjanbhai Mehta, III (1997) CPJ 31 (NC), and further argued that the compensation claimed by the Complainant exceeds Rs. 20 lakh which was more than the jurisdiction of the State Commission. He further argued that the State Commission, did not have the territorial jurisdiction to entertain the present Complaint against the Opposite Parties. The cause of action, if any, for the alleged deficiencies and negligence averred against the Opposite Parties Nos. 1 & 2 had admittedly arisen at Mumbai and no cause action arisen partly or wholly in Odisha. He relied upon the Judgments of the Hon'ble Supreme Court in the case National Textile Corporation & Ors. Vs Haribox Swalram & Ors. (2004) 9 SCC 786 and Kusum Ingots & Alloys Ltd. Vs Union Of India & Ors. (2004) 6 SCC 254. Thus the complaint was liable to be dismissed by the State Commission.

12. On merit; the learned counsel for the Opposite Parties argued that the patient suffered highly aggressive bone cancer. The doctors at TMH treated the patient as per standards. The learned counsel further argued that Osteosarcoma is a highly aggressive bone tumour affecting mostly children in the -5- adolescent group and prognosis is bad due to lung metastasis with chances of survival up to 5 years. Therefore even after best possible treatment, the death of a patient cannot be attributed to any medical negligence by the treating doctors or the hospital. He further submitted that based on the evidence of two medical experts (one expert was appointed by State Commission), the State Commission observed that the functioning of the Hospital was not "free from irregularities" which may have contributed to the suffering of the deceased Srutilekha Dash and without discussing the reasons, awarded Rs. 1 lakh as compensation to the Complainant No. 2.

13. I gave thoughtful consideration to the arguments advanced by the learned counsel of both sides and perused the Medical Record, the literature and the Order of the State Commission.

14. The incident happened in the year 1999 and we are now in the year 2020. Almost two decades have elapsed. The State Commission has already dealt with the preliminary objections on maintainability of the complaint (territorial and pecuniary jurisdiction). Therefore, I proceed to decide the matter on merit. The Complainant's grouse was that the patient was admitted to TMH in February, 1999, but the surgery was conducted after 6 months delay in September 1999. As per standard medical literature and text books, it is pertinent to note that the Osteosarcoma is a highly aggressive malignant tumour. Before the surgical treatment, the patient needs to stabilize with the few cycles of Chemotherapy. Depending upon the patient's clinical response the treating doctor decides the Chemotherapy schedule for "pre" (neoadjuvant) and "post" (adjuvant) operative stages. Generally, pre-operative cycles range from 3 to 5 sessions of chemotherapy. In the instant case it was decided to give five cycles of neoadjuvant

Chemotherapy between February, 1999 and August, 1999. Thus, the allegation of Complainant is not sustainable that surgery could have been done after 4 cycles of Chemotherapy and the unwanted 5 cycle of Chemotherapy which delayed the surgery th was not required. During the treatment, nothing prevented the Complaint No. 2 to seek 2 nd opinion from institution of his choice or any competent doctor, which he failed.

15. In the instant case, the Complainant neither led any expert evidence nor produced any medical literature to prove medical negligence. However, the State Commission obtained opinion of an Independent Expert Doctor – Dr. Rabin C. Mishra, Professor of Surgery & HOD, Acharya Harihar Regional Cancer Centre, Cuttack. The affidavit of evidence dated 18.10.2006 from Dr. Ajay Puri, Associate Professor (Bone & Soft Tissue Unit) of TMH is on record. The combined reading of both the expert opinions nothing is established about any lapses or failure of duty of care at TMH and does not corroborate the allegations of negligence raised by the Complainant No. 2. Thus, the State Commission rightly held that there was no medical negligence from the Opposite Parties.

16. Regarding the procurement of Prosthesis, the Complainant alleged that it was delayed by the TMH. It is apparent from the prescriptions that after the 4 cycle of Chemotherapy on 28.06.1999, Dr. Badhwar th wrote the prescription that " patient would require Prosthesis of appx. 9 mm diameter ". It means Dr. Badhwar noted the clinical findings and his advice. In my view, the Complainant misconceived about the treatment aspects. The said prescription was neither an "Indent" for placing an order to procure the Prosthesis nor suggestive of detailed specifications of the size of Prosthesis.

17. After administration of the 5 cycle of Chemotherapy in August, 1999, the patient was fit for th operation at the end of September, 1999. It is apparent from the challan of the supplier Howmedica (the Opposite Party No. 4) that on 27.08.1999 the Indent/Purchase Order for HMRS KOTZ Modular Prosthesis was placed by the TMH. The Prosthesis with all its parts of different configurations was received within 3 days by the Hospital on 31.08.1999. Thus, an allegation of complainant that there was delay in procurement of the Prosthesis because of non-payment of earlier dues by TMH is unsustainable. -6-

18. The KOTZ Modular Knee Prosthesis is a set of several different components including Str Anch, Extension PC, Femoral Joint, Proximal Tibial Fixation Plate, Bearings, Wedges, Clips, Bone Screws etc. These components come in different sizes /configurations. The sizes may usually vary with measurements taken on a clinical examination and the exact size can only be determined on the Operating Table by the operating surgeon. In the instant case on 28.06.1999, Dr. Badhwar on a clinical examination of the patient asked for the diameter of the main Prosthesis to be approximately 9 mm. However, the exact measurements taken during operation on the Operating Table indicated that the patient required Prosthesis of 10 mm diameter. Therefore, the Complainant's allegation about Prosthesis of a different size than that prescribed earlier was used which resulted in pain to the patient which had to be ultimately removed is not sustainable. It is pertinent to note that this was not a case where the Prosthesis with 9 mm diameter was not available at the time of operation. However, the operating Surgeon – Dr. Badhwar during surgery decided to use a Prosthesis with 10mm diameter. It was the wrong presumption of the Complainant that "oversized" Prosthesis would have caused pain to the patient.

19. The Complainant alleged that the Prosthesis procured in the name of Srutilekha Dash was not implanted while a used prosthesis originally implanted in another patient – Ritika Naik had been implanted . In my view , it was a baseless allegation that the Batch Codes of the Prosthesis procured for Srutilekha Dash also did not tally and match with the Batch Codes of the Prosthesis which were later removed from Srutilekha Dash at Christian Hospital, Cuttack. It is evident from the Manual / Literature published by Howmedica that the numbers inscribed on the different parts of the Prosthesis are generic in nature and reflect the Code Number of every part as 6465 -..-. The

handwritten challan of Howmedica revealed various parts of different sizes of the Prosthesis required during the surgery of Srutilekha Dash and the Howmedica prosthesis Code No. was 6465-0-020. The contention of the Complainant in this regard is just imaginary.

20. The allegation of the Complainant about complete mismanagement during the Surgery in the Operation Theatre as both the Orthopaedic Surgeon and the Plastic Surgeon were not present at the same time is also not sustainable. It should be borne in mind that the instant surgery was a major surgery and is to be performed in two stages by the two separate teams of doctors, each headed by the Senior Surgeons. The first part of the surgery is performed by the team of Orthopaedic Surgeons who do excision of the diseased bones and implantation of the Prosthesis, then the reconstruction of the tissues around the operated area is to be done by the second Team of Plastic Surgery. Therefore, there was no need of Plastic Surgeon to be present during 1 part of surgery. The Plastic surgeon is called once the resection of tissue is required st after the job is completed by the Orthopaedic Surgeon. Such allegation of the Complainant is based on conjectures and surmises; and is therefore vague.

21. The vague allegation that no water was available for the Plastic Surgeon for scrubbing. In TMH usually the Operation Theatre Complex consists of number of operation theatres and had never a problem of water. The scrubbing areas for several adjacent Operation Theatres are common. I do not think that could have materially affected the surgery of the instant patient. I further note that as per the Operation Record, the resection of the diseased bone, implantation of the Prosthesis and reconstruction surgery was successfully done and uneventful i.e., without any complications.

22. The treating doctors at TMH have attempted it for limb salvage which in the interest of Srutilekha Dash a young girl of 16 years of age. If infection occurs, then the better option would be that the Prosthesis be removed. On 16.12.1999 the patient was evaluated at TMH and advised immediate admission for removal of Prosthesis. However, patient's father instead of admission went back home and after almost 4 -7- months, in April, 2000 at Christian Hospital, Cuttack got the Prosthesis removed and the left leg got amputed. The amputation of leg shall not be construed as a result of "irregularities" in the functioning of the OP Hospital.

23. It should be borne in mind that simply proving the suffering of ailment by the patient after the surgery does not amount to medical negligence. The Hon'ble Supreme Court has recently held in the case S. K. Jhunjhunwala Vs. Dhanwati Kaur and Anr., (2019) 2 SCC 282 that a doctor or surgeon cannot assure that the outcome of any surgery would be beneficial. The court held that a professional might be held liable for negligence either if they do not possess the requisite skills that they claimed to have, or they don't exercise the skill which they have. While referring to the judgements, the court said that the human body is like a highly complex machine and a doctor could not assure full recovery of a patient. The only assurance that such a professional can give or can be understood to have given by implication is that he is possessed of the requisite skill in that branch of the profession which they are practising and while undertaking the performance of the task entrusted to them, they would be exercising their skill with reasonable competence, court added. In other case Achutrao Harbhau Khodwa Vs. State of Maharashtra, 1996 Vol 2 643 the Hon'ble Supreme Court has held "The skill of medical practitioner differs from doctor to doctor. The nature of the profession is such that there may be more than one course of treatment which may be advisable for treating a patient. Courts would indeed be slow in attributing negligence on the part of a doctor if he has performed his duties to the best of his ability and with due care and caution. Medical opinion may differ with regard to the course of action to be taken by a doctor treating a patient, but as long as a doctor acts in a manner which is acceptable to the medical profession and a court finds that he has attended on the patient with due care

skill and diligence and if the patient still does not survive or suffers a permanent ailment, it would be difficult to hold the doctor to be guilty of negligence."

24. To conclude, the doctors at TMH have made correct diagnosis of Osteosarcoma. There was no deviation from the duty of care as the cancer specialist / operating surgeon to decide the time of operation after appropriate chemotherapy cycles and use of proper implant during surgery. Thus the treatment plan was correct as per standard of practice. The cancer surgery consumes hours and needs team of doctors including plastic surgeon whose role starts only after the removal of cancerous lesion and thus, there was no need for plastic surgeon to remain personally present throughout the surgery. It is pertinent to note that the patient died after eight months of the surgery and it was not due to any infection or any deficiency in duty of care of the treating doctor. The patient died due to metastasis in the lungs which is known in the Osteosarcoma – the aggressive malignant tumour. The expert opinion did not comment on any deviation of treatment or negligence by the doctors at TMH.

25. Based on the above discussion, it cannot be attributed to medical negligence of the treating doctors or the TMH. The impugned order to the extent it is directed against Opposite Parties No. 1 and 2 cannot be sustained and is accordingly set aside. Resultantly, F.A. No. 115 of 2010 filed by the O.P.s is allowed and F.A. No. 53 of 2010 filed by the Complainant is dismissed. Consequently the Consumer Complaint is dismissed.

26. Considering the sufferings of 16 years young girl who died of highly aggressive bone cancer (Osteosarcoma) and the loss & agony of the bereaved parents who spent two decades in the litigation, with my sympathies for the parents of deceased, let Tata Memorial Hospital extend its charity and donate the amount deposited before this commission along with accrued interest to the Complainant No.2. -8- However, it shall not be construed as a precedent in any manner. The Registry is directed to disburse the amount to the Complainant No. 2 as stated above, within 4 weeks. .... DR. S.M. KANTIKAR PRESIDING MEMBER

<u>CASE NO. 13</u>

REVISION PETITION NO. 3878 OF 2010

(Against the Order dated 30/06/2010 in Appeal No. 126/2009 of the State Commission Andhra Pradesh)

UTI INFRASTRUCTURE TECHNOLOGY & SERVICES LTD. & ORS.

UNIT TRUST OF INDIA Surabhi Arcade,

UNIT TRUST OF INDIA AMC,

UTI TECHNOLOGY SERVICES LTD. Central Processing Centre...........Petitioner(s)

Versus

U. SANDHYA SREE & ANR.

UNIT TRUST OF INDIA Surabai Arcade,

UNIT TRUST OF INDIA AMC, Financial Centre

UTI TECHNOLOGY SERVICES LTD. Central Processing Centre,

SMT. K. BHAGYA SREE, W/O. SHRI K.V.G. PRASAD...........Respondent(s)

BEFORE: HON'BLE MR. C. VISWANATH,PRESIDING MEMBER

For the Petitioner : Mr. Parveen Mehdiratta, Advocate

For the Respondent : Mr. M.S. Vijaya Prasad, GPA Holder

Dated : 08 Jan 2021

ORDER

1. This Revision Petition is filed against the order passed by Andhra Pradesh State Consumer Disputes Redressal Commission, Hyderabad (in short, "the State Commission) dated 30.06.2010 in First Appeal No.126 of 2009.

2. Facts of the case are that Respondents/Complainants are daughter of Sri MBG Shastry, who made several investments with the Opposite Parties, vide distinctive certificates of investment. Unfortunately, the legal heirs of Sri Shastry could not take possession of all these certificates as some of them were missing. Complainant No.1 received a certificate bearing No.304000010802 having 14652.015 units. Complainant No.2 received certificate bearing No.304000010000798 having 9157.509 units. There was another certificate in the name of Sri MBG Shastri without any nomination. Complainant No.1 opted for conversion of units into 6.75% tax free bonds scheme and the UTI had converted 14652.015 units into bonds by considering 5000 units as 'A' category and 9652.015 units as 'B' category, and issued a bond certificate having 1565 bonds, for which Complainant No.1 had not given any option. Opposite Parties also sent a cheque for Rs.1,46,520.15 with respect to 14652.015 'B' category units. On a Complaint regarding non-receipt of payment with respect to 'A' category units, the Opposite Parties sent a separate cheque for Rs.10,000/-. Complainant No.1 alleged that as she had not received the redemption payment of initial units covering 5000 'A' category units, the Opposite Parties should have paid at least Rs.60,000/- instead of Rs.10,000/- for settlement of lost certificate. Complainant No.2 stated that she surrendered the original investment certificate with the Opposite Parties but the Opposite Parties had not made payment for the same. Complainant No.2 further alleged that the Opposite Parties admitted the existence of another certificate of investment having 18809.524 units held by their father Sri MBG Shastri but they had not made payments against these certificates also. Complainants filed a Complaint before the District Forum with following prayer: - "a) Opposite Party is to pay the Complainant No.1, Rs.2,06,520.15ps in total for full settlement of the surrendered Bond certificate and the lost certificate of investment considered for part settlement by opposite party. - 2- b) Opposite party is to pay the penal interest @ 16% per annum from 1 June, 2003, on the amount of Rs.2,06,520.15ps for the delay in settlement st of the Bond certificate and the lost certificate of investment. c) To release the 6.75% Tax free Bond Certificate jointly in favour of complainants that is having 1980 bonds worth Rs.1,98,00=00. d) To pay with penal interest of 16% per annum, the 1 instalment of st interest due in December, 2003, 2 instalment of interest due in July, nd 2004, 3 instalment of interest due in December, 2004, 3 instalment of rd th interest due in July, 2005 and to regularize. e) To pay Rs.5000/- towards the cost of this complaint. f) To order any relief or reliefs that the Hon'ble Forum may deem fit, proper and the complainants are entitled for."

3. Complaint was contested by the Opposite Parties by filing written statement. It was stated that the investment was made by Shri MBG Shastri, vide Membership No.304000010000801 and was allotted units under US-64 Scheme. The said scheme was consolidated into ID No.716141069. Opposite Parties further stated that as the Complainants have already availed repurchase under special package rate for Rs.5000 units, the relief sought by them was totally baseless and misconceived and the Complaint was liable to be dismissed.

4. The District Forum after hearing the Parties and perusing the material on record allowed the Complaint, vide order dated 12.09.2007 with the following observation:- "In the result, the complaint is allowed by directing the opposite parties to refund an amount of Rs.1,56,500/- with interest at 16% p.a. from 07-08-1999 till the date of realization to the complainants and also pay Rs.5,000/- towards costs of the complaint. The above order shall be complied within one month from the date of receipt of copy of this order."

5. Against the order of the District Forum, Opposite Parties filed an Appeal before the State Commission. The State Commission after hearing the parties, affirmed the order of the District Forum on merits. However, the State Commission reduced the rate of interest from 16% to 9%.

6. Aggrieved by the order of the State Commission, Petitioners/Opposite Parties have filed the present Revision Petition. Heard the Learned Counsel for the Petitioners and Mr. M.S. Vijaya Prasad, GPA holder on behalf of the Respondents/Complainants and carefully perused the record.

7. Learned Counsel for the Petitioners submitted that since the Respondents/Complainants failed to give any option in respect of their balance amount, the Petitioners converted all units into -3- Tax Free US-64 bonds carrying 6.75% interest and the Petitioners issued the respective bonds to the Respondents. Petitioners also paid the due amounts to the Respondents and the payments had been received by them.

8. Mr. M.S. Vijaya Prasad, GPA holder on behalf of the Respondents submitted that the Opposite Parties paid only Rs.10,000/- for settlement of lost certificate instead of Rs.60,000/-. He further submitted that the Opposite Parties failed to make payment of the investment certificate surrendered by Complainant No.2. It was also submitted that the orders passed by both the Fora below are justified and Revision Petition be dismissed.

9. Brief facts of the case are that father of the Complainants, Sri MBG Shastry, made several investments with the Opposite Parties, vide distinctive certificates of investment. Unfortunately, the legal heirs of Sri Shastry could not take possession of all these certificates as some of them were missing. Complainant No.1 received a certificate bearing No.304000010802 having 14652.015 units. Complainant No.2 received certificate bearing No.304000010000798 having 9157.509 units. There was another certificate in the name of Sri MBG Shastri without any nomination. Complainant No.1 opted for conversion of units into 6.75% tax free bonds scheme and the UTI had converted 14652.015 units into bonds by considering 5000 units as 'A' category and 9652.015 units as 'B' category, and issued a bond certificate having 1565 bonds, for which Complainant No.1 had not given any option. Opposite Parties also sent a cheque for Rs.1,46,520.15 with respect to 14652.015 'B' category units. On a Complaint regarding non-receipt of payment with respect to 'A' category units, the Opposite Parties sent a separate cheque for Rs.10,000/-. Complainant No.1 alleged that as she had not received the redemption payment of initial units covering 5000 'A' category units, the Opposite Parties should have paid at least Rs.60,000/- instead of Rs.10,000/- for settlement of lost certificate. Complainant No.2 stated that she surrendered the original investment certificate with the Opposite Parties but they had not made payment against that certificate also.

10. District Forum after hearing Parties and perusing the record, observed that the Opposite Parties had condensed 5000 units as "A" category valued at Rs.12/- per unit. The remaining 9652.015 units were valued at Rs.10/- per unit. The Opposite Parties mentioned that the number of units are 1.565 having a face value of Rs.100/-, the value of bond certificate amounting to Rs.1,56,000/-. If these bond certificates are discharged, the amount comes to Rs.1,56,000/-. Though the Opposite Parties stated that the Complainant had already availed repurchase under special package rate for Rs.5,000/- units, they failed to file any documents to show that the Complainants have already availed repurchase under special package rate. In the absence of any documents, The District Forum held that the contention of the Complainant had to be believed and the Opposite Parties have to refund an amount of Rs.1,56,000/- to the complainants with interest at 16% p.a. These facts and view of the District Forum were concurred by the State Commission.

11. On facts, there are concurrent findings of both the Fora below. However, the State Commission rightly modified the order of the District Forum reducing the amount of

interest from 16% to 9% p.a, as the interest awarded by the District Forum was on the higher side.

12. Jurisdiction of this Commission under Section 21 (b) is very limited. This Commission is not required to re-appreciate and reassess the evidences and reach to its own conclusion. The Court can intervene only when the petitioner succeeds in showing that the Fora below has -4- wrongly exercised its jurisdiction or there is a miscarriage of justice. It was so held by the Hon'ble Supreme Court in the case of Mrs. Rubi (Chandra) Dutta Vs. M/s United India Insurance Co. Ltd . (2011) 11 SCC 269 has held as under: - "13. Also, it is to be noted that the revisional powers of the National Commission are derived from Section 21 (b) of the Act, under which the said power can be exercised only if there is some prima facie jurisdictional error appearing in the impugned order, and only then, may the same be set aside. In our considered opinion there was no jurisdictional error or miscarriage of justice, which could have warranted the National Commission to have taken a different view than what was taken by the two Forums. The decision of the National Commission rests not on the basis of some legal principle that was ignored by the Courts below, but on a different (and in our opinion, an erroneous) interpretation of the same set of facts. This is not the manner in which revisional powers should be invoked. In this view of the matter, we are of the considered opinion that the jurisdiction conferred on the National Commission under Section 21 (b) of the Act has been transgressed. It was not a case where such a view could have been taken by setting aside the concurrent findings of two fora."

13. Same principle has been reiterated by Hon'ble Supreme Court in the case of Lourdes Society Snehanjali Girls Hostel and Ors. Vs. H & R Johnson (India) Ltd. and Ors. (2016 8 SCC 286 wherein Hon'ble Supreme Court has held as under:- "23. The National Commission has to exercise the jurisdiction vested in it only if the State Commission or the District Forum has failed to exercise their jurisdiction or exercised when the same was not vested in their or exceeded their jurisdiction by acting illegally or with material irregularity. In the instant case, the National Commission has certainly exceeded its jurisdiction by setting aside the concurrent finding of fact recorded in the order passed by the State Commission which is based upon valid and cogent reasons."

14. I see no reason to disagree with the concurrent findings of both the Fora below. There is no infirmity or illegality in the impugned order, warranting interference under Section 21 (b) of the Consumer Protection Act, 1986. Revision Petition is dismissed with no order as to costs. .... C. VISWANATH PRESIDING MEMBER

CASE NO. 14
REVISION PETITION NO. 4021 OF 2014

(Against the Order dated 22/09/2014 in Appeal No. 1235/2011 of the State Commission Punjab)

ANKUR SEEDS PVT. LTD............Petitioner(s)

Versus

RAM PRAKASH & ANR S/O BANWARILAL,

M/S KUKKAR TRADING COMPANY,...........Respondent(s)

REVISION PETITION NO. 4022 OF 2014

(Against the Order dated 22/09/2014 in Appeal No. 1236/2011 of the State Commission Punjab)

ANKUR SEEDS PVT. LTD............Petitioner(s)

Versus

HARI KISHAN & ANR. S/O DILSUKH RAM,

M/S KUKKAR TRADING COMPANY,...........Respondent(s)

REVISION PETITION NO. 4023 OF 2014 -1-

(Against the Order dated 22/09/2014 in Appeal No. 1237/2011 of the State Commission Punjab)

ANKUR SEEDS PVT. LTD. ....Petitioner(s)

Versus

BRIJLAL & ANR.

M/S KUKKAR TRADING COMPANY,...........Respondent(s)

REVISION PETITION NO. 4024 OF 2014 (Against the Order dated 22/09/2014 in Appeal No. 1720/2011 of the State Commission Punjab)

ANKUR SEEDS PVT. LTD...........Petitioner(s)

Versus

DHARAMVIR & ANR. S/O AMAR SINGH,

MUNSHI RAM ,S/O MADANLAL,...........Respondent(s)

BEFORE: HON'BLE MR. JUSTICE R.K. AGRAWAL,PRESIDENT HON'BLE DR. S.M. KANTIKAR,MEMBER

For the Petitioner :

For the Respondent : -2-

Dated : 08 Jan 2021

ORDER

Appeared at the time of arguments through video conferencing For

Petitioner : Mr. J. L. Bhoot, Advocate

For Respondent No. 1 : Mr. Pradeep Dahiya, Advocate

For Respondent No. 2 : NEMO

Pronounced on: 8 January 2021

ORDER

PER DR. S. M. KANTIKAR, MEMBER

1. By this Order, we propose to dispose of the above noted Revision Petitions involving similar question of law and fact arising out of common Order of the State Consumer Disputes Redressal Commission Punjab (hereinafter referred to as the "State Commission") dated 22.09.2014 in Appeal Nos. 1235, 1236, 1237 & 1720 of 2011.

2. The facts are that the Respondents/Complainants are the agriculturalists. They purchased the seeds developed and manufactured by Ankur Seeds Pvt. Ltd. (hereinafter referred to as the "Opposite Party No. 1") and Rashi Seeds (P) Ltd. (hereinafter referred to as the "Opposite Party No. 3") through their respective dealers. The Opposite Party No. 3 has not been made a party in the instant Revision Petitions. The Complainants purchased the seeds on assurance by the dealers of the Petitioner that the seeds were of good quality and would yield crop of about 10 quintals per acre and that the crop from the said seeds would be immune to "Leaf Curl Virus", other diseases and insects etc. As per instructions, they sowed the seeds and also used right quantity of pesticides and fertilisers. However, the growth of crop was not proper, it gave very less fruits bearing and suffered from "Leaf Curl Virus". The Complainant and the respective dealers admitted that there was less growth of crop and less yield. The Complainant filed a Complaint with the Agriculture Officer, who visited the site and observed in his report that the loss caused to the crop was due to "Leaf Curl Virus" and that the farmers had suffered monetary loss. However, the Petitioner failed to pay any compensation to the respective Complainants. Being aggrieved, the Complainants approached the District Consumer Disputes Redressal Forum, Firozpur (hereinafter referred to as the "District Forum") for the compensation.

3. The Opposite Parties in their respective Written Version admitted the sale of seeds to the Complainants. It was, however, denied that any assurance as to yield was given. The Opposite Parties pleaded that yield of crop depends upon so many external and environmental factors like -3- agriculture practice, application of seed rate, climatic condition, water intervals, sowing of seeds in depth, attack of pests and diseases, doses of fertilizers/pesticides, soil and water, etc. It was further alleged that as per the report of the Agriculture Officer, plants were suffering from "Leaf Curl Virus", which is caused by white fly transmitted virus and it has nothing to do with the quality of seed.

4. The District Forum, Ferozepur vide respective Orders, allowed the Complaints and awarded compensation to the respective Respondents/Complainants. Being aggrieved by the Orders of the District Forum, the Petitioner/Opposite Party No. 1 preferred Appeals before the State Commission Punjab, which were dismissed vide common Order dated 22.09.2014 concurred with the Order of the District Forum. Thus, these present Revision Petitions.

5. The learned Counsel for the Petitioner vehemently argued that this Commission allowed number of similar Revision Petitions filed by the different Seed Cos. and dismissed the Complaints. In his support, the Counsel relied upon the following judgments of this Commission: i. Mahyco Vegetable Seeds Ltd. Vs. Ishwarbhai Baburao Thakare & Ors. , R.P. No. 4319 of 2012, decided on 05.01.2016; ii. Maharashtra Hybrid Seeds Co. Ltd. Vs. Garapati Srinivas Rao & Anr. , R.P. No. 2602 of 2008 & Ors., decided on 12.02.2014; iii. Mahyco Vegetable Seeds Ltd. vs. B. Yedukondalu & Ors. , R.P. No. 2272 of 2010 & Ors., decided on 27.04.2011; iv. Syngenta India Ltd. vs. P. Chowdaiah & Ors. , R.P. No. 1451 of 2011 & Ors., decided on 31.07.2013; v. Mahyco Monsanto Bio Tech (India) Ltd. vs. Doddabasappa & Ors. , R.P. No. 3800 of 2006, decided on 10.04.2012; vi. Mahyco Seeds Ltd. vs. G. Venkata Subba Reddy & Ors. , III (2011) CPJ 99 (NC); vii. Syngenta India Ltd. (earlier Novartis India Ltd.) vs. Velaga Narasimha Rao & Ors. , IV (2010) CPJ 119 (NC); viii. Sonekaran Gladioli Growers vs. Babu Ram , II (2005) CPJ 94 (NC); ix. M/s Rasi Seeds Pvt. Ltd. vs. Hari Kishan & Ors. , R.P. No. 403 of 2013, decided on 29.03.2016; x. M/s. Rasi Seeds Pvt. Ltd. vs. Ram Prakash & Ors. , R.P. No. 404 of 2013, decided on 29.03.2016 and xi. Indian Farmers Fertilizers Co-operative Ltd. vs. Jagdish , R.P. No. 2143 of 2014, decided on 09.04.2015

6. We have gone through the recent Orders passed by the coordinate Bench of this Commission in Revision Petitions Nos. 403 of 2013 & 404 of 2013, wherein the Revision -4- Petitions were allowed and Complainants were dismissed. It is pertinent to note that in the above Revision Petitions filed by M/s Rashi Seeds Pvt. Ltd., the Complainants - Ram Prakash and Hari Kishan were Respondent no. 1 in the Revision Petitions respectively, who were the Opposite Party No. 3 in the Original Consumer Complaints filed before the District Forum, Firozpur. The coordinate Bench allowed both the Revision Petitions by observing as below: " 10. We have gone through the brochure of OP No.2 placed on record. The brochure states that OP No.2 has established its name in northern India because it has the following features: "1. Best ability for every kind of soil and environmental conditions. 2. Less hoeing cost for prevention of weed. 3. Lesser need of irrigation 4. Production of good quality and good cost in the market. 5. Best ability for cotton and wheat crop cycle 6. Easy to keep" It also assures that seeds Rasi 134 are choice of million of farmers because it has : "1. Good height and dispersion 2. Effective prevention from grasshopper boll weevil (Pied, American boll weevil, Pink boll weevil) 3. Maximum yielding power 4. Continuous appearance of Flower, Stalk." 11. The brochure also give helpful advice for increase of production of rasi boldguard hybrid cotton varieties with regard to inspection of soil and water prior to sowing, preparation of bed of seed, the distance to be maintained, use of fertilizer. It also contains an advice regarding the pesticides to be used for jassid control, white fly control, spodoptra control and for wilt and tirak. Nowhere in the brochure, do we find any mention that seeds were resistant to whitefly infestation and the resultant "Leaf Curl Virus" or any guarantee of minimum yield 12. xxxx 13. There is no cogent evidence on record to show that the complainants took preventive steps to protect the crop from white flies which are the causes of Leaf Curl Virus disease, which obviously was the cause for less yield of the crop. The Fora below have ignored the above aspect of the case and have relied primarily on oral evidence of -5- the respondents/complainants instead of the documents on record. The Fora below have relied primarily on the oral evidence of the respondent complainants instead of documents on record to conclude that the seeds manufactured by OP2 were defective and more susceptible to "Leaf Curl

Virus" in comparison to other varieties of seeds. The brochure of OP-2 nowhere states that the seeds are resistant to "Leaf Curl Virus" and the complainants had the choice to purchase other variety of seeds if they were aware that they were resistant to this disease. Hence, we allow the revision petitions, set aside the impugned orders and dismiss the complaints. " (extracts from the Order in R.P. No. 403 of 2013 dated 29.03.2016)

7. On the basis of the foregoing discussion, we don't differ with the decision of the coordinate Bench of this Commission and set aside the impugned Order of the State Commission. Consequently, the respective Complaints are dismissed. However, there shall be no order as to costs. ....J R.K. AGRAWAL PRESIDENT .... DR. S.M. KANTIKAR MEMBER

<u>CASE NO. 15</u>
REVISION PETITION NO. 4021 OF 2014

(Against the Order dated 22/09/2014 in Appeal No. 1235/2011 of the State Commission Punjab)
ANKUR SEEDS PVT. LTD............Petitioner(s)

Versus

RAM PRAKASH & ANR S/O BANWARILAL,

M/S KUKKAR TRADING COMPANY,...........Respondent(s)

REVISION PETITION NO. 4022 OF 2014

(Against the Order dated 22/09/2014 in Appeal No. 1236/2011 of the State Commission Punjab)
ANKUR SEEDS PVT. LTD. ....Petitioner(s)

Versus

HARI KISHAN & ANR. S/O DILSUKH RAM,

M/S KUKKAR TRADING COMPANY,...........Respondent(s)

REVISION PETITION NO. 4023 OF 2014 -1-

(Against the Order dated 22/09/2014 in Appeal No. 1237/2011 of the State Commission Punjab)
ANKUR SEEDS PVT. LTD...........Petitioner(s)

Versus

BRIJLAL & ANR.

M/S KUKKAR TRADING COMPANY,...........Respondent(s)

REVISION PETITION NO. 4024 OF 2014

(Against the Order dated 22/09/2014 in Appeal No. 1720/2011 of the State Commission Punjab)
ANKUR SEEDS PVT. LTD............Petitioner(s)

Versus

DHARAMVIR & ANR. S/O AMAR SINGH,

MUNSHI RAM ,S/O MADANLAL, ...Respondent(s)

BEFORE: HON'BLE MR. JUSTICE R.K. AGRAWAL,PRESIDENT HON'BLE DR. S.M. KANTIKAR,MEMBER

For the Petitioner :

For the Respondent : -2-

Dated : 08 Jan 2021

ORDER

Appeared at the time of arguments through video conferencing

For Petitioner : Mr. J. L. Bhoot, Advocate

For Respondent No. 1 : Mr. Pradeep Dahiya, Advocate

For Respondent No. 2 : NEMO

Pronounced on: 8 January 2021

ORDER

PER DR. S. M. KANTIKAR, MEMBER

1. By this Order, we propose to dispose of the above noted Revision Petitions involving similar question of law and fact arising out of common Order of the State Consumer Disputes Redressal Commission Punjab (hereinafter referred to as the "State Commission") dated 22.09.2014 in Appeal Nos. 1235, 1236, 1237 & 1720 of 2011.

2. The facts are that the Respondents/Complainants are the agriculturalists. They purchased the seeds developed and manufactured by Ankur Seeds Pvt. Ltd. (hereinafter referred to as the "Opposite Party No. 1") and Rashi Seeds (P) Ltd. (hereinafter referred to as the "Opposite Party No. 3") through their respective dealers. The Opposite Party No. 3 has not been made a party in the instant Revision Petitions. The Complainants purchased the seeds on assurance by the dealers of the Petitioner that the seeds were of good quality and would yield crop of about 10 quintals per acre and that the crop from the said seeds would be immune to "Leaf Curl Virus", other diseases and insects etc. As per instructions, they sowed the seeds and also used right quantity of pesticides and fertilisers. However, the growth of crop was not proper, it gave very less fruits bearing and suffered from "Leaf Curl Virus". The Complainant and the respective dealers admitted that there was less growth of crop and less yield. The Complainant filed a Complaint with the Agriculture Officer, who visited the site and observed in his report that the loss caused to the crop was due to "Leaf Curl Virus" and that the farmers had suffered monetary loss. However, the Petitioner failed to pay any compensation to the respective Complainants. Being aggrieved, the Complainants approached the District Consumer Disputes Redressal Forum, Firozpur (hereinafter referred to as the "District Forum") for the compensation.

3. The Opposite Parties in their respective Written Version admitted the sale of seeds to the Complainants. It was, however, denied that any assurance as to yield was given. The Opposite Parties pleaded that yield of crop depends upon so many external and environmental factors like -3- agriculture practice, application of seed rate, climatic condition, water intervals, sowing of seeds in depth, attack of pests and diseases, doses of fertilizers/pesticides, soil and water, etc. It was further alleged that as per the report of the Agriculture Officer, plants were suffering from "Leaf Curl Virus", which is caused by white fly transmitted virus and it has nothing to do with the quality of seed.

4. The District Forum, Ferozepur vide respective Orders, allowed the Complaints and awarded compensation to the respective Respondents/Complainants. Being aggrieved by the Orders of the District Forum, the Petitioner/Opposite Party No. 1 preferred Appeals before the State Commission Punjab, which were dismissed vide common Order dated 22.09.2014 concurred with the Order of the District Forum. Thus, these present Revision Petitions.

5. The learned Counsel for the Petitioner vehemently argued that this Commission allowed number of similar Revision Petitions filed by the different Seed Cos. and dismissed the Complaints. In his support, the Counsel relied upon the following judgments of this Commission: i. Mahyco Vegetable Seeds Ltd. Vs. Ishwarbhai Baburao Thakare & Ors. , R.P. No. 4319 of 2012, decided on 05.01.2016; ii. Maharashtra Hybrid Seeds Co. Ltd. Vs. Garapati Srinivas Rao & Anr. , R.P. No. 2602 of 2008 & Ors., decided on 12.02.2014; iii. Mahyco Vegetable Seeds Ltd. vs. B. Yedukondalu & Ors. , R.P. No. 2272 of 2010 & Ors., decided on 27.04.2011; iv. Syngenta India Ltd. vs. P. Chowdaiah & Ors. , R.P. No. 1451 of 2011 & Ors., decided on 31.07.2013; v. Mahyco Monsanto Bio Tech (India) Ltd. vs. Doddabasappa & Ors. , R.P. No. 3800 of 2006, decided on 10.04.2012; vi. Mahyco Seeds Ltd. vs. G. Venkata Subba Reddy & Ors. , III (2011) CPJ 99 (NC); vii. Syngenta India Ltd. (earlier Novartis India Ltd.) vs. Velaga Narasimha Rao & Ors. , IV (2010) CPJ 119 (NC); viii. Sonekaran Gladioli Growers vs. Babu Ram , II (2005) CPJ 94 (NC); ix. M/s Rasi Seeds Pvt. Ltd. vs. Hari Kishan & Ors. , R.P. No. 403 of 2013, decided on 29.03.2016; x. M/s. Rasi Seeds Pvt. Ltd. vs. Ram Prakash & Ors. , R.P. No. 404 of 2013, decided on

29.03.2016 and xi. Indian Farmers Fertilizers Co-operative Ltd. vs. Jagdish , R.P. No. 2143 of 2014, decided on 09.04.2015

6. We have gone through the recent Orders passed by the coordinate Bench of this Commission in Revision Petitions Nos. 403 of 2013 & 404 of 2013, wherein the Revision -4- Petitions were allowed and Complainants were dismissed. It is pertinent to note that in the above Revision Petitions filed by M/s Rashi Seeds Pvt. Ltd., the Complainants - Ram Prakash and Hari Kishan were Respondent no. 1 in the Revision Petitions respectively, who were the Opposite Party No. 3 in the Original Consumer Complaints filed before the District Forum, Firozpur. The coordinate Bench allowed both the Revision Petitions by observing as below: " 10. We have gone through the brochure of OP No.2 placed on record. The brochure states that OP No.2 has established its name in northern India because it has the following features: "1. Best ability for every kind of soil and environmental conditions. 2. Less hoeing cost for prevention of weed. 3. Lesser need of irrigation 4. Production of good quality and good cost in the market. 5. Best ability for cotton and wheat crop cycle 6. Easy to keep" It also assures that seeds Rasi 134 are choice of million of farmers because it has : "1. Good height and dispersion 2. Effective prevention from grasshopper boll weevil (Pied, American boll weevil, Pink boll weevil) 3. Maximum yielding power 4. Continuous appearance of Flower, Stalk." 11. The brochure also give helpful advice for increase of production of rasi boldguard hybrid cotton varieties with regard to inspection of soil and water prior to sowing, preparation of bed of seed, the distance to be maintained, use of fertilizer. It also contains an advice regarding the pesticides to be used for jassid control, white fly control, spodoptra control and for wilt and tirak. Nowhere in the brochure, do we find any mention that seeds were resistant to whitefly infestation and the resultant "Leaf Curl Virus" or any guarantee of minimum yield 12. xxxx 13. There is no cogent evidence on record to show that the complainants took preventive steps to protect the crop from white flies which are the causes of Leaf Curl Virus disease, which obviously was the cause for less yield of the crop. The Fora below have ignored the above aspect of the case and have relied primarily on oral evidence of -5- the respondents/complainants instead of the documents on record. The Fora below have relied primarily on the oral evidence of the respondent complainants instead of documents on record to conclude that the seeds manufactured by OP2 were defective and more susceptible to "Leaf Curl Virus" in comparison to other varieties of seeds. The brochure of OP-2 nowhere states that the seeds are resistant to "Leaf Curl Virus" and the complainants had the choice to purchase other variety of seeds if they were aware that they were resistant to this disease. Hence, we allow the revision petitions, set aside the impugned orders and dismiss the complaints. " (extracts from the Order in R.P. No. 403 of 2013 dated 29.03.2016)

7. On the basis of the foregoing discussion, we don't differ with the decision of the coordinate Bench of this Commission and set aside the impugned Order of the State Commission. Consequently, the respective Complaints are dismissed. However, there shall be no order as to costs. ....J R.K. AGRAWAL PRESIDENT .... DR. S.M. KANTIKAR MEMBER

CASE NO. 16
REVISION PETITION NO. 439 OF 2015

(Against the Order dated 10/06/2014 in Appeal No. 782/2012 of the State Commission Punjab)

AMANDEEP HOSPITAL MODEL TOWN,...........Petitioner(s)

Versus

DARSHAN SINGH & 3 ORS. S/O SAUDAGAR SINGH

M.D. INDIA HEALTHCARE SERVICES PRIVATE LIMITED THROUGH ITS AUTHORIZED OFFICER MOHALI PUNJAB.

ICICI LOMBARD, HEALTH INSURANCE HAVING THROUGH ITS BRANCH MANAGER/ M.D.

THE CHAND BHAN, MULTIPURPOSE COOPERATIVE AGRICULTURE SERVICE SOCIETY LIMITED..........Respondent(s)

BEFORE: HON'BLE MR. JUSTICE R.K. AGRAWAL,PRESIDENT HON'BLE DR. S.M. KANTIKAR,MEMBER -1-

For the Petitioner :

For the Respondent :

Dated : 08 Jan 2021

ORDER

APPEARED AT THE TIME OF ARGUMENTS THROUGH VIDEO CONFERENCING

For Petitioner : Mr. Raktim Gogoi, Advocate

For Respondents : Mr. Gagan Gupta, Advocate for R-1

Mr. Yogesh Malhotra, Advocate for R-3 NEMO

for R-2 & R-4

Pronounced on: 8 January 2021

ORDER

PER DR. S. M. KANTIKAR, MEMBER

1. The present Revision Petition is against the impugned Order dated 10.06.2014 passed by the Punjab State Consumer Disputes Redressal Commission, Chandigarh (hereinafter referred to as the "State Commission") whereby the First Appeal filed by Petitioner was dismissed and the Order dated 25.04.2012 passed by the District Consumer Disputes Redressal Forum, Faridkot (hereinafter referred to as the "District Forum") was upheld, while inter alia upholding that there was nothing on record to show that the Petitioner was not an enlisted hospital under the Scheme and the act of Petitioner amounting to fleecing the patients.

2. For the convenience, the Parties are referred to the positions as stated in the Original Complaint filed before the District Forum.

3. Brief facts of the case are that the Complainant Darshan Singh was a member of The Chand Bhan Multipurpose Cooperative Agriculture Service Society Ltd – the Opposite Party No.4 (hereinafter referred to as the 'Society'). He got himself insured with ICICI Lombard, Health Insurance (the Opposite Party No. 2) under the Scheme named "Bhai Ghanya Sehat Sewa Scheme" (hereinafter referred to as the "Scheme") vide Policy No. 4016/00004117. The Scheme was valid for the period 01.02.2010 to 31.01.2011. Under the Scheme, the insured Complainant -2- was entitled to get free treatment in empaneled hospitals. For some spinal cord problems, from 30.05.2010 to 11.06.2010 Complainant was admitted in Amandeep Hospital – the Petitioner / the Opposite Party No. 3 and spent Rs. 3,50,000/-. The complainant alleged that at the time of admission the Petitioner /Opposite Party No.3 had promised that it would give all the benefits under the Scheme and later on refused to give those benefits. Also the Insurance Company the Opposite Party No. 2 did not reimburse the treatment expenses. Being aggrieved, the Complainant filed a Complaint against the Opposite Parties i.e. Insurance Company, the Hospital and the Co-op Society.

4. The Hospital/ Opposite Party No. 3 filed a Written Version and denied the allegations. It was contended that the hospital was a partner hospital with Bhai Ghanya Sehat Sewa Scheme up to 30.09.2009 only. Thereafter, the Opposite Party No. 3 never signed any fresh MOU with concerned authorities for the new scheme which commenced from 01.02.2010 till 31.01.2011. The Complainant was admitted during that period; therefore the Opposite Party No. 3 was not liable to give cashless facility to the Complainant.

54

5. The Opposite Parties No.1 and 2 have neither appeared nor filed any reply despite service of notice. The District Forum, after hearing the Complainant and the Opposite Parties Nos. 3 & 4 passed an ex-parte order against the Opposite Parties Nos. 1 & 2. District Forum ordered the Opposite Party No. 3 to refund Rs. 1,50,000/- to the Complainant on account of medical treatment and Rs. 30,000/- as compensation on account of mental agony within 30 days from the date of receipt of the copy of the order. It observed: 11. We have perused the evidence adduced by the complainant, by the opposite party No. 3 in this regard. Nowhere it has come on record that on the day of admission of the patient on the day of complainant having fallen ill i.e 26.4.2010 and thereafter having undertaken various investigations and treatment etc. The complainant was admitted in the hospital of the opposite party No. 3 on 3.5.2010 to 11.6.2010. Thus, from 3.5.2010 to 11.6.2010 is the period which is very important for us to know whether the hospital i.e opposite party No. 3 was the enlisted hospital or not. Nothing has come on record to prove the stand of the opposite party No. 3 i.e it was not a enlisted hospital. On the contrary, the counsel for the complainant in order to assist the Forum has taken out the print from the Internet showing the list of cashless hospitals in District Amritsar under Bhai Ghanyha Sehat Sewa Scheme and name of the hospital still exist as an empaneled hospital at Sr. No.21 of the said list. This list has been downloaded on 18.4.2012 . The counsel for the opposite party No. 3 could not bring anything on record to rebut the list so dated 18.4.2012 printed. 12. In view of the aforesaid facts and circumstances the complaint filed by the complainant is allowed. The amount of bills which were filed by the complainant Ex. C- 4 to Ex. C- 59 is Rs. 1,83,095/- but as the limit of treatment of a member in the Bhai Ghanya Sehat Sewa Scheme is Rs. 1,50,000/- as mentioned in the Guide Book and List of Network Hospitals Ex. C- 3 but the complainant has not filed the complete Guide Book and only filed the cover note of this Book so we take the assistance of earlier decided case titled as "Harbans Singh Versus Nagpal Hospital and others" decided on 28.3.2012 in which the complete Guide Book and List of Network Hospitals was filed by the opposite parties in which it is clearly mentioned that in one calendar year one family is entitled to avail the cashless facility maximum up to Rs. 1,50,000/- only and not actual expenditure of Rs. 1,83,095/- as per the bills attached. (relevant extracts of paras 11 & 12 of the District Forum's Order) -3-

6. Being aggrieved, the Opposite Party No. 3 appealed to the State Commission. The State Commission, after hearing both the sides and perusal of records, dismissed the Appeal with following observation: 9. It is an admitted fact that the name of opposite party No.3- Hospital is appearing in the guidebook and in the list of network hospitals issued by the Sheme. In order to substantiate its plea that it ceased to be a partner hospital with the Scheme with effect from 30.9.2009, it proved on record notice dated 8.6.2010 Ex. R- 2, which was sent by it to the Scheme and others. The notice was so given for deleting its name from the list of partner hospitals of the Scheme on the ground that the MOU had not been signed by it after 30.9.2009 and such MOU for the Scheme, which commenced from 1.2.2010 to 31.1.2011, was never signed by it. It also proved the letter dated 17.8.2010 written to it by opposite party No. 2- Insurance Company as Ex. R- 3. Vide that letter, it was informed that the name of the hospital has been removed from the list of network of hospitals for cashless hospitalization and that public notice to that effect has already been given in the newspaper "Punjabi Tribune" on 6.5.2010. From this evidence it stands proved that on the day the complainant was admitted in this hospital, it was not a partner hospital under the Scheme. 10. That may be so , but the complainant has come with a specific plea that at the time he was admitted this opposite party had promised that it would give all the benefits under the Scheme and later on refused to give those benefits. That plea was duly substantiated by the complainant by means of his affidavits Ex. C- 1, Ex. C- 7 and Ex. C- 61. No doubt, the opposite party pleaded in its written reply that such a promise was never extended to the complainant but it has failed to prove that fact. No doubt, affidavit of Amandeep Kaur, Proprietor/

Director of this hospital is proved as Ex. R-1 but that is not a valid affidavit in the eyes of law as only the written reply has been given the form of an affidavit. She has not specifically deposed about the facts. Therefore, the evidence produced by the complainant that such a promise was extended to him at the time of his admission has remained unrebutted. By virtue of that promise this opposite party is estopped from taking up the plea that it is not liable to reimburse the complainant for the medical expenses incurred by him. It was duty bound to disclose to the complainant at the time of admission that it had ceased to be the partner hospital of the Scheme. Had that information been given he might have gone to some other empanelled hospital for his treatment. The said act of opposite party No. 3 is nothing but an act of fleecing the patients. The District Forum did not commit any illegality or infirmity while passing the impugned order against this opposite party. We do not find any merit in this appeal and the same is hereby dismissed. (paras 9 & 10 of the State Commission's Order)

7. Being aggrieved by the Order of the State Commission, the Opposite Party No. 3 has filed the present Revision Petition.

8. We have heard both the Parties. Perused the material on record.

9. The record shows the Complainant's hospitalization claim was for date 3.5.2010 to 11.6.2010, whereas the Petitioner Amandeep Hospital was ceased to be an empaneled hospital from 30.9.2009. We note that both the fora have not considered the terms and conditions of the Insurance Policy and decided the matter ex-parte against the Principal Insurer M.D. India Healthcare Services Pvt. Ltd. (Opposite Party No. 1) and ICICI Lombard, Health Insurance (Opposite Party No. 2). In our considered view, the evidence of Principal Insurer is necessary before deciding the instant matter. Moreover, both the Fora have failed to observe that why the -4- name of Amandeep Hospital (Petitioner) was reflecting in the Guide Book/ brochure of the Insurance Company under empaneled hospitals which ceased to be an empaneled hospital from 30.9.2009.

10. In the interest of justice, and for holistic and comprehensive adjudication of the case on merit in the forum of original jurisdiction (District Forum), we set aside the Orders of both the fora below and remand the matter back to the District Forum. The Insurance Companies (Opposite Parties Nos. 1 & 2) are allowed one (more) opportunity to file their Written Version before the District Forum.

11. The Opposite Parties Nos. 1 & 2 are sternly advised to conduct their case professionally before the District Forum.

12. All parties are directed to appear before the District Forum on 22.02.2021.

13. The District Forum is requested to take the Written Version of the Opposite Parties Nos. 1 & 2 on record, if duly filed, to give opportunity to the Complainants to file their rejoinder thereto, and to proceed further with the adjudication of the case in the normal wont as per the law.

14. The District Forum (Commission) is requested to decide the matter within three months from today. 15. The Revision Petition so disposed. 16. The Registry is directed to send a copy of this Order to the District Forum within ten days. ....J R.K. AGRAWAL PRESIDENT .... DR. S.M. KANTIKAR MEMBER

<u>CASE NO. 17</u>
REVISION PETITION NO. 3945 OF 2011

(Against the Order dated 31/10/2011 in Appeal No. 3/2011 of the State Commission West Bengal)

MANAGER, INDUSLAND BANK LTD. & ANR.

The Branch Manager, Indusland Bank Ltd

The Branch Manager, Indusland Bank Ltd H/O Sahadev Mondal...........Petitioner(s)

Versus

ABANI KANTA DAS & ANR. S/o Sri Anil Kumar Das

Sri Badal Samanta, S/o Late Amulya Samanta ....Respondent(s)

BEFORE: HON'BLE MR. C. VISWANATH,PRESIDING MEMBER

For the Petitioner : Mr. Rana Ranjit, Advocate

For the Respondent : For the Respondent No.1 : Mr.Somraj Gangopadhyay, Advocate (Ex-parte vide order dated 25.07.2013)

For the Respondent No.2 : NEMO (Ex-parte vide order dated 20.01.2015) Dated : 11 Jan 2021 ORDER -1-

ORDER

1. The present Revision Petition has been filed by the Petitioners against order dated 31.10.2011 of the West Bengal State Consumer Disputes Redressal Commission (for short "State Commission") in FA/3/2011 wherein the Appeal filed by the Petitioners was dismissed.

2. 2. Case of the Complainant is that the Complainant purchased a ten-wheeler truck of Ashok Leyland Ltd. bearing registration no. WB29/6162, chassis no. WDE-545847, and engine no. DWE 406960 financed by OP No. 1 through OP No. 2. The Complainant entered into an agreement with OP No. 1 and accordingly OP No. 1 and 2 sanctioned a loan of Rs.9,15,000/-. As per the terms and conditions of the agreement, the Complainant deposited a sum of Rs.82,687/- with Opposite Parties Nos.1 and 2 as margin money. The Complainant was supposed to repay a sum of Rs.11,57,700/- in 47 instalments @ Rs.24,720 w.e.f. 24.02.2005. Thereafter, when it came to the notice of the Complainant that the Registration Certificate bore the name of Opposite Party No.3 as a joint registered owner, on enquiry, Opposite Party No. 3 informed him that he had incurred an expenditure of Rs.45,000/- from his own pocket in order to get the loan sanctioned in favour of the Complainant and as and when the Complainant would repay the same, he would take necessary steps to remove his name from the Registration Certificate. Later, although the Complainant paid Rs.45,000/- to Opposite Party No.3 in two instalments, Opposite Party No.3 took no steps to delete his name from the Registration Certificate. On 05.04.2008, Opposite Party No.3 detained the vehicle by force and removed its tyres to render it defunct. According to the Complainant, Opposite Parties, in collusion with each other, seized the vehicle on 01.05.2008. On 01.05.2008, Opposite Party No.2 sent a letter to the Complainant to repay Rs.1,05,000/-, although the Complainant did not owe any money to Opposite Parties Nos. 1 and 2. Complainant had so far paid Rs10,27,610 to Opposite Parties Nos. 1 and 2. A sum of Rs.40,000/- which the Complainant got as accident claim on 27.09.2006, had already been adjusted against his loan by Opposite Parties Nos. 1 and 2. Complainant sent a legal notice to Opposite Parties No.2 on 23.08.2008, but he did not receive any reply. In view of the above, the Complainant filed a Complaint before the District Forum with the following prayer: - "1. O.P. No. 1 and 2 should be directed to return the truck to the complainant in a moveable condition. 2. The complainant should be given at least a six months time to repay the left over amount of loan, towards O.P. No. 1 and 2. 3. O.P. No. 1, 2 and 3 should be directed to pay Rs.5 lacs as compensation as the complainant has lost Rs.50,000 per month when the vehicle was seized. 4. O.P. No. 3 should be directed to transfer his co-Ownership, regarding the vehicle completely in the name of the complainant. 5. To direct the O.P. No.1, 2and 3 to pay Rs.1 lac as compensation for causing harassment and mental agony. 6. and to pass such further order or orders as your Honour may deem fit and proper."

3. The case was contested by OP No. 2 who denied all the allegations of the Complainant. It was stated that out of the 47 installments, the Complainant paid only 37 installments and the remaining installments had not been paid. The Complainant paid only Rs.9,11,400/- out of a total amount of Rs.11,57,700/-. The Complainant owed Rs.3,71,096/- towards loan repayment and despite reminders had not cleared his dues. According to the terms and conditions of the agreement, Opposite Parties Nos.1 and 2 were entitled to take possession of the vehicle. It was further stated that Opposite Party No. 3, being co-owner of the vehicle as well as co-borrower, voluntarily handed over

possession of the vehicle to Opposite Parties Nos. 1 and 2, who disposed off the vehicle after proper valuation at the highest available market price and appropriated the same against the loan amount. Opposite Parties Nos.1 and 3 did not file any written version in this case. OP No. 2 was present to contest the case during the initial stage but subsequently, remained absent on consecutive dates, and the case was decided ex-parte against all the Opposite Parties. The District forum after hearing the Counsel for the Complainant and perusing the record passed the following order: - "that the case be allowed ex-parte against OP No. 1, 2 and 3. OP No. 1 and 2 are directed jointly or severally to return the balance amount (i.e. Rs. 8,00,000/- - amount of sale proceeds which OP No. 2 appropriated with the loan amount) to the complainant. However, we allow the OP No. 1 and 2 to recover the arrear amount of monthly installments, if any along with interest @ 8% p.a. over the amount from the date of default till the date of auction; but they are not entitled to levy any other charge on this amount. OP No. 1 and 2 are further directed to pay the balance amount to the complainant within 30 days from the date of this order. In default, complainant is at liberty to execute this order in accordance to the law. Considering the facts and circumstances of this case, we make no order as to costs."

4. Aggrieved by the order of the District Forum, Appeal was filed by OP No. 1 and 2 before the State Commission. The State Commission dismissed the Appeal as under:- " Going by the foregoing discussion, it is ordered that the appeal is dismissed on contest without any cost and the judgment passed by the Ld. Forum below is hereby affirmed. The office is directed to send down the LCR along with a copy of this judgment to the Ld. Forum below forthwith."

5. Heard the Learned Counsels for the Petitioners and Respondent No.1 and carefully perused the record. Brief facts of the case are that the Respondent No.1 purchased a ten-wheeler truck of Ashok Leyland Ltd. truck bearing registration No.WB29/6162, chassis No.WDE-545847, and engine No.DWE 406960 which was financed by Petitioner No.1 through Petitioner No.2. Respondent No.1/Complainant entered into an agreement with Petitioner No.1 and accordingly Petitioner No. 1 and 2 sanctioned a loan of Rs.9,15,000/-. As per the terms and conditions of the agreement, Respondent No. 1 deposited a sum of Rs.82,687/- to Petitioner Nos.1 and 2 as margin money. Respondent No. 1 was supposed to repay a sum of Rs.11,57,700/- in 47 instalments @ Rs.24,720/- w.e.f. 24.02.2005. The Registration Certificate bore the names of Respondent Nos. 1 and 2 as joint registered owners. Respondent No.2 had incurred an expenditure of Rs.45,000/- in order to get the loan sanctioned to Respondent No.1. As and when Respondent No.1 would repay the loan, Respondent No.2 told the Complainant that necessary steps would be taken to delete his name from the Registration Certificate. According to Respondent No.1, though he had paid Rs.45,000/- to Respondent No. 2 in two instalments, Respondent No. 2 took no steps to delete his name from the Registration Certificate. On 05.04.2008, Respondent No. 2 detained the vehicle by force and removed its tyres to render it useless. On 01.05.2008, Petitioner No. 2 asked Respondent No.1 to repay Rs.1,05,000/-. The Opposite Parties seized the vehicle on 01.05.2008.

6. The Counsel for the Petitioners contended that the truck was handed over voluntarily by one of the co-borrowers due to default in payment of the loan installments and thereafter, the truck was sold in accordance with the terms of the agreement to realize the dues. As per the Petitioners' Counsel, the agreement provided for seizure of the vehicle in case of default in payment of loan installments and the Petitioners, having seized the vehicle in accordance with such terms, cannot be held liable for deficiency in service.

7. Learned Counsel for Respondent No.1/Complainant contended that Respondent No. 2 illegally and in collusion with the Petitioners seized the vehicle. He further contended that the money owed to Respondent No. 2 was already paid in two installments and

Respondent No. 2, in spite of his promise to take steps to remove his name from the Registration Certificate, failed to do so. Respondent No. 2 could not have, on his own, and without the consent of Respondent No 1, delivered the vehicle to the Petitioners.

8. It is seen that the Complainant paid major portion of the loan taken from the Petitioners/Opposite Parties Nos. 1 and 2. Several receipts of having made payment have also been produced by Respondent No.1. Respondent No. 2/Opposite Party No.3, though registered as co-owner and co-borrower of the loan, had not paid any amount to the Petitioners towards repayment of the loan. Neither the loan application form nor the copy of the agreement have been placed on record by the Petitioners. It is not understood as to why Respondent No.2/Opposite Party No.3 took possession of the vehicle on 05.04.2008 and removed its tyres and later on 01.05.2008 said to have voluntarily handed over the possession of the vehicle to the Petitioners. Even Rs.45,000/- spent by Opposite Party No.3, which according to him makes him entitled to be the co-owner of the vehicle, has been subsequently paid according to the Complainant. This contention of the Complainant has remained uncontested as Respondent No.2/Opposite Party No.3 did not contest the case, though notice was served upon him. The Petitioners could not place any evidence as to any notice having been given to the Complainant for seizure of the vehicle nor any notice of auction of the vehicle. No evidence has been produced to show that the vehicle was handed over voluntarily. The District Forum rightly held "we do not see any reason to accept the contention of Opposite Party No.2 that they did not take possession of the vehicle in question by force." The State Commission observed that the vehicle was auctioned without issuing any prior notice to the Complainant. Law is settled that illegal and forceful means cannot be adopted by Banks to seize any property. Due notice had to be given for seizure of the vehicle and following the established procedure the vehicle could be seized and later auctioned. There are concurrent findings of both the Fora rejecting the contention of the Petitioners that no illegal means were used to seize the vehicle and that there is no evidence on record to show that the vehicle was voluntarily delivered to them. The Petitioners in collusion with Respondent No.2/Opposite Party No.3 adopted illegal and unfair means in seizure of the vehicle which amounts to unfair trade practice.

9. Jurisdiction of this Commission under Section 21 (b) is very limited. This Commission is not required to re-appreciate and reassess the evidences and reach to its own conclusion. The Court can intervene only when the petitioner succeeds in showing that the Fora below has wrongly exercised its jurisdiction or there is a miscarriage of justice. It was so held by the Hon'ble Supreme Court in the case of Mrs. Rubi (Chandra) Dutta Vs. M/s United India Insurance Co. Ltd . (2011) 11 SCC 269 has held as under: - "13. Also, it is to be noted that the revisional powers of the National Commission are derived from Section 21 (b) of the Act, under which the said power can be exercised only if there is some prima facie jurisdictional error appearing in the impugned order, and only then, may the same be set aside. In our considered opinion there was no jurisdictional error or miscarriage of justice, which could have warranted the National Commission to have taken a different view than what was taken by the two Forums. The decision of the National Commission rests not on the basis of some legal principle that was ignored by the Courts below, but on a different (and in our opinion, an erroneous) interpretation of the same set of facts. This is not the manner in which revisional powers should be invoked. In this view of the matter, we are of the considered opinion that the jurisdiction conferred on the National Commission under Section 21 (b) of the Act has been transgressed. It was not a case where such a view could have been taken by setting aside the concurrent findings of two fora."

10. Same principle has been reiterated by Hon'ble Supreme Court in the case of Lourdes Society Snehanjali Girls Hostel and Ors. Vs. H & R Johnson (India) Ltd. and Ors. (2016 8 SCC 286 wherein Hon'ble Supreme Court has held as under:- "23. The

National Commission has to exercise the jurisdiction vested in it only if the State Commission or the District Forum has failed to exercise their jurisdiction or exercised when the same was not vested in their or exceeded their jurisdiction by acting illegally or with material irregularity. In the instant case, the National Commission has certainly exceeded its jurisdiction by setting aside the concurrent finding of fact recorded in the order passed by the State Commission which is based upon valid and cogent reasons."

11. In view of the foregoing discussion, I agree with the concurrent findings of both the Fora below. There is no infirmity or illegality in the impugned order, warranting interference under -5- Section 21 (b) of the Consumer Protection Act, 1986. Revision Petition is therefore dismissed with no order as to costs. .... C. VISWANATH PRESIDING MEMBER

CASE NO. 18
FIRST APPEAL NO. 993 OF 2015

(Against the Order dated 06/11/2015 in Complaint No. 28/2014 of the State Commission Rajasthan)
M/S. MANGLAM BUILD-DEVELOPERS LTD. & 2 ORS. THROUGH THE DIRECTOR, DR. N.K. GUPTA THE CHAIRMAN MANGLAM BUILD-DEVELOPERS LTD., MR. RAMBABU AGARWAL THE MANAGING DIRECTOR, ...Appellant(s)

Versus

AVIRAL MATHUR & ANR. S/O. MR. YOGESHAR DAYAL MATHUR, MRS. SAPNA MATHUR W/O. MR. AVIRAL MATHUR, ...Respondent(s)
BEFORE: HON'BLE MR. ANUP K THAKUR,PRESIDING MEMBER
For the Appellant : For the Appellants : Mr. Sukumar Pattjoshi, Sr. Adv. with Mr. Sunil Mund, Advocate
For the Respondent : For the Respondents : Mr. Debesh Panda, Advocate with Mr. Naman Maheshwari, Advocate
Dated : 12 Jan 2021

ORDER

1. This First Appeal No.993 of 2015 has been filed challenging the order dated 06.11.2015 of the Rajasthan State Consumer Disputes Redressal Commission, Jaipur (for short, 'State Commission') in C.C. No.28 of 2014. The impugned order, for ease of reference, is reproduced below: "19. The present complaint of complainants is allowed jointly and severally against the opposite parties as follows: (a) The Opposite Parties shall pay to the complainants consolidated amount of Rs.2 Lacs (Rupees Two Lacs Only) as compensation for the defects and deficiencies in the construction." (b) We restrain the opposite parties from extending the Club House facilities created for the residents of Manglam Arpan, the Villas to any of it's projects viz. Manglam Arpan Residency, the Premium Residential Apartments. (c) We further direct the Opposite parties to:- (i) to construct 6' feet high boundary wall on the fourth remaining side of the campus. (ii) to construct the 30' feet and 40' feet wide CC road at the entrance and in the entire campus. (iii) to provide/fix glasses in the MS railing in the stairs. (iv) The opposite parties shall also pay to the complainants Rs.11,000/- (Rupees Eleven Thousand Only) as cost of proceedings. The compliance of the order shall be made within one month."

2. C.C. No.28 of 2014 had been filed, as noted in the impugned order, alleging the following deficiency and defects in the villa: "a) Vitrified tiles have been provided in Drawing and Dining Room and Kitchen instead of Marble flooring; b) Interlocking pavers not provided; c) Kitchen Garden not provided; d) MS Railing with glass not provided; e) Electrical circuits not provided at suitable places; f) Provision for AC not kept in the room; g) Internet connection was not provided; h) DTH installation was not provided; i) Power backup was not provided as promised; j) Bitumen entrance road provided in place of cc road; k) Security arrangements not inadequate; l) Surrounding Wall around campus was not constructed; m) Sewage Treatment Plan was not provided;

n) Floating Terrace not provided; o) Club House not functioning; p) Landscape Garden was not provided;

3. Besides these defects the complainants alleged that the opposite party has developed another project-Manglam Arpan Residents-Premium Residential Apartments. The complainant alleged that Club House facility provided for the Manglam Arpan Villa is being shared with the residents of the apartments, while both these projects are different and also no common entrance for these projects is permissible". And making the following prayer for reliefs: "a) Pass an order directing the Respondents not to allow anybody else to enter the club house of Manglam Arpan, the Villas except the residents and their guests. b) Pass an order directing the Respondents to rectify and provide all the services/facilities as promised specifically in the Brochure within a maximum time period of three months. bb) In the alternative, if the Respondents fail to provide such services/facilities, direct the Respondents to pay a compensation of Rs.20,66,000 (Twenty lacs sixty-six thousand) towards the loss of the value and utility in the said property. c) Pass an order directing the Respondents to reimburse Rs.1,27,000/- (One lac twenty seven thousand) for out of pocket expenses incurred by the Complainants. d) Pass an order directing the Respondents to pay damages to the tune of Rs.12,00,000/- (twelve lacs) for the mental harassment and suffering caused to the Complainants. e) Pass an order directing the Respondents to reimburse the costs of the proceedings to the Complainants. f) Pass any other order it deems fit in the interest of justice, equity and good conscience."

4. A brief look at the facts reveals that the respondents/complainants (complainants hereinafter) had, on 16.1.2013 , booked villa no. 17 in Manglam Arpan on a plot measuring 165 sq. yards. The total consideration was Rs.62 Lakh as settled and agreed between the parties in the Agreement to Sell (agreement hereafter). Initial payment of Rs.11 Lakh (Rs.9.7 Lakh vide cheque no.695528 dated 25.1.2013 and Rs.1.3 Lakh in cash on 26.2.2013) was made against receipts except for cash receipt of Rs.30,000/-. Further, payments of Rs.2 Lakh in cash on 13.3.2013, Rs.45 Lakh vide cheque no.030103 on 31.1.2013, Rs.2 Lakh in cash on 16.7.2013 and then Rs.1 Lakh vide cheque no.198950 on 27.11.2013, aggregating Rs.61 Lakh, was made till the time for filing of the consumer complaint. Per the plaint, 5% of the BSP (Basic Sale Price) was to be paid only after the complainants were fully satisfied with the Villa and other facilities. The complainants have been residing at this Villa since April, 2013 .

5. The matter was heard on 19.11.2020 . Counsels sought and were given permission to file two page synopsis of main arguments made during their oral submissions along with citations, if any. These were submitted in the first week of Dec. 2020 .

6. Learned Senior Counsel for the appellants began by raising the following issues: (i) Whether after having taken possession of the Villa, it was permissible to raise grievances regarding defects, given that the complainants had purchased an already constructed villa and had thus done so with their eyes wide open; (ii) Whether the complainant, being one individual occupying one villa from out of 97 villas and 47 apartments in a housing complex could seek reliefs affecting all other residents, through an individual consumer complaint; (iii) a sub-issue was whether the State Commission could have granted both reliefs which were, in-fact, sought as alternative to each other.

7. Reference issue (i), counsel argued that there were no grievances of the complainant till the time of filing of the consumer complaint. This was clear from the text of the complaint itself: the first interaction between the parties took place on 16.1.2013 , agreement to sell was signed on 25.1.2013 and the complainants have been residing in the villa since 19.4.2013 . Learned counsel then drew attention to para 12 of the complaint, arguing that clearly, made up grievances had been listed, from sr. (a) till (q), ranging from flooring, kitchen, driveway to sewage, floating terrace, security, power back up, six feet high wall surrounding the campus, were made in this consumer complaint filed on 19.3.2014 . In other words, argued the counsel, the complainant was

in occupation from 19.4.2013 and then filed his complaint only on 19.3.2014 i.e. after a full one year. This itself spoke volumes about the integrity of the plaint.

8. He drew attention to para 12 (o) of the consumer complaint to make the point that this was in relation to the club house and the allegation was that the club house was not functional till the time of filing of the complaint. However, the tentative date of completion of the whole project was 31.03.2012; therefore, the complainants, having booked the villa in January 2013 and been in occupation since April 2013 , clearly knew that this was the case and had yet signed the agreement. They had done so with eyes wide open. If so, how were the complainants concerned that the club house was to be completed tentatively within 31.03.2012. It was argued therefore that this had to be classified and treated as a non-existent grievance.

9. Learned counsel then drew attention to the prayer clause of the consumer complaint (supra). Reference prayer (a) seeking an order not to allow anybody other than the villa residents and their guests to enter the club house of Manglam Arpan, he argued that the complainant, as an individual who had visited in January 2013 and occupied in April, 2013 , could not possibly seek such a relief. Afterall, he was not an original allottee; rather, he had seen what he was purchasing and could not raise this issue now.

10. Similarly, regarding prayer (b) seeking a direction to rectify and provide all the services/facilities as promised specifically in the brochure within a maximum time period of three months, learned counsel argued that the things mentioned in the brochure could not be enforced by the complainant in this manner, in view of the fact that a separate agreement dated 25.1.2013 had been signed with the complainant and that he was fully aware of the status of things as on that date. He then drew attention to the alternative prayer (bb): this sought direction, as an alternate to prayer (b), to the OPs to pay a compensation of Rs.20,66,000/- towards the loss of the value and utility in the said property. Since prayer (b) itself was not for the complainant to raise, any consideration of this was clearly unwarranted, submitted the learned counsel.

11. Counsel then referred to the impugned order of the State Commission, para 19 thereof, to draw attention to the reliefs granted to the complainant. Regarding para 19 (a) directing OPs to pay to the complainants a consolidated amount of Rs.2 Lakh as compensation for the defects and deficiencies in the construction, learned counsel drew attention to the agreement to sell dated 25.1.2013 , clause 10.1 thereof which clearly stated that all the building plans, layouts, specifications etc. were tentative and subject to variations and modifications as decided by the company/architect. He reiterated that the complainant had signed this agreement with eyes wide open. Clause 17 of the same agreement dealt with quality of construction and clearly provided that after possession, the purchaser (complainant) shall not be entitled to make any claim regarding any item of work, the material used for construction etc. and the seller (OP) shall not be liable for any claim whatsoever. The point emphasized by the counsel was that the complainant had waived such rights after admittedly seeing and finding things to be to his satisfaction before signing the said agreement. It was therefore not understood as to how he had filed a consumer complaint straight away without even taking up these issues with the OPs. In this regard, he drew attention to paras 16 and 18 of the impugned order wherein it has been held that the complainants have been able to prove inferior quality of construction of walls, non providing of marble in kitchen, drawing room and dining room etc. and thus proved that things were not as per the brochure, and that therefore the OPs had cheated and defrauded the complainants: Learned Counsel argued that it was not clear from a plain reading of the order as to how the State Commission had come to this conclusion. He drew attention to clause 4 of the agreement in which it has been clearly stated that all other agreements and/or arrangements etc. which were in any way contradictory to or inconsistent with this agreement, shall have no effect. He argued that this agreement was a concluded contract; therefore the issues raised in the complaint flowing from brochure etc., simply could not be raised. He invoked a citation in support

viz. an order of the Hon'ble Calcutta High Court, dated 4.5.1984, in the case of C.V. Enterprises vs. Braithwaite & Co. Ltd. and Ors., AIR 1984 Cal 306: the point was that the State Commission could not have enforced the brochure of the project in the complaint as it had seemingly done, the same having no relevance after the agreement to sell dated 25.1.2013 which was a concluded contract between the parties and which would henceforth govern their relations.

12. Drawing attention to para 19 (b) of the impugned order restraining the OPs from extending Club House facilities created for the residents of Manglam Arpan to residents of any of it's other project(s) viz. Manglam Arpan Residency, the Premium Residential Apartments, learned counsel argued that qua the club house, complainants' right therein was governed by clause 9 of the agreement viz. that the complainant had specifically agreed to pay Rs.50,000/- as onetime payment towards the lifetime membership of the club, that the same was compulsory and was towards the establishment of the structural facilities of the club and was neither transferable nor refundable. He argued that the correct question to be asked is whether the OP had abridged the complainants' right as enshrined in this clause 9; the answer was clearly in the negative.

13. Counsel further drew attention to para 19 (c) of the impugned order vide which the State Commission had directed the OPs (i) to construct 6 feet high boundary wall on the fourth remaining side of the campus, (ii) to construct 30 feet x 40 feet wide CC road at the entrance and in the entire campus, (iii) to provide/fix glasses in the MS railing in the stairs, and (iv) pay Rs.11,000/- as cost of proceedings. He pointed out as there was a common entrance for both the projects, the direction to construct a 6' feet high boundary wall on the fourth remaining side seemed clearly infirm. As for the direction to construct 30' X 40' feet CC road at the entrance and in the entire campus, he argued that this was obviously for use of all the residents and could not have been decided on the basis of an individual consumer complaint. In this regard, he also drew attention to some photographs (at pages 125-126), showing the common gate and the internal metal road. At page 129, he also showed the boundary provided by the OPs which comprised wire mesh on pillars rather than a wall as directed in the impugned order. He argued that the agreement did not mention a brick wall; further, the complainant did not even reside on this road and therefore it was not clear as to why he had made this demand in the complaint. He added that in fact the residents had welcomed this wire mesh wall and drew attention to statements of these residents, annexed with the appeal (Annexure-A10). His argument was that in view of this, the State Commission could not have imposed a wall on the basis of an individual complaint. As for stair case railing, he submitted that glasses have already been fixed by the OP.

14. Learned counsel for the respondents/complainants began with the submission that the Commission may not consider any document which had not been placed before the State Commission and further submitted that his arguments would be confined to the four corners of the complainants' pleadings.

15. He drew attention to additional documents filed vide I.A. No.5231 of 2020 dated 25.8.2020 , drawing attention to letter dated 15.4.2013 from Jaipur Development Authority to the OPs, conveying in respect of plot no. R1 Yozana Arpan, approval of building plan of the proposed residential complex. He then drew attention to lease deed of JDA dated 13.3.2013 and the agreement to sell dated 25.1.2013 . His submission was that when the complainants had taken the villa, the apartments project was nowhere in the picture. The same was sanctioned later, and now, the OP is arguing that the club was meant for everyone, both the villas as well as the apartment residents. This then is the main dispute, submitted the learned counsel for the complainants.

16. Referring to affidavit evidence of the OPs, he drew attention to para 10 thereof which states that it was true that the OPs had issued brochure Ex.OP-W2 & 3 and that the work was done according to the brochure and that the complainant on his own had ascribed wrong interpretation to it for which the OP was not responsible. Learned counsel

submitted that it was only today during arguments that it was heard from the learned counsel for the OP that there was one license held by the OPs and two projects under the said license. This was not the situation before the State Commission. This being so, this alleged fact cannot now be considered at the appellate stage.

17. He then drew attention to the consumer complaint itself and to the arguments of the counsel for the OPs denying the reliefs claimed as being non-maintainable. Reference para 10 of the complaint, he submitted that this clearly states that at the time of booking, the OPs had handed over a brochure specifically designed for Manglam Arpan, the villas. Thus, per the brochure, it was clear that all the facilities mentioned therein were to be enjoyed only by the residents of the villas and to the exclusion of all others. Para 11 of the complaint stated that Manglam Arpan Residency, Premium Residential Apartments was a separate project, with separate brochure, separate boundary and separate entrance. As such, making available the club house to the residents of Manglam Arpan Residency, Premium Residential Apartments, was not permissible. In fact, instead of two club/community centers as shown in the brochure, OPs had cut their number down to one club house and one community which was insufficient to cater to the needs of 97 villas. It is this that is the chief dispute, argued the counsel. He then referred to the prayer clause of the complaint: clause (a) sought direction not to allow anybody else to enter the club house; clause (b) sought direction to rectify and provide all the services/facilities as promised specifically in the brochure within three months and clause (bb), in the alternate, sought a compensation of Rs.20,66,000/- towards the loss of the value and utility in the complainants' property. His submission was that these reliefs had to be seen in the context explained by him at the outset viz. the complainant had paid for a villa under a different impression of what they were buying from the OPs and the OPs had let them down.

18. Learned counsel then drew attention to the reply and the affidavit evidence of the OPs. He read out para 10 and 11 thereof to make the submission that when the complainant had signed lease deed dated 13.3.2013 , the apartment project was non-existent and that for the OP to claim, as it had, that it was but one project under one licence, was untenable, as the two projects were separate and had different brochures. He drew attention further to para 12, 8 line thereof, which the status that "the OP has not made any deficiency in construction and every work has been done according to the brochure" to argue that it is OP's own admission that he has carried out work as per the brochure. Further, in para 13, the same point regarding security has been reiterated; again in para 15, it has been clearly stated by the OP that he has complied with the condition as mentioned in the brochure. So, counsel for OP could not now argue that the brochure and the promises therein stood superseded by the agreement between the OP and the complainant.

19. Learned counsel drew attention to order of the National Commission dated 18.7.2016: vide this order, at the time of admission of this appeal, the Commission, upon perusing the brochure supplied to the complainants at the time of booking the villa, had directed stay of the operation of directions of the State Commission contained in para (c) (i), (ii) and (iii). The counsel argued that all that the complainants want is that reliefs be provided as per the brochure which was relied upon by them at the time of purchase of the villa. He drew attention to the specifications contained in the brochure furnished with the appeal to observe that in the "Specifications", it did not mention "MS railing with glass". He argued that this showed that the brochure submitted with this Appeal was different from the brochure on which the complainants had relied. To further drive this point home, he referred to para 12 (d) of the complaint which mentions MS railing with glass.

20. He then drew attention to para 2 of the impugned order of the State Commission: this had noted that the OPs had developed another project-Manglam Arpan Residents-Premium Residential Apartments and that the Club House facility provided for the

Manglam Arpan villa was being shared with the residents of the apartments. In para 5, the State Commission had noted that the complainants, in support of their allegations, had filed affidavits, photographs of the defects and deficiencies and also a brochure. In para 6, it had been noted that the dispute regarding common entrance for the residents of the two projects had since been resolved, as the OP had decided not to keep any opening of the apartment project towards the villa project. In para 9 of the impugned order, it has been noted that it was an admitted fact that the OP had given a brochure to the complainants wherein certain specifications of the villa and other facilities to be provided had been shown. Learned counsel for the complainant argued that as per it's own affidavit, OP stood by his own brochure and therefore there was no need to discuss this anymore as it was an admitted position. He then read out para 13 of the impugned order wherein the situation regarding deficiencies alleged in the complaint and their status and the position of the OP has been discussed in detail. Learned counsel drew attention to an opinion regarding construction of road in Arpan Residency, filed with the appeal by the OP, submitting that this was a new document and had been introduced without even an application before the Commission and was therefore not acceptable. Drawing attention to para 13 (k) of the impugned order, counsel drew attention to the noting of the State Commission that the counsel for the OP had admitted that three sides of the project was surrounded by 6 feet high boundary wall and that there was some dispute with adjoining land owner and the wall of the fourth side would be built as soon as the dispute was resolved. It was on this basis, the counsel argued, that the National Commission had granted stay of the impugned order. It was not known whether the dispute has been resolved or not. In para 15 of the impugned order, regarding the club facility, the State Commission had found after discussion that the facility was available only to the villa owners and could not be shared with others. He then referred to the operational part of the State Commission's order submitting that it was a well-considered order which was just and proper.

21. Finally, learned Counsel for the complainants drew attention to section 12 of the Consumer Protection Act, 1986 to submit that this provided for filing of a consumer complaint by (a) the -8- consumer, (b) any recognized consumer association, (c) one or more consumers with same interest and (d) the central or the State Government. Section 14 provided that if, after proceeding under section 13, the consumer forum was satisfied that any of the allegations contained in the complaint about the services are proved, it shall issue an order to the OP directing one or more of the following things listed therein. His legal argument was that what was important was a finding of allegation of deficiency to have been established, regardless of who had made the allegation and in what capacity. Once an allegation was found to have been proved, the District Forum/State Commission/National Commission, as the case may be, was duty bound to decide the penalty, as per section 14. With this the learned counsel concluded his arguments.

22. Learned counsel for the OPs rebutted this argument, in respect of jurisdiction, arguing that the complainants could raise only those issues which affected them, not those which affected others. As far as the submission that the OP had, before the State Commission, admitted that work was carried out in terms of the specifications in the brochure, he argued that if this was so, nothing remained in this complaint. In respect of paras 10, 11 and 12 of the original complaint which were referred to by the counsel for the complainants, he drew attention to OPs' reply at paras 10 and 11 to say that it was obvious that the complainants had interpreted the brochure in their own way for which OPs could not be held responsible and that both the projects Manglam Arpan Residence-Premium Residential Apartments and the villas were projects of the OPs and that since the flats and villas were sold separately, different brochures had been printed. However, the scheme was the same and the facilities were common. Clearly, argued the counsel, complainants had misunderstood the meaning of the club house and community center.

DISCUSSION AND ORDER

23. It can be said that the gist of the case of the appellants/OPs, shorn off all rhetoric, is that the complainant was an individual who had bought and moved into his villa in April 2013, with his eyes wide open, under a specific agreement dated 25.1.2013 . This being so, the complainants could not file and maintain a consumer complaint qua the common items/concerns of all the other residents of the project. In particular, the complainant's grievance qua the club house as being only for the exclusive use of the villas residents, to the exclusion of all others, cannot stand. As per the agreement (supra), the complainant was provided the facility of a club house, and he had paid a fee for it. In the same way, others including apartment owners had also paid a fee for the use of the club house. It was therefore not understood how the complainant, in his individual capacity, was claiming exclusiveness of the club house only for the villas residents. Further, the learned counsel argued that the complainant could not cite the brochure(s) of the project as these were not relevant in his case: This was so because as far as the complainant was concerned, he visited the site, the villa, liked what he saw, signed an agreement, and was given possession of this, within a few months. The complainant clearly did all this with his eyes wide open. It was therefore not for him to now refer to what all had been promised in the brochure(s) and start making demands based on that.

24. The gist of arguments on behalf of the respondents/complainants was that the State Commission's impugned order was evidence based and therefore could not be assailed. He argued that sections 12 and 14 of Consumer Protection Act, 1986 read together, holistically, did not debar the State Commission from passing orders if it came to a finding that an allegation, whether made by an individual or by an association or through a joint complaint, could pass orders awarding compensation etc. as per section 14. He emphasized that in the scheme of things, it was hardly important as to how a consumer complaint had been field; what was important that if an allegation had been made and had been found to be proved, consequences would follow and consumer forum would be duty bound to pass orders as provided in sec 14 of CPA 1986. This therefore rebutted the core argument of the OPs that an individual could not seek a common grievance in his individual consumer complaint.

25. Having heard all the arguments, and carefully perused the record, I am of the considered view that the instant appeal against the impugned order of the State Commission deserves consideration and can be partly allowed. It is accordingly so allowed as explained hereafter. 25. The impugned order of the State Commission (supra) is in two parts. In the first part, para 19(a), the OP has been directed to pay a consolidated amount of Rs. 2 Lakh as compensation for the defects and deficiencies in the construction. I agree with the learned counsel for the complainants that this order was based on the evidence furnished. Being evidence based, the same is upheld. Further, it is only just that the complainants are recompensed for the amount having not been paid to them within 30 days of the impugned order. Therefore, I consider it just that the amount of Rs. 2 lakh be paid with simple interest of 6% per annum from the date of the impugned order till the date of payment.

26. I do not however agree with the rest of the impugned order of the State Commission viz. para 19(b) restraining OP from extending the club house facilities to others, and para 19(c) (i) directing the OPs to construct 6' feet high boundary wall on the fourth remaining side of the campus and para 19(c)(ii) directing the OPs to construct 30' X 40' CC road at the entrance and in the entire campus. These reliefs are addressing what are clearly common grievances about common facilities, not the individual grievance of the complainants. There is much merit in the argument that for the proper adjudication of these common grievances, an individual complainant's complaint was not the proper way and that it was necessary to have involved all other residents also, of at least the villas if not of both the villas as well as the apartments. This is a self-evident proposition. Whereas the complainant may feel greatly inconvenienced by the fact that

the club house is also open to apartment residents, by the absence of a boundary wall on the fourth side barring entry of the apartment residents to the club house and a concrete road of the promised dimension in the entire campus, it is not necessary at all that these views would also be shared by all the other villa residents. There is nothing in the complaint petition to show that there was even a claim that all other villa residents were of the same view. Indeed, if this had been the case, the complainant would then have filed a joint complaint or have come through the Association of villa owners. Similarly, there is nothing in the impugned order to show that this aspect of the matter had at all been considered.

27. Further, while it is true that the complainants are submitting their case on the basis of what had been promised in the brochure made available, there is much merit in the argument of the counsel for the OP that what is or is not admissible to the complainant is squarely determined by the agreement dated 25.1.2013 signed by the complainant with eyes wide open. It has to be appreciated that the complainants had signed this agreement, after applying their mind to the aspects of community living in a villa in a project which had 96 other villas and that they were not the original allottees; rather, they came in January 2013 , saw the villa, were satisfied with what they saw and were told, and then, with eyes wide open, signed the agreement. This agreement itself had spelt out clearly that it is this agreement alone henceforth which would govern the relationship between the complainant and the OP. Indeed, this agreement was a concluded contract, as argued by the learned senior counsel for the OP. It would be useful to reproduce clause 4 of the Agreement to make this aspect abundantly clear: "4. The purchaser has applied for allotment of Villa No. 17 in the above said scheme "Manglam's Arpan" and the seller has agreed to allot to the purchaser Villa/Shop in the said Scheme on the following terms & conditions. All other agreements and/or arrangements or letters , assurances written, oral or implied hereto, sales brochures, newspapers advertisements ,etc. before made and which are in any way contradictory to or inconsistent with this agreement shall have no effect. The sellers hereby agrees to sell Purchaser hereby agrees to purchase on terms &conditions mentioned in this Agreement." It was therefore not for the complainants to refer to the brochure that may have attracted initial allottees and base their claims thereupon. It was not for the complainants, for instance, to make statements such as in para 12 of the complaint viz. "That despite the continuous and repeated requests by the Complainants and other residents since December 2012 to the local Site Engineer Mr. Mohammad Hussain and other employees of Respondent 1 along with requests to made to Respondent 3 to undertake and complete the work as assured in the Brochure, none of the following work has been undertaken or performed till now…" Clearly, the complainants could not have laid any claim to what was promised in the brochure in view of the agreement they had signed on 25.1.2013 ; further, they could certainly not have claimed anything, on behalf of themselves as well as on behalf of other residents, and that too since December 2012, when they were nowhere in the picture. The legal argument advanced by the learned counsel for the complainants during arguments that it did not matter whether the complaint was made by an individual or how the complaint was made , and that, once the State Commission found a deficiency, it was duty bound to pass an order under sec14 of CPA 1986, is, in my opinion, an unreasonable inference. A complaint has to derive it's merit from what it claims on it's own behalf. A narrative which goes beyond what falls in the domain of the individual complainant can still have relevance but confined strictly to what directly affects the complainant, not beyond that.

28. In view of the discussion above, this First Appeal No.993 of 2015 is partly allowed and decided, with the following directions: (i) order of the State Commission in para 19 (a), directing the OPs to pay to the complainants a consolidated amount of Rs.2 lakh as compensation for defects and deficiencies in construction, is upheld; (ii) This amount of Rs.2 lakh shall carry an interest @ 6% p.a. from the date of the impugned order of the

State Commission, till the date of actual payment; (iii) Rest of the order of the State Commission relating to common facilities and costs is set aside. (iv) In the facts of the case, there shall be no order as to costs. .... ANUP K THAKUR PRESIDING MEMBER

CASE NO. 19
REVISION PETITION NO. 2405 OF 2013

(Against the Order dated 15/03/2013 in Appeal No. 1364/2009 of the State Commission Gujarat)

SHREE DHAIN AUTO TRANSPORT CORPORATION ....Petitioner(s)

Versus

UNITED INDIA INSURANCE COMPANY LTD. ....Respondent(s)

BEFORE: HON'BLE MR. C. VISWANATH,PRESIDING MEMBER

For the Petitioner : Mr. Hemant Gupta, Advocate

For the Respondent : Ms. Nanita Sharma, Advocate

Dated : 13 Jan 2021

ORDER

1. The present Revision Petition has been filed by the Petitioners against order dated 15.03.2013 of the Gujarat State Consumer Disputes Redressal Commission, Ahmedabad (for short "the State Commission") in First Appeal No.1364/2009 whereby Appeal filed by the Respondent was allowed.

2. The case of the Complainant/Respondent is that he purchased Eicher vehicle from V.G. Automobiles, bearing Registration No.GJ 6 X 8858, Engine No.20575898, Chasis No.205013100, for an amount of Rs.5,55,000/-. Vehicle was insured with the Petitioner/Opposite Party from 22.05.2002 to 21.05.2003, vide Policy No.18100/02209/2002 dated 22.05.2002, for a sum of Rs.6,78,000/-. The vehicle met with an accident on 03.07.2002 at Bhilwara Road near Jharwala Village, and got badly damaged. The Complainant had consulted V.G. Automobiles, who had given an estimate of Rs.5,55,000/. On the basis of the said estimate, Complainant filed Insurance Claim with the Petitioner on 19.07.2002, claiming an amount of Rs.5,55,000/-. Petitioner/Opposite Party got the vehicle inspected and informed the Complainant that as per the Survey Report, labour charges for repair would be Rs.21,700/- alongwith Rs.1,61,611 towards replacement cost of parts with Rs.11,500/- deduction for salvage. Claiming deficiency in service on the part of the Opposite Party, the Complaint filed Complaint before the District Forum with the following prayer: - -1- 1. 2. 3. (1) The Hon'ble Forum may grant the following reliefs in favour of the Complainant: The amount of Rs.5,55,000/- being the damages caused to the vehicle business may be awarded with interest @ 18% per annum till the realization of claim amount. Rs.1,00,000/- may be awarded for mental torture and agony. The expenses of the complaint may be awarded."

3. The Complaint was contested by the Petitioner/Opposite Party by filing written statement. It was stated that that the Complaint was not maintainable. On merit, Opposite Party appointed a Surveyor and as per the Survey Report, the damaged vehicle was to be repaired requiring Rs.21,700/- for labour charges and Rs.1,61,611/- towards replacement of parts. As per the claim manual, when the damage to the vehicle is 75% or more, the claim can be considered on total loss basis.

4. The District Forum after hearing the Learned Counsel for the Parties and perusing the record, allowed the Complaint in part and directed the Petitioner/Opposite Party as follows: - "The complaint is partly allowed. The opponents are directed to pay Rs.5,44,912.00 (rupees five lacs forty four thousand nine hundred twelve only) with 9% interest, from 23.8.2002 i.e. the date of report of Shri Mahendra R. Patel the opponent's surveyor since the claim has not been repudiated till realization. The opponents are further directed to pay Rs.3,000.00 (rupees three thousand only) for mental agony and

inconvenience and another sum of Rs.1,500.00 (rupees one thousand five hundred only) towards the cost of this proceedings. This award be complied with within one month from the d ate of receipt of copy hereof. On payment of the money awarded, the Complainant shall give the vehicle to the Opponent."

5. Aggrieved by the order of the District Forum, Petitioner/Opposite Party filed an Appeal before the State Commission. State Commission allowed the Appeal and set aside the order passed by the District Forum and granted compensation of Rs.1,61,611/- with 9% interest till realization. Further Rs.3,000/- for mental agony and inconvenience and Rs.1500/- towards cost of other expenses was also given. Against this order of the State Commission, the Petitioner/Complainant filed the present Revision Petition.

6. Heard the learned Counsel for the Petitioner as well as the Respondent and carefully perused the record. Learned Counsel for the Petitioner submitted that the State Commission failed to appreciate that the Surveyor had submitted the report without dismantling the vehicle, and therefore, the said report could not be relied. Surveyor had also overlooked the estimate prepared by V.G. Automobiles, authorised dealer of Eicher vehicles. It was also -2- 3. submitted that the impugned order had been passed on conjectures and surmises, without application of judicial mind. Learned Counsel further submitted that the order passed by the State Commission was a non-speaking order, without any reasoning.

7. Learned Counsel for the Respondent submitted that the impugned order passed by the State Commission was justified because the District Forum failed to take into consideration the Surveyor's Report, which is an important document. It was submitted that there was no expert report of Automobile Engineer or any other expert which could bypass the Surveyor Report. She submitted that the Revision Petition is liable to be dismissed.

8. Regarding maintainability, whether the Complainant can be said to be a consumer as defined in Section 2(1)(d) of the Consumer Protection Act or not, it has been held by this Commission in Harsolia Motors v. National Insurance Co. Ltd. I, (2005) CPJ 27 (NC) decided on 03.12.2004 that since an Insurance Policy is taken for reimbursement or for indemnity of the loss which may be suffered on account of insured perils, the services of the insurer cannot be said to have been hired or availed for a commercial purpose. This Commission does possess the requisite jurisdiction to entertain a Consumer Complaint wherever a defect or deficiency in the services rendered by an insurer is made out. In view of the above, the Complaint is held maintainable.

9. It is an admitted fact that the vehicle met with an accident on 03.07.2012. The vehicle was a new one, only 2 months old. The only dispute in the matter relates to the quantum of loss. Surveyor appointed by the Insurance Company assessed the loss at Rs.1,61,611/- plus labour charges, whereas the claim filed by the Complainant was Rs.5,55,000/-, cost of repair of the vehicle estimated by M/s V.G. Automobiles, authorised dealer of Eicher. Though the Surveyor had mentioned about the estimate of repair submitted by M/s V.G. Automobiles, there is no discussion at all on this estimate. The Surveyor ought to have given reasons for disagreeing with the estimate. Moreover, in the Survey Report it is clearly mentioned that the assessment was carried out without dismantling the vehicle and there were chances of an additional estimate after dismantling the same. The District Forum observed 'that the surveyor who is expert in branch of assessing damages is required to give reasons as to on what basis and for what reasons claim of the Complainant was not justified. In such absence, the Surveyor's Report cannot be accepted.' The District Forum therefore rightly allowed the Complaint. The State Commission, however, without going into the estimate, has gone by the Surveyor's Report, which is very sketchy and shallow.

10. In view of the foregoing discussion, the orders of the State Commission are set aside, upholding the orders of the District Forum. Respondent/Opposite Party is directed to

comply with the orders within eight weeks from today. .... C. VISWANATH
PRESIDING MEMBER

CASE NO. 20
APPEAL EXECUTION NO. 1 OF 2021

(Against the Order dated 17/12/2020 in Complaint No. 147/2019 of the State Commission Chandigarh)

DARA ESTATES PRIVATE LIMITED & 2 ORS. THROUGH ITS MANAGING DIRECTOR,

RAHUL, MANAGING DIRECTOR, C/O DARA ESTATE PRIVATE LIMITED,

ASHOK KUMAR, DIRECTOR, C/O DARA ESTATE PRIVATE LIMITED,...........Appellant(s)

Versus

HIMANSHU SHARMA S/O SHRI NARAYAN SHARMA,...........Respondent(s)

BEFORE: HON'BLE MR. C. VISWANATH,PRESIDING MEMBER

For the Appellant : MR. JALAJ AGRAWAL

For the Respondent :

Dated : 14 Jan 2021

ORDER

AE/01/2021 is an Execution Appeal filed by Dara Estates Pvt. Ltd. & Ors., against the order of the State Consumer Disputes Redressal Commission, UT Chandigarh in EA/147/2019 dated 17.12.2020. According to the Learned Counsel for the Appellants, the State Commission, vide order dated 13.07.2017 ordered to pay an amount of Rs.22,51,945/- along with interest. Earlier AE/19/2020 was filed in this Commission. The Appellants submitted that they were prepared to clear the entire dues along with interest -1- @ 18%. The issuance of non-bailable warrants of arrest of Mr. Ashok Kumar, Respondent No.3 was deferred, in view of the assurance given by Learned Counsel for the Appellants that both Mr. Rahul Kumar and Ashok Kumar would appear before the State Commission on the date fixed i.e. 25.02.2020. It is submitted that on 25.02.2020 they appeared before the State Commission and deposited post-dated cheques of Rs.13,00,000/- to the Decree Holders. It is also submitted that the cheques could not be honoured, which by itself is an offence under the provisions of Negotiable Instruments Act and somehow they managed to give an amount of Rs.7,00,000/- to the Decree Holders. Again bailable warrants were issued against the Appellants due to non-appearance, vide orders dated 20.08.2020 and 19.11.2020. This shows that the Appellants are in the habit of not appearing before the State Commission on the dates fixed. On 17.12.2020, the State Commission noted that the Appellants failed to comply with the order under execution and sought more time for compliance. The State Commission also noted that the Judgment Debtors are trying to delay the proceedings. The State Commission also directed to secure the Judgment Debtors through non-bailable warrants of arrest for the date fixed. The Judgment Debtors have not fully complied with the order of the State Commission. They are also frequently absenting from hearing before the State Commission. In view of the conduct of the Appellants, State Commission has issued the above directions. I see no reason to interfere with the orders of the State Commission in EA/147/2019 on 17.12.2020. Appeal Execution No.01 of 2021 is dismissed. ....
C. VISWANATH PRESIDING MEMBER

CASE NO. 21
CONSUMER CASE NO. 1904 OF 2018

HARESH BATHIJA & ANR. ....Complainant(s)

Versus

OZONE PROJECTS PRIVATE LIMITED ....Opp.Party(s)

BEFORE: HON'BLE MR. JUSTICE R.K. AGRAWAL,PRESIDENT

For the Complainant : For the Complainants : Mr. Prateek Chandra, Advocate Mr. Yash Sinha, Advocate With Complainant in person

For the Opp.Party : For the Opposite Party : Mr. Anish R. Shah, Advocate

Dated : 14 Jan 2021

ORDER

1. The present Consumer Complaint has been filed under Section 21(a)(i) of the Consumer Protection Act, 1986 (for short "the Act") against Ozone Projects Private Limited through its Managing Director, Mr. S. Vasudevan (hereinafter referred to as the 'Builder').

2. The facts of the case as enumerated in the Complaint are that in response to an advertisement of the Builder proposing to develop and sell Residential Apartments in their Project 'The Metrozone' located at Koyambedu, Chennai (hereinafter referred to as 'Project') and the assurance given by the Representative of the Builder that the Project would be ready for occupation by November, 2012, Mr. Haresh Bathija and his wife Kiran Dhameja (hereinafter referred to as 'the Complainants') purchased one Flat from the Builder in their Project for the use of his parents by availing Housing Loan from the HDFC Bank.An 'Agreement for Sale' was entered between the Parties on 30.11.2010 to purchase the Schedule D Property being an undivided share (UDS) of 564 sq.ft. in the Schedule C Property together with all other rights for a consideration of 22,56,000/-.A Construction Agreement dated 30.11.2010 was also executed between the Parties for purchasing a Flat, i.e., Unit No. H-202 in Tower H/2 measuring an area of 2062 sq. ft. with one car parking at a cost of 1,21,76,070/-.The total sale consideration agreed was fixed at 1,49,05,152/-.As per Construction Agreement, the Builder was to handover the possession of the flat within 2 years from the date of Agreement, i.e., by 30.11.2012.The Complainant deposited a sum of 1,38,55,893/-, i.e., more than 90% of the sale-consideration with the Builder despite that the Builder failed to deliver the possession of the flat within the stipulated period.The Complainants requested the Builder to adjust the compensation for delayed possession amounting to 3,73,710/- as on October 2013 from the balance outstanding amount payable against the cost of the flat.The Builder agreed and sought few days' time to arrive at the -1- 2. actual outstanding amount.Despite that after repeated requests and reminders, Builder failed to confirm the balance outstanding amount to the Complainants.The Complainants deposited a sum of 14,10,974/- towards the completion of internal plastering installment on 22.10.2013.It is alleged that despite depositing more than 90% of the total purchase consideration as on 22.10.2013, Builder failed to handover the possession of the Flat even after 5 years of the Construction Agreement.The Complainant sent a Legal Notice to the Builder on 26.09.2016 demanding payment of 42,07,000/- towards compensation for the delay in handing over the possession of the Flatin terms of Clause 7 of the Agreement executed between the Parties. The Builder sent a statement on 28.09.2016 whereby compensation was calculated at 8,74,975/-.The Builder sent Reply to the Legal Notice sent by the Complainant asking him to meet for amicable settlement.But the Complainant did not convince with the reply and preferred to file a Consumer Complaint before the Tamilnadu State Consumer Disputes Redressal Commission at Chennai.Vide Order dated 07.08.2018, the State Commission returned the Complaint to the Complainant for presenting the same before the proper forum. Consequently, alleging Unfair Trade Practice and deficiency in service on the part of the Builder for not handing over the possession of the flat within stipulated period despite receiving more than 90% of the sale consideration and not paying the compensation for delay in possession as per Clause 7 of the Construction Agreement, the Complainant has filed the present Complaint before this Commission seeking following prayer:- " i) Direct the Opposite Party to deliver the possession of the Residential Unit after completing in all respects in

a liveable condition with all amenities, facilities including roads, water/electricity/sewerage connections, not limited to herein, and as represented and projected by the Opposite Party in its "Brochure" together with all necessary governmental clearances, within the time frame as may be stipulated by this Hon'ble Commission; ii) Direct the Opposite Party to pay compensation to the Complainants herein amounting to 1,16,31,116/- which is 15/- per sq. ft. per month for delay in delivery of the flat with interest @18% p.a. thereon towards delay in payment of above said compensation as agreed by the Opposite Party together with future agreed compensation and interest till the date of making such payment by the Opposite Party herein and 18% interest on the amount paid by the Complainants herein; iii) Direct the Opposite Party to pay compensation of 10,00,000/- towards for mental agony, torture, hardship & depression caused and monetary loss caused on account of 'Deficiency of Service' committed by the Opposite Party besides Unfair & Restrictive Trade Practice adopted by the Opposite Party;. iv) Alternative cost of Rental accommodation amounting to 13,20,000/- at the rental rate of 20,000/- per month for a period of 65 months commencing from Feb 2013 till August 2018 and further alternatives cost of rental accommodation till the date of Order/Decree by this Hon'ble Commission; and -2- 2. 3. 4. v) That the Opposite Party is liable to pay the differential amounts in the Stamp duty and Registration fee as per the revised market rates of lands in Urban as per the provisions of Revised Guideline Value in Tamil Nadu as the Opposite Party has failed to complete the registration and handing over of possession as on date; vi) The Opposite Party be directed to pay the Complainants herein all legal costs at least a sum of 1,00,000/- including court fees, lawyer professional fees, travel and lodging expenses incurred by the Complainants herein in the proceedings filed before this Hon'ble Commission; vii) Pass such other Order or Orders as this Hon'ble Commission may deem fit and proper in the facts and circumstances of the case and thus, render justice. "

3. The Opposite Party Builder contested the Complaint by filing its Written Statement and denied the contents of the Complaint.It was stated that the Complainant had violated the Arbitral Clause of the Agreement by filing the present Complaint.It was stated that as per the Construction Agreement dated 30.11.2010 the anticipated date of delivery was within 2 years but the same was subject to force majeure and several unforeseeable circumstances. It was also submitted that as per Clause 4(e) and (f) of the Construction Agreement, the Complainant was bound to make the payment as per Schedule and to keep the Opposite Party Builder free from any loss due to non-payment of the installment on time.The Complainant did not make the payment as per Schedule and there was cumulative delay of more than 765 days in remitting 'Milestone Payments'.'Milestone Payments' means once the mutually agreed stage of construction is reached, a demand will be raised by the Builder seeking payment for the milestone achieved. As per the demand notices, 10 days' time was provided from the date of intimation of achieving each milestone to the Complainant. Although as per Clause 5(b) of the Construction Agreement, Opposite Party Builder was entitled to terminate the Agreement in case of breach of the payment terms by the Complainant, yet they neither terminated the Agreement nor charged any escalation charges from the Complainant but extended all possible support to the Complainant. The Complainant remained silent for about 4 years and suddenly asked for compensation for delay in terms of Clause 7 of the Construction Agreement. It was submitted that as per Clause 7(2) for grant of damages, the installments were to be paid as per the Payment Schedule, which the Complainant had not adhered to.

4. It was also submitted that the delay in handing over the possession was neither willful nor wanton but due to the reasons which were beyond their control.They got the plan approved from State Government in April 2009, which was valid for 3 years but due to short supply of construction material, restrictions imposed by the State Government on other State -3- 4. 5. 6. 7. 8. labours they could not complete the Project within three

years.Considerable time was lost in obtaining statutory approvals for getting Revised Planning Permission from the Government Authorities.

5. It was further submitted that the Builder obtained Completion Certificate from the Government Authorities in January 2016 for Tower H in which the Complainant had booked his Unit.Possessions of several apartments in Tower H have been handed over to the respective owners from January 2016 and they have settled in satisfactorily without any complaints.Complainants' flat was ready for fit out by January 2016 and for delivery by August 2016 but despite informing to the Complainants for getting the possession after paying 10% balance amount, the Complainants were unwilling to pay the outstanding amount and taking the possession of the Flat.It was also submitted that as a goodwill gesture, they offered to waive off 8,74,975/- towards the delay interest payable by the Complainants, though the delay was neither wilful nor wanton, and requested the Complainant to pay 2,52,447/- and get their sale deed registered and take possession of the Flat.Despite that the Complainants did not pay the balance amount but demanding an exorbitant sum of 42,07,000/- towards delay in handing over the possession of the Flat and this would show that the Complainant was not interested in taking possession of the Flat.Learned Counsel for the Opposite Party Builder relied upon the Judgment of the Hon'ble Supreme Court in "Bangalore Development Authority vs. Syndicate Bank" [(2007) 6 SCC 711] in which it was observed that having enjoyed the full appreciation of the Flat value and not being put to any penalty of paying the escalation cost, the Complainant is not entitled for any interest.He submitted that there is no deficiency in service on their part and prayed that the Consumer Complaint be dismissed.

6. I have heard Mr. Prateek Chandra, learned Counsel for the Complainants, Mr. Anish R. Shah, learned Counsel for the Opposite Party Builder, perused the Consumer Complaint, Written Statement and the material available on record.

7. During the proceedings, IA No. 7861 / 2019 was filed by the Complainants seeking a direction to the Opposite Party Builder to deliver the possession of Flat, i.e., Unit No. H202 in the building situated at No. 44, Pillaiyar Koil Street (Jawaharlal Nehru Road), Anna Nagar, Chennai – 600040.On 05.12.2019, Complainant handed over a cheque of 2,52,447/- to Mr. Anish R. Shah, learned Counsel for the Opposite Party and the Builder was directed to hand over the possession of the flat in question, i.e., Unit No. H202, in a habitable condition to the Complainant on 12.12.2019 and the IA No. 7861 / 2019 was disposed off.As such the only question with regard to compensation to be awarded to the Complainants for delay in delivery of the possession, remains to be decided..

8. Mr. Prateek Chandra, learned Counsel for the Complainants submitted that they are entitled for the compensation for delay in possession as per Clause 7 of the Construction Agreement, which reads as under:- "(b) The Developer shall handover possession of the Residential Unit to the Allottee(s) after the same is ready for occupation and subject to payment of all the amounts due under this Agreement. In the event of delay in handing over possession of the residential unit beyond the time period specified above, not attributable to any of the reasons stated above, the Developer shall pay to the Allottee(s) 15/- per sq. ft. per month till such time possession of the residential unit is handed over or intimated to the Allottee, whichever is earlier, subject to the Allottee(s) having paid all the instalments as per the Payment Schedule. In the event of such delay exceeding 6 months, the Developer shall pay to the Allottee(s), interest at the rate of 10% per annum, pro-rated for the further periods of such delays. The interest shall be calculated on all amounts received by the Developer from the Allottee(s), excluding the taxes and deposits. Such penalty shall be applicable only if the Allottee(s) has / have made all payments to Developer as per the Payment to Developer as per the Payment Schedule."

9. Per contra, Mr. Anish R. Shah, learned Counsel for the Opposite Party Builder submitted that the Complainants are not entitled for any compensation for delay in offer of possession as they had not followed the schedule of payment and the delay had

occurred due to obtaining statutory approvals which were beyond their control.However, they have already adjusted 8,74,975/- towards delay compensation in the balance amount payable by the Complainants and offered the possession of the flat to the Complainant vide letter dated 26.12.2016 to take the possession of the Flat after paying balance amount but the Complainants did not come-forward to take the possession.

10. Having gone through the material available on record, evidence adduced by the Parties as well as the oral submissions made by both the Parties, I am of the view that under the facts and circumstances of the case, the Complainants are entitled for interest @8% p.a. on the deposited amount towards compensation for delay in handing over the possession of the flat. Even though, the Opposite Party Builder had sent a letter of offering possession of the Flat on 26.12.2016 but on account of certain issues, the possession was not delivered/taken.This Commission vide Order dated 05.12.2019 had directed the Opposite Party Builder to hand over thepossession of flat, i.e. "Unit No. H202" to the Complainants in a habitable condition on 12.12.2019. For ready reference the Order dated 05.12.2019 is reproduced below:- " IA No. 7861 of 2019 This Application has been filed by the Complainants, seeking a direction to the Opposite Party to deliver the possession of flat, i.e. "Unit No. H202", in the building situated at No. 44, Pillaiyar Koil Street (Jawaharlal Nehru Road), Anna Nagar, Chennai-600040. -5- 10. 11. We have heard Mr. Haresh Bhatija, Complainant No.1, who has appeared in person, and Mr. Anish R. Shah, learned Counsel for the Opposite Party. Learned Counsel for the Opposite Party invited our attention to Annexure A-1 at page 16, filed along with the Application, wherein a demand of Rs.2,52,447/-, after deducting the delay compensation of Rs.8,74,975/-, was made by the Opposite Party in order to give the possession of the flat in question. Mr. Haresh Bhatija, Complainant No.1, states that he has handed over a cheque of Rs.2,52,447/- to Mr. Anish R. Shah, learned Counsel for the Opposite Party, today. The cheque be received by the learned Counsel for the Opposite Party and the possession of flat in question, i.e. "Unit No. H202" be delivered to the Complainants in a habitable condition on 12.12.2019. The Application stands disposed of."

11. It would be appropriate in the interest of Justice that the Opposite Party Builder be directed to pay compensation for delayed delivery of possession in the form of interest @8% p.a. from the date of delivery of possession as specified in the Agreement till the date of Order vide which Opposite Party Builder was directed to deliver the possession of the Flat.Accordingly, the Opposite Party Builder is directed to pay interest @8% p.a. to the Complainants with effect from 30 November 2012 (date of delivery of possession) to 05 th December 2019 (date of Order directing Opposite Party to deliver the possession) within th a period of six weeks from the date of receipt a copy of this Order.It is made clear that the amount of 8,74,975/- already received by the Complainants as compensation, will be adjusted by the Opposite Party Builder against the amount calculated in terms of this Order. ....J R.K. AGRAWAL PRESIDENT

CASE NO. 22
CONSUMER CASE NO. 987 OF 2017

SURENDER SINGH & ANR. S/o. Sh Hardwari Lal,
Sushila Singh W/o. Sh Surender,...........Complainant(s)

Versus

M/S. VARDHMAN BUILDTECH PVT. LTD. Through Its Managing Director,...........Opp.Party(s)
BEFORE: HON'BLE MR. JUSTICE R.K. AGRAWAL,PRESIDENT HON'BLE DR. S.M. KANTIKAR,MEMBER
For the Complainant : For the Complainant : Mr. Abhinav Ramkrishna, Advocate
For the Opp.Party : For the Opposite Party :

Ex Parte vide Order dated 01.11.2017

Dated : 14 Jan 2021

ORDER

1. The present Consumer Complaint has been filed under Sections 21, 2(c) read with Section 12(1)(c) of the Consumer Protection Act, 1986 (for short "the Act") by the Complainants, in the representative capacity, agitating their joint personal as well as collective grievance of about 600 buyers, against the Opposite Party, M/s. Vardhman Buildtech Pvt. Ltd. (hereinafter referred to as the 'Builder') for the inordinate delay in handing over possession of the Flats booked by them in the Project launched by the Builder in the name and style of "Vardhman Springdale, Daruhera (VSD)". Since the interest of the Complainants and other flat buyers in the aforesaid project is the same and identical reliefs have been claimed on behalf of all the Complainants, IA No. 4886 / 2017, an Application under Section 12(1)(c) of the Act has also been filed with the Complaint to treat the Complaint as a class-action Complaint. Vide Order dated 1 Nov. 2017, IA No. 4886/2017 was allowed and the st Complaint was treated as filed under Section 12(1)(c) of the Act.

2. According to the Complainants, the facts of the case are that the Opposite Party Builder launched a residential Project 'Vardhman's Springdale Dharuhera' (hereinafter referred to as the Project).Complainants booked a 3 BHK Flat No. 503, 5 Floor, Tower – H, th admeasuring 1640 sq. ft. in the said Project for a total sale consideration of 40,22,000/-. A Builder Buyer Agreement was executed between the Parties on 19.10.2012. As per Builder Buyer Agreement, the Construction of the Tower was to be completed by December 2015 and possession was to be offered within 30 days thereafter for interior and fit outs.It is the say of the Complainants that they had made the payments of more than 23,82,019/- as per demands of the Opposite Party Builder despite that the Builder had failed to compete the construction and did not provide possession for interior and fit outs on or before December 2015 as per terms of the Builder Buyer Agreement.Alleging unfair trade practice and deficiency in service on the part of the Opposite Party Builder, the Complainants has filed the present Complaint with following prayer:- " a) Direct the Opposite Parties to complete construction work of the entire project 'Vardhman Springdale Daruhera' including the flat of the Complainants bearing Flat No. 503 on 5 Floor of Tower H in the project Vardhman's Springdale Dharuhera, th admeasuring 1640 sq. ft. Consisting of 3 bedrooms, drawing/dinning, kitchen, toilets in the Project Vardhman's Springdale Dharuhera and handover possession to each flat buyer with all amenities within stipulated time as it may deem fit to this Hon'ble Commission; b) Award interest at the rate of 18% per annum to each buyer for the period of delay in handing over the possession of the flat on the amount paid by each buyer respectively. c) Award Cost of litigation & mental harassment which may be quantified to 4,00,000/- (Rupee Four Lakh only).. "

3. Despite service of Notice neither any one appeared on behalf of the Opposite Party Builder nor any Written Version was filed on their behalf.Accordingly, vide Order dated 1 Nov. st 2017 the Opposite Party Builder was proceeded ex-parte and their right to file Written Statement was forfeited.They even did not choose to file any Application to set aside the ex-parte Order.

4. We have heard Mr. Abhinav Ramkrishna, learned Counsel for the Complainant and perused the material available on record as well as the Written Submissions filed by the Complainant on 01.10.2018.

5. Mr. Abhinav Ramkrishna, learned Counsel appearing for the Complainants strenuously submitted that the Complainant had paid all the amounts as demanded by the Builder from time to time.It was assured to the Complainant that the entire Project would be completed and possession would be delivered by December, 2015. However, the Builder has failed to deliver the possession for interior and fit outs within the stipulated period of time which tantamount to deficiency in service on their part and as such the

Complainants are entitled for the reasonable compensation for the delay in delivery of possession, mental agony and harassment. Further, placing reliance upon the Judgment of the Hon'ble Supreme Court in the case 'Karnataka Housing Board' Vs. K.A. Nagamani – (2019) 6 SCC 424 - , he vigorously contended that the Complainants are entitled to an interest @15% p.a on the deposited amount of 23,82,019/- on completion of 2½ years from the date of commencement of the construction, i.e., from 03.02.2013 and @9% p.a. from December 2015 onward. He further submitted that the Builder be directed to complete the entire Project within the period of one year and to hand over the possession of the booked flats, complete in all respects and free from all encumbrances. Alternatively, if the Builder is not in a position to complete the Project and deliver the possession of the allotted Flats, they may be directed to refund the deposited amounts along with interest @ 9% p.a. from the date of respective deposit till the date of realization. Besides, a sum of 2,00,000/- towards cost of litigation and mental harassment.

6. A perusal of the Complaint reveals that the Complainants had booked a 3 BHK Flat No. 503, 5 Floor, Tower-H admeasuring 1640 sq. ft. with the Opposite Party Builder for a th total sale consideration of 40,22,000/- out of which they had paid a substantial amount of 23,82,019/-. As per the Complaint, the Builder Buyer Agreement was executed between the parties on 19.10.2020. As per the conditions embodied in the Builder Buyer Agreement, the Opposite Party Builder was under an obligation to provide possession for interior and fit-outs on or before 31.12.2015. However, the Builder has failed to keep their promises of timely delivery of possession of the booked flats.

7. Despite the notices being served on the Complaint as well as on the Application filed u/s 12(1)(c), for the reasons best known to them, the Opposite Party neither put appearance nor filed their Written Version in support of their defense.Hence, the facts averred in the Complaint remain unrebutted. Under these circumstances, the questions regarding reasons for delay in completing the Project and as to when the Builder will be in a position to complete the entire Project also remain unanswered.

8. In the case of Emmar MGF Land Ltd. & Ors. vs. Amit Puri - [II (2015) CPJ 568 (NC)] , this Commission has held that after the promised date of delivery, it is the discretion of the Complainant whether to accept the offer of possession, if any, or to seek refund of the amounts paid by him with some reasonable compensation and it is well within his right to seek for refund of the principal amount with interest and compensation.

9. Further, in the case of Kolkata West International City Pvt. Ltd. Vs. Devasis Rudra - II (2019) CPJ 29 SC, the Hon'ble Apex Court has observed as under :- "…..It would be manifestly unreasonable to construe the contract between the parties as requiring the buyer to wait indefinitely for possession. By 2016, nearly seven years had elapsed from the date of the agreement. Even according to the developer, the completion certificate was received on 29 March 2016. This was nearly seven years after the extended date for the handing over of possession prescribed by the agreement. A buyer can be expected to wait for possession for a reasonable period. A period of seven years in beyond what is reasonable. Hence, it would have been manifestly unfair to non-suit the buyer merely on the basis of the first prayer in the reliefs sought before the SCDRC. There was in any event a prayer for refund. In the circumstances, we are of the view that the orders passed by the SCDRC and by the NCDRC for refund of moneys were justified."

10. In the instant case also, the Complainants cannot be made to wait indefinitely for possession of their Flat, when there is absolutely no response from the Opposite Parties and the Complainants are entitled for refund of the principal amount with interest. Accordingly, keeping in view the ratio laid down by the Hon'ble Supreme Court in DLF Homes Panchkula Pvt. Ltd Vs. D.S. Dhanda - II (2019) CPJ 117 (SC) , that compensation under multiple heads cannot be awarded, we are of the considered view that simple interest in the form of compensation @ 8% p.a. would meet the ends of justice together with costs of 50,000/-.

11. In the result, this Complaint filed under Section 12(1)(c) of the Act i.e., for the benefit of all Consumers/Complainants is allowed in part directing the Opposite Party to refund the deposited amount to the Complainants with compensation in the form of simple interest @ 8% p.a. from the respective dates of deposit till the payment is made together with costs of 50,000/. This amount is directed to be paid within four weeks from the date of receipt of a copy of this order, failing which, the amount shall attract interest @ 10% p.a. for the same period. ....J R.K. AGRAWAL PRESIDENT .... DR. S.M. KANTIKAR MEMBER

CASE NO. 23
FIRST APPEAL NO. 549 OF 2020

(Against the Order dated 13/02/2020 in Complaint No. 27/2019 of the State Commission Chhattisgarh)

NATIONAL INSURANCE CO. LTD............Appellant(s)

Versus

RAM SURAT PASWAN S/O. LATE SHRI RAM AWADH PASWAN, R ....Respondent(s)

BEFORE: HON'BLE MRS. JUSTICE DEEPA SHARMA,PRESIDING MEMBER

For the Appellant : MR. ANKUR JAITLY

For the Respondent :

Dated : 15 Jan 2021

ORDER

JUSTICE DEEPA SHARMA
(ORAL) THROUGH VIDEO CONFERENCING

The present Appeal, under Section ---51(1) of the Consumer Protection Act, 2019 (for short "the Act") has been filed by the Appellant against the order dated 13.02.2020 of the State Consumer Disputes Redressal Commission, Chhattisgarh (for short "the State Commission") in Complaint No.27 of 2019 whereby the Complaint of the Respondent/Complainant was allowed and the following directions were given: "23. Therefore, the complaint of the complainant is initially accepted and passed the direction in order, that:

1. The Opposite Party Insurance Company is directed to pay the amount of 23,92,500/- (twenty three lakh ninety two thousand five hundred only) to the complainant within 45 (forty five) days;

2. The Opposite Party Insurance Company is also directed to pay the interest yearly 6 per cent calculated on 23,92,500/- (twenty three lakh ninety two thousand five hundred only) from the date of institution of case dated 30.05.2019.

3. The Opposite Party Insurance Company is directed to paythe compensation on mental agony, 10,000/- (rupees ten thousand) and the cost of the litigation 3,000/- (rupees three thousand) to the complainant."

4. The brief facts of the case are that the Complainant had purchased a vehicle no.CG 07 BA/8577 and the same was insured with the Appellant against theft. During the validity of the insurance policy, on the intervening night of 7 and 8 October 2017, the vehicle got th th stolen from the roadside. An FIR of theft was registered on 09.10.2017 and the Appellant was also immediately informed of the theft and the claim was also filed. The claim of the Respondent was, however, repudiated by the Appellant on the ground that the Complainant was guilty of violation of Clause 5 of the terms and conditions of the

policy. Aggrieved, the Respondent/Complainant filed the Complaint before the State Commission.

5. The case of the Complainant before the State Commission was that his vehicle when being driven on road developed some fault, probably in the clutch plate and therefore, the vehicle could not be driven further. The vehicle was then parked on the roadside and a search for mechanic was made. However, it was found that the vehicle had been stolen. 4. Thereafter, the Complainant approached the Opposite Party for claim of insured vehicle. The claim was repudiated only on the ground of violation of the Clause 5 of the insurance policy.

6. Parties led their evidences before the State Commission. The State Commission after appreciating the evidences on record and hearing the arguments of learned counsel for the parties and going through the case laws relied upon by the parties has held as under: "19. The claim submitted by the complainant has been rejected by the Opposite Party Insurance Company due to breach of condition point no.5 of the insurance contract, according to which the complainant himself will be responsible for the loss incurred because the complainant has not been taken adequate security measures, for which it is said that the complainant is responsible for that loss. The First Information Report (annexed hereto Annexure C-6) and O.P.-2) lodged by driver Nathuram Juganlal Dewang stated in brief that: "on 06.10.2017, as on instructions of the owner, I was directed, came to Nagpur, so after reaching in Nagpur I met his friend on 07.10.2017, when that time after meeting he said, got to Bhandara to load the sand dust on truck. At the behest of him, I have been decided to depart from Nagpur in the evening at 05/06, then, I carried out the vehicle from that place of his house, but while going to Bhandara, I stopped the truck just after crossing the bridge pulia at around 6/00 hrs due to mechanical problem occurred in truck, may be the clutch plate defunct, I parked the truck on road side. After gap of some time I made a phone call to a friend of the owner of the vehicle, requested him to come down because the vehicle at now is technically given some problem and stopped at road side. That after sometime the friend of the owner of the vehicle came at that side, there from informed to the owner of the vehicle on phone. At around 6:30 pm, I along with that person left to search the mechanic, after locking the vehicle, but due to the night, no mechanic was there available or found due to darkness in the night at that time then we both went back to nearby dhaba for taking of dinner and he suggested me to stay here, don't be bother, we will be sure to find the mechanic in tomorrow morning. He again suggested me to stay here in the night. That on 08.10.2017 at around 7:00 am in the morning, when I went by auto to the place where the truck was parked on road side, have seen, no truck was there parked that mean theft, I made effort by hard to search the vehicle but did not find it anywhere, so I made a phone call to Mangesh Channe and narrated about missing of the vehicle from there and requested him to come here. When that time we started search drive in surrounding areas there where nearby road but the trick was not found then informed the owner of this vehicle on phone. "Thus, it is clearly mentioned in lodging of the first information report – the driver went to find a mechanic by locking the vehicle. So the driver locked the vehicle and kept the key in safe. It has been raised a question by the defendant that the vehicle was left wihout locking the truck vehicle and keys was leave on dash board so the vehicle was stolen but it is not true because after locking of truck vehicle the key was deposited, further the Opposite Party said the complainant deposited only one key to the insurance company. That in other hand the report of the Sai consultant extracted on page number 6 of the report there two key received by the Opposite Party insurance company. It is mentioned, even if the insurance company did not receive two keys, from the complainant plaintiff, so the question is raised the said insurance company why did not asked for demand of keys in his written letter dated 12.01.2018, 06.03.2018 and 07.06.2018. The Opposite Party insurance company was not clarifying about this raising point. It is clear from the First Information Report that

the vehicle was left safely by the complainant and the keys of the vehicle were also given to the insurance company by the complainant. Thus the complainant has not violated the condition no.5 of the insurance terms and condition. 20. The justice illustration presented by the non-applicant insurance company is a different from the facts of this case, so it does not get the benefit to the non-applicant insurance company. 21. In view of the above averments, we have now come to the conclusion that the complainant has been successful in certifying that after locks the vehicle left from there after parking of the vehicle on safe stand, after that both the keys of the vehicle was submitted to the insurance company. Thus insurance policy condition number 5 has not been violated by the complainant. In such a situation, the service has not been discharge in proper that mean lack of service incurred by the Opposite Party insurance company by cancelling the claim of the complainant, so the complainant is entitled to receive the claim amount. 22. The complainant submitted a copy of the insurance policy terms and condition Exhibit C-2, there is mentioned I.D. value of vehicle in total of 25,20,000/- (twenty five lakh and twenty thousand) and there in written statement of the insurance company at para no.3 mentioned about the vehicle utilized in total of 5 months, so for this use of vehicle the cost of the vehicle shall be reduce in ratio of 5% plus 1500/- (rupees one thousand five hundred) that mean the cost of the vehicle after reduce shall be valued 23,92,000/- (twenty three lakh ninety two thousand five hundred only), the complainant is entitled to receive the claim amount. 23. Therefore, the complaint of the complainant is initially accepted and passed the direction in order, that:- The Opposite Party insurance company is directed to pay the amount 23,92,000/- (twenty three lakh ninety two thousand five hundred only) to the complainant within 45 (forty five) days; The Opposite Party insurance company is also directed to pay the interest yearly 6 per cent -4- 5. -6- calculated on 23,92,000/- (twenty three lakh ninety two thousand five hundred only) from the date of institution of case dated 30.05.2019; (3) The Opposite Party insurance company is directed to pay the compensation on mental agony, 10,000/- (rupees ten thousand) and the cost of the litigation 3,000/- (rupees three thousand), to the complainant." 6. Learned Counsel for the Appellant has challenged these findings of the State Commission on the ground that the proper precautions were not taken when the vehicle was parked on the road. It is submitted that the vehicle had mechanical defects and therefore, could not have been moved from the road and that the claim submitted by the Complainant is false.

7. I have heard the arguments of learned Counsel for the Appellant and perused the record.

8. It is observed that the Appellant had taken only one ground in its repudiation letter that is breach of clause 5 of the terms and conditions of the insurance policy and no other. Clause 5 is reproduced as under: "5. The insured shall take all reasonable steps to safeguard the vehicle insured from loss or damage and to maintain it in efficient condition and the Company shall have at all time free and full access to examine the vehicle insured or any part thereof or any driver of employee of the insured. In the event of any accident or breakdown, the vehicle insured shall not be left unattended without proper precautions being taken to prevent further damage or loss and if the vehicle insured be driven before the necessary repairs are effected, any extension of the damage or any further damage to the vehicle shall be entirely at the insured's own risk.

9. In the case of Galada Power and Telecommunication Ltd. Vs. United India Insurance Company Limited & Another, 2016 14 SCC 161, the Hon'ble Supreme Court has observed that the Insurance Company cannot proceed beyond the reasons specified in the repudiation letter. The Apex court has held as under: "12. It is evincible, the insurer had taken cognizance of the communication made by the appellant and nominated a surveyor to verify the loss. Once the said exercise has been undertaken, we are disposed to think that the insurer could not have been allowed to take a stand that the claim is hit by the clause pertaining to duration. In the absence of any mention in the letter of repudiation and also from the conduct of the insurer in appointing a surveyor, it can

safely be concluded that the insurer had waived the right which was in its favour under the duration clause. In this regard, Mr. Mukherjee, learned senior counsel appearing for the appellant has commended us to a decision of High Court of Delhi in Krishna Wanti v. Life Insurance Corporation of India[1], wherein the High Court has taken note of the fact that if the letter of repudiation did not mention an aspect, the same could not be taken as a stand when the matter is decided. We approve the said view."

10. A similar view was taken by the Hon'ble Supreme Court in the case of "Saurashtra Chemicals Limited vs. National Insurance Company Limited, 1 (2020) CPJ 93 SC" which is as under: "22. Hence we are of the considered opinion that the law as laid down in 'Galada' on issue (2) still hodls the field. It is a settled position that an insurance company cannot travel beyond the grounds mentioned in the letter of repudiation. If the insurer has not taken delay in intimation as a specific ground in letter of repudiation, they cannot do so at the stage of hearing of the consumer complaint before NCDRC."

11. Thus, the Hon'ble Supreme Court has clearly held that the only plea, as a defence, which can be taken by the Insurance Company is the one mentioned in the repudiation letter. Admittedly, in this case, the repudiation letter only mentions the breach of condition no.5 of the insurance policy wherein it is mentioned that the insured is not entitled for the benefit under this contract if he had not taken adequate security measures. The evidences on record which is the statement of the Complainant in the form of affidavit and another documents on record clearly show that the Complainant had taken adequate measures while leaving the vehicle on roadside. The Complainant had clearly stated that he locked the vehicle while leaving it on the roadside. There is no evidence on record to show the contra. The surveyor's report clearly shows that the Complainant had handed over the two keys of the vehicle to the surveyor. This corroborates the testimony of the Complainant that he had properly locked the vehicle and then took the keys with him at the time of leaving the vehicle on the roadside. The findings of the State Commission, therefore, are based on the cogent evidences on record. I found no illegality or perversity in the impugned order. The present Appeal has no merit and the same is dismissed in limine. ....J DEEPA SHARMA PRESIDING MEMBER

CASE NO. 24
FIRST APPEAL NO. 1401 OF 2018

(Against the Order dated 10/05/2018 in Complaint No. 8/2007 of the State Commission Himachal Pradesh)

ORIENTAL INSURANCE CO. LTD. THROUGH MANAGER, ...Appellant(s)

Versus

HIMACHAL PHARMACEUTICALS LTD. THROUGH ITS MANAGING PARTNER, SH. B.M. SOOD,...........Respondent(s)

FIRST APPEAL NO. 1498 OF 2019

(Against the Order dated 10/05/2018 in Complaint No. 8/2007 of the State Commission Himachal Pradesh)

M/S. HIMACHAL PHARMACEUTICALS LIMITED KANDRORI THROUGH ITS MANAGER PARTNER, SH. B.M. SOOD............Appellant(s)

Versus

ORIENTAL INSURANCE- COMPANY LIMITED THROUGH ITS SR. DIVISIONAL MANAGER TO BE SERVED THROUGH THE DIVISIONAL MANAGER ....Respondent(s)

BEFORE: HON'BLE MR. C. VISWANATH,PRESIDING MEMBER

For the Appellant :

For the Insurance Company Mr Mithilesh Sinha, Advocate

For the Respondent :

For Himachal Pharmaceuticals Mr Yaduinder Lal, Advocate
Dated : 18 Jan 2021

ORDER

1. The present cross Appeals are filed by the Appellants under Section 19 of the Consumer Protection Act, 1986 against the order passed by the Himachal Pradesh State Consumer Disputes Redressal Commission, Shimla (for short 'the State Commission') in CC No. 08 of 2007 dated 10.05.2018. First Appeal no. 1401 of 2018 has been filed by the Appellant/ Insurance Company with a delay of 54 days as per the report of the Registry, however, as per the Appellant/Insurance Company the delay is 53 days. First Appeal No.1498 of 2019 has been filed by M/s Himachal Pharmaceuticals Limited with a delay of 401 days, as per report of the Registry. However, as per the Appellant/Complainant, the delay is of 364 days. For the reasons stated in both the applications and in the interest of justice, the delay is condoned.

2. Complainant is a partnership firm engaged in manufacturing and sale of Pharmaceuticals Drugs at its factory in Kandrori, Kangra District, Himachal Pradesh. The unit was started after obtaining loan from Oriental Bank of Commerce, Pathankot. Complainant obtained a Standard Fire and Special Risks Policy, valid from 13.04.2005 to 12.04.2006. According to the Complainant, the unit suffered extensive damage due to fire which broke out on 25.10.2005. On receiving information of the fire, the Opposite Party appointed a Surveyor, who visited the spot on 28.11.2005. The Surveyor assessed the loss at Rs.1,07,447.47. However, the Complainant filed a claim of Rs.20,19,689/- alongwith Rs.2 lakhs for mental agony and Rs.35,000/- for litigation cost. In spite of voluminous correspondence between the Parties, claim of the Complainant was not settled. Therefore, the Complainant filed Complaint before the State Commission with following prayer: That this complaint may kindly be allowed and this Commission may kindly be pleased to direct the opposite party – insurance company to pay to the complainant; The indemnification amount of Rs.20,9,689/- along with interest at the rate of 18% per annum with effect from 25.10.2005 till the date of actual payment; A sum of Rs.2,00,000/- as compensation for mental torture and harassment suffered by the complainant; A sum of Rs.35,000/- as cost of litigation.

3. The case was contested by the Opposite Party who contended that the Complainant had been a defaulter in making payment to the Oriental Bank of Commerce, Pathankot, and therefore, had been declared NPA in 2004. It was admitted that fire took place in the Complainant's unit on 25.10.2005 and Mr Duggal Gupta, Surveyors Private Limited was deputed to assess the loss. He submitted report on 15.01.2007 assessing the loss at Rs.1,07,447.47 and a cheque for Rs.1,06,905/- was issued in the name of the Complainant's banker, Oriental Bank of Commerce. There was no deficiency in service on the part of the Opposite Party and therefore the Complaint be dismissed.

4. The Consumer Complaint was decided by the State Commission on 28.08.2009, as follows: "32. In the light of the above discussion, we are of the view that in the ordinary course of things, claim of the complainant should have been settled expeditiously by the opposite party – insurance company and it cannot be made to shift the burden or to wash off its hands by raising the plea that the complainant failed to provide necessary documents to the surveyor appointed to assess the loss. If this was the situation, nothing prevented the opposite party to have the closed the file. 33. It hardly needs to be emphasized in this context that as a limb of the welfare state, wholly owned and controlled by the Government of India who also have pervasive control over it, all actions of opposite party are expected to be just, reasonable and fair besides being not arbitrary. It was for the opposite party to have ensured that the surveyor appointed by it facts in a swift, just and expeditious manner to deal with the assessment and submit it report. According to us, claim of the complainant should have been settled within six months after the date of fire. Accordingly, we hold that the complainant is entitled to sum claimed Rs.20,19,689/- towards indemnification of the loss suffered by it along

with interest @ 12% per annum from 01.04.2006 till the date of payment/ deposit whichever is earlier. In addition to this, complainant is held entitled to compensation for harassment etc., which we quantify at Rs.50,000/-. Besides, this opposite party is directed to pay Rs.20,000/- as punitive damages, as also Rs.10,000/- as cost of litigation. Complaint is allowed in these terms".

5. Aggrieved by the order of the State Commission, the Opposite Party filed Appeal No.474 of 2009 before this Commission, wherein the order of the State Commission was set aside and the matter remanded to the State Commission for taking decision afresh.

6. Learned Counsel appearing on behalf of both the Parties were heard and after carefully perusing the record, the State Commission in CC no. 8 of 2007 passed the following order: "17. In view of the findings upon point no .1, complaint is partly allowed and it is ordered that opposite party would indemnify the complainant to the tune of Rs.10.00 lakh only along with interest @ 9% per annum with effect from 16.07.2007 till realisation. In addition it is further ordered that opposite party would pay compensation for mental torture and harassment to the tune of Rs.25,000/- to the complainant. In addition it is further ordered that opposite party would pay litigation costs to the complainant to the tune of Rs.10,000/-. It is further ordered that opposite party would be legally entitled to adjust the advance payment of cheque to the tune of Rs.1,06,905/- paid to the loanee back if the cheque has been enchased by the loanee bank. Letter sent by Mr B M Sood, Managing Director of complainant company dated 26.10.2005 Annexure 2, report of Up-pradhan Annexure A – 3 and Nakal Report no. 15 dated 26.10.2005 would form part and parcel of order".

7. Aggrieved by the order of the State Commission, Cross Appeals have been filed by both the Parties. Heard the Learned Counsels for the Parties and carefully perused the record.

8. 8. Learned Counsel for the Complainant stated that Taxol is a generic name of Paclitaxel which is a final product and not a product at research or intermediate stage. He further stated that the Surveyor had neither valued nor calculated the loss suffered by the unit. Learned Counsel for the Opposite Party stated that the fire brigade was not called to douse the fire and also that the Complainant's unit was declared as NPA, as they did not pay dues to the Bank which financed the unit. The State Commission had not given any reason for rejecting the Surveyor's report. The impugned order be, therefore, set aside and their Appeal allowed.

9. Brief facts of the case are that the Complainant is a partnership firm engaged in the manufacture and sale of pharmaceuticals and had obtained a Standard Fire and Special Risks Policy from the Opposite Party, valid from 13.04.2005 to 12.04.2006. Fire broke out in the unit on 25.10.2005 and the Opposite Party was informed of the same on 26.10.2005. A report was also lodged with the Police.

10. Complainant informed the Surveyor that the fire brigade was not called after the incident. The Complainant stated that the fire occurred when their chemist was working in the laboratory and the person present on the spot controlled and extinguished the fire within half an hour. It is not understood as to how fire which allegedly led to extensive damage, was brought under control by a person present on the spot in 20 to 30 minutes, without calling for the fire brigade. The Complainant informed the Opposite Party on 26.10.2005 that the estimated loss was to the tune of Rs.8-10 lakhs. Police Report filed by Mr Brij Mohan Sood quoted the same figure. This has also corroborated by the report of Up-pradhan. The State Commission observed that the Complainant himself by his own admission held that the loss occurred to his unit was to the tune of Rs.8-10 lakh only. The Complainant was therefore entitled for damage to the tune of Rs.10 lakh.

11. However, later the Complainant, made a claim for Rs.20,19,689/- and thereafter filed a Complaint seeking compensation for the loss suffered by the unit. A Surveyor was appointed by the Opposite Party and he submitted his report on 15.01.2007 assessing the loss at Rs.1,07,447.47. Based on the report of the Surveyor, the Opposite Party offered a

sum of Rs.1,07,447.47 to the Complainant which was not accepted by them. In his report the Surveyor stated that the actual loss suffered by the Complainant did not tally with the claim loss and the stock statements were not submitted after the unit was declared as NPA on 31.07.2004. The loss had been calculated on the basis of the record and hence, there was no deficiency in service on the part of the Opposite Party.

12. Regarding maintainability of the Complaint, the Learned Counsel for the Opposite party contended that the Complainant had been declared as NPA since 2004 and the present Complaint was not maintainable. The Insurance Policy was issued in favour of the Complainant which was valid from 13.04.2005 to 12.04.2006 and the fire incident had occurred on 25.10.2005, during the validity of the Policy. The Insurance Company had received the premium and hence, the Insurance Company was bound to indemnify the Complainant.

13. In FA no.474 of 2009, this Commission, vide order dated 22.09.2016, observed that the State Commission should have carefully gone into the details of the report submitted and then recorded their findings. The State Commission, vide order dated 10.05.2018, however, arrived at its findings merely based on the submissions of the Complainant as well as the report of the Up-Pradhan. Based on the admission and reports of the Complainant and Up-Pradhan, the State Commission awarded Rs.10 lakh along with interest and certain other cost to the Complainant. These admissions and statements cannot be considered as a valid basis for arriving at a decision. The State Commission, without analysing the issues raised has erred in solely relying on the submission of the Complainant, corroborated by a non-official Pradhan, ignoring the detailed Surveyor Report available on record. The order of State Commission therefore, deserves to be set aside.

14. I have carefully gone through the report of the Surveyor. The Complainant could not clarify the fact as to whether Taxol was extracted by their own concern or brought from others. Copies of the purchase bills or Taxus Extract or for leaves from which it was extracted were also not provided. In the absence of documentary evidence/ purchase and sale bills, the Surveyor was unable to arrive at the quantity and value of stocks which was destroyed in the fire. As regards Methoxsalene, insured could not establish quantity of this item available before the loss occurred due to fire. The Surveyor further observed that Chrysarobin did not appear in the details of stocks on hand as on 25.10.2005, as per information provided on the day of their visit and was found incorporated thereafter manually by the insured. Sufficient evidence was not provided for the purchase of raw material or semi-finished product of the chemicals. The Respondent also did provide any further evidence to the State Commission to analyse the loss suffered and, the State Commission sought to rely merely on the statement of the Complainant, Nakal Report and the estimate given in the report submitted by the Up-Pradhan, which hardly have any evidentiary value.

15. Learned Counsel for the Complainant during the course of arguments insisted that Taxol was a final product and was not at research stage, but could not produce any documentary evidence to show any licence to manufacture or sell Taxol. This argument, however does not seem to have been taken up in the past, as even this Commission, vide its order dated 22.09.2016, was given to understand that it was at research stage. However, this Commission has already held that the product whether at the research stage or at the final stage, had to be evaluated in a proper manner.

16. In " Sri Venkateswara Syndicate Vs Oriental Insurance Company Limited & Anr., 2009 (8) SCC 507, the Hon'ble Apex Court held as under: The assessment of loss, claim settlement and relevance of survey report depends on various factors. Whenever a loss is reported by the insured, a loss adjuster, popularly known as loss surveyor, is deputed who assess the loss and issues report known as surveyor report which forms the basis for consideration or otherwise of the claim. Surveyors are appointed under the statutory provisions and they are the link between the insurer and the insured when the question

of settlement of loss or damage arises. The report of the surveyor could become the basis for settlement of a claim by the insurer in respect of the loss suffered by the insured. There is no disputing the fact that the Surveyor/Surveyors are appointed by the insurance company under the provisions of Insurance Act and their reports are to be given due importance and one should have sufficient grounds not to agree with the assessment made by them.

17. It is very clear from the above judgment of the Apex Court that the report of the Surveyor is an import document and a basis for consideration of the claim. There should, however, be -5- sufficient grounds available on record to disregard the assessment made by the Surveyor. In the present case, the Surveyor had very clearly discussed the entire damage caused to the property and the stocks of the Complainant and specially dealt in detail with the three chemicals, whose loss could not be assessed. He had very clearly mentioned that even the basic details required for arriving at the loss suffered could not be satisfactorily provided and explained by the insured. Further, during the opportunity provided to the Complainant both at the State level and during the course of arguments in this Commission also, no further evidence was placed on record which could throw further light on the damage and the loss suffered by the Complainant in terms of the quantity and value of the stocks of these chemicals.

18. In view of the above, the order of the State Commission is set aside and the Opposite Party/Insurance Company is directed to pay Rs.1,07,447.47 net assessment made by the Surveyor for the loss suffered along with 9% interest from the date of filing of the Complaint till the date of payment. If any amount has already been paid and received by the Complainant, the same be adjusted from the amount to be paid and for that amount interest shall not be awarded from the date of such payment. Both the Appeals are accordingly disposed. There shall be no order as to costs.

19. The order be complied within a period of eight weeks. .... C. VISWANATH PRESIDING MEMBER

<u>CASE NO. 25</u>
FIRST APPEAL NO. 323 OF 2018

(Against the Order dated 03/01/2018 in Complaint No. 460/2015 of the State Commission West Bengal)

PRANABESH DAS & ANR. REP. THROUGH SRI. SRIBASH CHANDRA ROAD, P.S.-DUM DUM. KOLKATA-700030

SINCHITA DAS. REP. THROUGH SRI. SRIBASH CHANDRA DAS. W/O. PRANABESH CHANDRA DAS............Appellant(s)

Versus

M/S. CANOPY PROJECTS LTD. REP. THROUGH ITS DIRECTORS, AMITHABH KEJRIWAL, VIKASH BAGRI, AND REKHA MAHESHWARI............Respondent(s)

BEFORE: HON'BLE MR. C. VISWANATH,PRESIDING MEMBER

For the Appellant : Mr. Arunava Mukherjee, Advocate

For the Respondent : Mr. Dinesh Sabarwal, Advocate

Dated : 18 Jan 2021

ORDER

1. This Appeal is filed against the order dated 06.12.2017 of the West Bengal State Consumer Disputes Redressal Commission, Commission, Kolkata (hereinafter referred to as "the State Commission) in CC/460/2015.

2. Case of the Appellants/Complainants is that on 15.02.2007 they entered into an agreement with the Respondent/Opposite Party for purchase of a developed plot, measuring 7.5 Cottah, for a consideration of Rs.22,50,000/-, out of which Complainants

paid Rs.20,25,000/- on different dates. As per the Agreement, the plot was to be developed in two Phases, Phase I was to be completed by December, 2006 and Phase II by December, 2007, but the Opposite Party failed to do so. Complainants sent a legal notice dated 22.06.2015 to the Opposite Party. Opposite Party replied to the legal notice, vide letter dated 03.07.2015, wherein they admitted having received an amount of Rs.20,25,000/-and also agreed to refund the entire amount. On 18.07.2015, Opposite. Party sent an email containing offer of settlement. Since the terms of settlement were not acceptable to the Complainants, on 03.09.2015 they approached the Consumer Affairs Department for redressal of their grievance. On 29.9.2015, the Opposite Party agreed to refund the principal amount of Rs.20,25,000/- on the next date i.e. 15.10.2015, but the Opposite Party failed to make payment. Claiming deficiency in service on the part of the Opposite Party, Complainants filed Consumer Complaint before the State Commission with the following prayer to: "i) The opposite party to handover the developed plot of land as per agreement or failing which refund the amount of Rs.20,25,0000/- which has been paid by the Complainants, the details have already been given in para 4 & 6 plus interest @ 16% till date of payment calculated as on 25.10.2015 as Rs.21,78,960/-. To pay the compensation towards mental torture, damage and cost Rs.10,000/-. Any other order or orders as your Honour deem fit."

3. Complaint was contested by the Opposite Party/Respondent on the ground that the Opposite Party could not develop the plot in time, since State of West Bengal initiated vesting proceedings against them. Since the matter was subjudice in Calcutta High Court, nature of the land could not be changed by the Opposite Parties.

4. State Commission, after hearing Learned Counsel for the Parties and perusing the record, allowed the Complaint and directed the Respondent/Opposite Party as follows: - "The OP is directed to hand over and to execute the Deed of Conveyance in respect of the plot as per Agreement for Sale dated 15.02.2007 in favour of the Complainants within 60 days from date on receipt of balance consideration amount of Rs.2,25,000/-, failing which the OP must refund Rs.20,25,000/- along with interest thereon @ 12% p.a. from the date of payment till its full realization. The OP is further directed to pay compensation of Rs.1,00,000/- and litigation cost of Rs.10,000/- aggregating Rs.1,10,000/- within 30 days from date otherwise the amount shall carry interest @ 9% p.a. from date till its realization."

5. Not satisfied with the order of the State Commission, Complainants have filed present Appeal. Heard Learned Counsel for the Parties and carefully perused the record. Learned Counsel for the Appellants submitted that the State Commission erred in giving an option to the Respondent to give the plot or refund the amount with interest. It was also submitted that the interest granted by the State Commission was on lower side and the interest should have been awarded @ 16%.

6. Learned Counsel for the Respondent submitted that the Appellants in their Complaint before the State Commission made a prayer for allotment of the plot. They cannot seek the relief before this Commission beyond their prayer in the Complaint. Therefore, the impugned order is justified and the Appeal be dismissed.

7. Admitted facts of the case are that on 15.02.2007 Appellants/ Complainants entered into an Agreement with the Respondent/Opposite Party for purchase of a developed plot, measuring 7.5 Cottah, for a consideration of Rs.22,50,000/-, out of which Complainants paid Rs.20,25,000/- on different dates. As per the Agreement, the plot was to be developed in two Phases, Phase I was to be completed by December, 2006 and Phase II by December, 2007, but the Opposite Party failed to do so. The Complainants sent a legal notice dated 22.06.2015 to the Opposite Party. The Opposite Party replied to the legal notice, vide letter dated 03.07.2015 wherein they admitted having received an amount of Rs.20,25,000/-and also agreed to refund the entire amount. On 18.07.2015, the Opposite Party sent an email containing offer of settlement. Since the terms of settlement were not acceptable to the Complainants, on 03.09.2015 they approached

Consumer Affairs Department for redressal of their grievance. On 29.9.2015, the Opposite Party agreed to refund the principal amount of Rs.20,25,000/- on the next date i.e. 15.10.2015, but the Opposite Party failed to make payment.

8. The Complainants/Appellants themselves made a prayer before the State Commission that the Opposite Party be directed to handover the developed plot of land as per the Agreement, failing which refund the amount of Rs.20,25,000/-State Commission allowed the Complaint and directed the Opposite Party/Respondent to hand over and to execute the Deed of Conveyance in respect of the plot as per the Agreement for Sale dated 15.02.2007 in favour of the Complainants within 60 days from date on receipt of balance consideration amount of Rs.2,25,000/-, failing which the OP was directed to refund Rs.20,25,000/- along with interest thereon @ 12% p.a. from the date of payment till its full realization. The Appellants in their prayer before the State Commission sought developed plot of land failing which to give refund of amount deposited with interest, apart from compensation for mental torture. Appellants cannot change their stand in the Appeal and they cannot pick and choose. The order of the State Commission is in accordance with the prayer in the Complaint.

9. For the foregoing discussion, I am of the view that the order passed by the State Commission is fully justified. Appellants failed to show any illegality or irregularity in the impugned order warranting interference in the appellate jurisdiction. Appeal is dismissed with no order as to costs. .... C. VISWANATH PRESIDING MEMBER

<u>CASE NO. 26</u>
FIRST APPEAL NO. 780 OF 2020

(Against the Order dated 06/12/2019 in Complaint No. 21/2015 of the State Commission Andhra Pradesh)

NEW INDIA ASSURANCE CO. LTD. DELHI LEGAL HUB,...........Appellant(s)

Versus

M/S. COASTAL AGRO INDUSTRIES LTD REEP. BY ITS AUTHORISED SIGNATORY, MVV KAUTIILIYA, ...Respondent(s)

BEFORE: HON'BLE MR. C. VISWANATH,PRESIDING MEMBER

For the Appellant : MR. MAIBAM N. SINGH

For the Respondent :

For the Respondent/ Caveator Mr B Suyodhan, Advocate

Dated : 18 Jan 2021

ORDER

1. The present Appeal has been filed against the order dated 06.12.2019 of the Andhra Pradesh State Consumer Disputes Redressal Commission, Vijayawada ('the State Commission') in CC no. 21 of 2015.

2. IA no. 6935 of 2020 is an application for Condonation of Delay. According to the Registry, there is a delay of 260 days, though the Appellant has not mentioned any number in his application. The impugned order of the Andhra Pradesh State Consumer Disputes Redressal Commission at Vijayawada is dated 06.12.2019. The order was received by the Counsel for the Appellant on 30.12.2019. As per the averments made in the application for Condonation of Delay, there was a delay in seeking legal advice and thereafter on 23.03.2020, lock down was declared. Hon'ble Supreme Court in Suo Moto Writ Petition no. 3 of 2020, vide its order dated 23.03.2020, has extended the time for filing any petitions/ applications/ suits/ appeals/ all other proceedings irrespective of the limitations prescribed under general law or special laws whether condonable or not with effect from 15.03.2020 till further order to be passed. In view of the above, the delay is condoned and IA No. 6935 of 2020 is allowed.

3. Case of the Complainant/ Respondent is that he has been carrying on agro industries business. A BMW M3 Coupe car bearing registration no. AP 13 R 0009, was purchased

from M/s Hetero Labs Limited, Hyderabad for an amount of Rs.57,04,000/-. The Complainant took an Insurance Policy - "Private Car Enhancement Cover Policy" bearing no. 62060331120300003714 for a sum of Rs.58,80,000/- valid from 09.01.2013 to 08.01.2014, from the Appellant/ Opposite Party. On 16.02.2013, when the officials of the Company were proceeding to Bangalore from Hyderabad in the car, at Shamshabad, Ranga Reddy District, the car hit a stone in the middle of the road at 11.00 p m, resulting damage to the car. Immediately the Complainant took the car to the authorised workshop, M/s Kun Motoren, Khairatabad who found that the engine was damaged. The Complainant informed the Opposite Party about the said incident. Thereafter the Opposite Party appointed a Surveyor – Vijaya Surveyors and Assessors for inspection and assessment of the loss. The Surveyor inspected the car and permitted the Complainant to get the repairs carried out. The vehicle was repaired, including replacement of the engine and the car was made road worthy. The Complainant paid the entire repair charges of Rs.23,20,352/- to M/s Kun Motoren (Motors) Khairatabad, Hyderabad The Surveyor inspected the car again on 21.09.2013 and submitted his final report. The Opposite Party had appointed another Surveyor Shri A Chandrasekhara Rao in March or April 2014 to give his technical opinion on the damage and the admissibility of the claim. The Opposite Party repudiated the claim vide letter dated 25.02.2015, nearly after two years from the date of the accident. Thereafter the Complainant sought copy of the Surveyor Reports through RTI, which was duly supplied. Aggrieved by the repudiation of his claim complaint was filed before the State Commission for redressal of his grievances with the following prayer: To pay claim of the Complainant of Rs.35,22,866/- (Rs.23,20,245/- + Rs.12.02,621/-) with interest of 24% per annum from the date of the complaint till realisation; To award an amount of Rs.5,00,000/- towards compensation for mental agony and suffering, and the OP 1 and 2 are liable to pay the same; To grant costs Rs.30,000/- for the complainant; To grant such further and other incidental relief's as the Complainant be found entitled as deem just and proper.

4. The Opposite Party resisted the Complaint. The Opposite Party contended that the Complainant without giving information to them had given the car for repair, denying the opportunity to make an on the spot inspection of the accident. The Complainant gave intimation of the claim on 18.02.2013 to the Opposite Party. M/s Vijaya Surveyors and Assessors conducted post repair inspection and submitted their report on 20.09.2013 and 21.09.2013. The Surveyor assessed the loss at Rs.20,36,459/- and salvage value at Rs.2.00 lakh. The contention of the Complainant was that the car was damaged due to hitting a stone, when oil leaked out and the engine stopped. The Surveyor's report did not come to a positive conclusion that the damage to engine was covered by insured peril or not. As the Surveyor failed to arrive a specific recommendations, the Opposite Party appointed a second Surveyor for ascertaining the cause of the accident and damage to the car. The Surveyor noticed that a sump was created by wilfully hammering the engine. The Surveyor further observed that a protective panel duly protecting the engine from outside panel was intact. He gave a report stating that the claim of the Complainant was fraudulent in nature and not caused by external means. Based on the report of the second Surveyor, the Insurance Claim had been repudiated.

5. The State Commission after hearing both the parties and based on record and evidence, allowed the Complaint in part directing the Opposite Party to pay an amount of Rs.23,21,824/- with interest @ 9% per annum from the date of the Complaint, i.e., 07.07.2015 till the date of realisation; Rs.50,000/- towards mental agony and Rs.10,000/- towards cost to the Complainant.

6. Aggrieved by the order of the State Commission, the Opposite Party/ Appellant filed the present Appeal before this Commission. It is an admitted fact that the Insurance Policy was taken and the car met with an accident during the Policy period. The Respondent/ Complainant took the vehicle to the authorised dealer of BMW Car, at Hyderabad and

got it repaired. Surveyor was appointed by the Opposite Party who inspected the car before and after the repair and agreed with the Respondent/ Complainant that the engine was damaged due to hitting of a stone and the engine stopped suddenly after the engine oil leaked. Not satisfied with the report of the Surveyor, the Insurance Company appointed another Surveyor who reported that the claim of the Respondent was fraudulent in nature and not caused due to an act of insured peril. The Opposite Party repudiated the claim of the Complainant based on the report of the second Surveyor.

7. Learned counsel for the Appellant argued that the second Surveyor appointed was an investigator and the Company was well within its right to appoint an investigator,if not satisfied with the report of the first Surveyor. Since the second Surveyor was also a technical expert and the Insurance Company had relied on his report that the claim of the insured was fraudulent in nature and not proximately caused due to the act of insured peril, the claim was repudiated.

8. Learned Counsel appearing on behalf of the Respondent/ Complainant stated that the vehicle was duly repaired after seeking permission for carrying out the same from the Surveyor and at the authorised dealer of BMW Car in Hyderabad. Since the car got damaged by hitting a stone, oil had leaked and the engine suddenly stopped. The vehicle was towed to the authorised work-shop and after thorough verification it was identified that the engine was damaged. The Appellant/ Opposite Party had wrongly repudiated their claim.

9. The vehicle met with an accident due to hitting a stone due to which the engine got damaged and stopped due oil leakage from the car. The Respondent informed M/s Kun Motoren, Khairatabad, the authorised BMW dealer/ work-shop who in turn sent a recovery van to take the car to the work-shop. The authorised dealer got the vehicle inspected and identified that the engine was damaged. The authorised dealer estimated the cost of repairs at Rs.27,15,989/-. The Respondent sent claim intimation to the Opposite Party within two days on 18.02.2012. The Appellant appointed Surveyor– Vijaya Surveyors and Assessors on 22.02.2013 for inspection and assessment of loss caused to the Complainant's car. The Surveyor duly inspected the car and took the photographs before the repairs were carried out. After repair, the Surveyor again inspected the car on 21.09.2013 and submitted a final report. The Appellant appointed a second Surveyor to inspect the vehicle and report, vide letters dated 10.03.204 and 08.04.2014. The second Surveyor submitted his report on 02.06.2014. The authorised dealer issued the repair bill for Rs.23,21,824/-. The Appellant repudiated the claim of the Respodnent, vide its letter dated 25.02.2015.

10. Learned Counsel for the Appellant stated that the Surveyor did not come to a positive conclusion about the damage to the engine and had failed to arrive at a specific recommendation for payment of the claim. The Surveyor/ Investigator were appointed by them because the first Surveyor did not arrive at a specific recommendation. I have carefully perused the report of the first Surveyor. It is very clear that the vehicle got damaged due to accident caused by hitting a big stone, the oil leaked and the vehicle stopped suddenly. As seen from the preliminary report submitted by the Surveyor, " car ran over the big stone which hit the sump of the engine, resulting the engine oil was dried out and vehicle was stopped with noise………….. Hence, informed this matter to BMW authorised work-shop………………….., after thorough inspection identified that the engine was damaged………….. I have inspected the car on 23.02.2013 and many occasions conducted final survey" . He concluded that " after considering the above points, I am strongly feel that engine was damaged due to hitting of big stone and oil was leaked out it was happened accidentally. Hence, I am recommending the same to insurers consideration ". In fact by their own admission the Appellant stated that the first Surveyor merely reiterated the narration of the Complainant. No evidence has been placed on record to show scope for any suspicion and the reasons for discarding the report of the first Surveyor and appointing another Surveyor/ Investigator. The

Appellant did not even care to inform the Respondent about the appointment of a second Surveyor/ Investigator. The second Surveyor noted that a sump was created by willful act of making a hole with a hammer. This appears to be height of imagination, that engine of a BMW car would be destroyed in that manner. The second Surveyor also noted that there was no possibility of damage to the engine by hitting a stone, in view of the protected panel of the car. The second Surveyor came to the conclusion: " Thus after conducting a detailed investigation and inspection of the vehicle under claim, and its engine etc., the undersigned opines that the insured's claim is fraudulent in nature and not proximately caused due to the act of an insured peril, i.e., accident by external means. The insured's claim may be repudiated as per the terms and conditions of the policy".

11. The State Commission has noted the Chief Examination of PW 2: " It is just and necessary to state that the undercover of the vehicle, is to protect the air friction, wind blow noise and water spill into the vehicle from bottom but it cannot protect any accidental damages to it. Even assuming but not conceding that there is a protected panel, that will be only for some other purpose other than protection engine. The opposite party did not choose to cross examine PW 2, to falsify this aspect. The 2 Surveyor's nd report did not completely ruled out the possibility of damage of the engine, if the car came into contact with a big stone. In such circumstances, the report given by the 1 Surveyor st cannot be discarded".

12. As seen from the above, the report of the second Surveyor/Investigator could not be relied upon. The Appellant appears to have appointed the second Surveyor only to subvert the opinion of the first Surveyor and to obtain a favourable report. The first Surveyor had categorically held that the engine got accidentally damaged due to hitting of a stone and leakage of oil and recommended the case of the Insurer to the Insured. The State Commission after a detailed examination of witnesses arrived at a considered view that the Respondent was entitled to recover repair charges from the Opposite Party. Order passed by the State Commission is fully justified. Appellants failed to show any illegality or irregularity in the impugned order warranting interference in the appellate jurisdiction. Appeal is dismissed with no order as to costs. .... C. VISWANATH PRESIDING MEMBER

CASE NO. 27
REVISION PETITION NO. 1175 OF 2017

(Against the Order dated 03/02/2017 in Appeal No. 600/2013 of the State Commission Rajasthan)

SURESH KUMAR SHARMA S/O. SH. KALYAN SAHAI SHARMA, ...Petitioner(s)

Versus

ORIENTAL INSURANCE COMPANY LIMITED THROUGH BRANCH MANAGER,...........Respondent(s)

REVISION PETITION NO. 3981 OF 2017

(Against the Order dated 03/02/2017 in Appeal No. 600/2013 of the State Commission Rajasthan)

ORIENTAL INSURANCE CO. LTD............Petitioner(s)

Versus

SURESH KUMAR SHARMA W/O LATE NARAYAN TANDON, ...Respondent(s)

BEFORE: HON'BLE MR. C. VISWANATH,PRESIDING MEMBER

For the Petitioner :

For the Respondent :

Dated : 18 Jan 2021

ORDER

RP/1175/2017

For the Petitioner : Mr. Nimit Mathur, Advocate
For the Respondent : Mr. Amreeta Swarup, Advocate
RP/3981/2017
For the Petitioner : Mr. Amreeta Swarup, Advocate
For the Respondent : Mr. Nimit Mathur, Advocate

ORDER

1. Revision Petition No.1175/2017 has been filed by the Petitioner/Complainant and Revision Petition No.3981/2017 has been filed by the Petitioner/Opposite Party against the order dated 03.02.2017 in First Appeal No.600/2013 of the Rajasthan State Consumer Disputes Redressal Commission, Jaipur (for short "the State Commission").

2. Case of the Complainant is that the Complainant got his Honda City Car bearing registration No.RJ-06-CB-6381 insured with the Opposite Party/Insurance Company, vide Policy No.242400/31/2012/000243 valid from 06.04.2011 to 05.04.2012 for a sum of Rs.7,60,000/-, by paying premium amount of Rs.17,788/-. On the night of 11.04.2011 the car met with an accident within the limits of Police Station Mandal, District Bahilwara, when a vehicle came on wrong side, without giving light. The vehicle fled after hitting and badly damaging the car of the Complainant. The vehicle was taken to authorized dealer, Jaipur Pink City Motors Pvt. Ltd. for repair. As the Complainant suffered minor injuries and no other person was injured in the accident, FIR was not registered. Intimation of the accident was given to the Opposite Party immediately. Authorised dealer issued estimate for repair of the vehicle to the tune of Rs.8,84,079/-, as the vehicle was totally damaged. The Complainant filed Insurance Claim before the Opposite Party for Rs.7,60,000/-, being IDV of the vehicle. Opposite Party sent a letter to the Complainant for settlement of the claim at Rs.2,93,000/-. Complainant replied, vide letter dated 09.02.2012, to the Opposite Party seeking payment of IDV value of the vehicle i.e. Rs.7,60,000/-, but the Opposite Party did not settle the claim within the prescribed time. Therefore, the Complainant filed Consumer Complaint before the District Forum with following prayer: - "1. That as the vehicle of complainant damaged totally, the complainant be allowed Rs.7,60,000/- being IDV Value of service with interest @ 18% per annum till payment from the respondent insurance company. 2. That Rs.1,50,000/- as compensation for physical and mental agony be allowed to the complainant from respondent Insurance Company. 3. That totally damaged vehicle of complainant is lying at Pink City Motors Pvt. Ltd., Jaipur and parking charges for the same @ Rs.100/- per day till payment of claim amount be allowed separately.4. That the cost of case with Advocate's fee be allowed. 5. That any other relief for which complainant is legally entitled be allowed to the complainant from respondent Insurance Company."

3. Complaint was contested by the Opposite Party by filing written statement. It was stated that on receiving intimation, Mr. K.C. Sharma, Surveyor was appointed immediately, who found that the vehicle was not having more than 70% damage and the vehicle did not come under the category of total loss. The vehicle was repairable at a cost of Rs.2,96,446.99/-. An amount of Rs.2,96,446.99 towards repair was offered to the Complainant, which he refused to accept. The Complainant violated the terms & conditions of the agreement, therefore this Complaint is triable by the Civil Court, and not maintainable in the Consumer Forum. There are complicated questions involved in this matter, which can be decided only by the Civil Court and the Complaint is not maintainable in the Consumer Forum.

4. It is relevant to mention that another Complaint being CC/165/2012 was also filed by Ridhi Sidhi Eco Logistic Pvt. Ltd. for separate cause of action. The District Forum, however, clubbed both the Complaints together and after hearing Learned Counsel for the Parties and going through the record, dismissed both the Complaints as not maintainable by a common order dated 27.05.2013, with following observation: - "As

such, these complaints filed by complainants against respondent are rejected and each of the complaints is dismissed with cost of Rs.5,000/- (rupees five thousand)."

5. Ridhi Sidhi Eco Logistic Pvt. Ltd. did not file any Appeal against the order of the District Forum. However, the Complainant (Petitioner in RP/1175/2017) filed an Appeal before the State Commission. State Commission allowed the Appeal directing the Opposite Party/Insurance Company to make payment of the claim assessed by the Surveyor alongwith interest @ 10% p.a. from the date of presentation of the complaint, with cost of Rs.11,000/-.

6. Aggrieved by the impugned order, Complainant as well as Opposite Party/Insurance Company have filed cross Revision Petitions before this Commission.

7. Heard the learned Counsel for the Parties and carefully perused the record. Learned Counsel for the Complainant contended that the State Commission had erred in allowing the Complaint on the basis of Surveyor Report, in spite of the fact that there was total damage to the car and the Complainant had produced estimate to that effect, issued by Pink City Honda. He further submitted that the Survey Report dated 01.07.2011 was arbitrary and erroneous as the Surveyor had deliberately undervalued the loss suffered by the Complainant. It was also submitted that the Surveyor had assessed the depreciated value of the parts at Rs.4,79,862/- without any detail or reasons.

8. Learned Counsel for the Respondent submitted that the Surveyor assessed damage to the vehicle as less than 70% and an amount of Rs.2,96,446.99/- was offered to the Complainant for repair which the Complainant refused to accept. He submitted that the Respondent/Opposite Party was still ready and willing to pay this amount to the Petitioner. There are complicated questions involved in this matter, which can be decided only by the Civil Court and the Complaint is not maintainable in the Consumer Forum.

9. Briefly stated, facts of the case are that the Petitioner/Complainant got his car insured with the Respondent for a sum of Rs.7,60,000/-, from 06.04.2011 to 05.04.2012. On the night of 11.04.2011, the car met with an accident. It was taken to Jaipur Pink City Motors Pvt. Ltd, an authorised dealer, who estimated the cost of repair at Rs.8,84,079/-, as the vehicle was totally damaged. The Petitioner filed insurance claim before the Opposite Party for Rs.7,60,000/-, being IDV of the vehicle. As the Surveyor appointed by the Respondent estimated the repair cost at Rs.2,96,446.99, the Respondent offered Rs.2,96,446.99 to the Petitioner, which was not accepted and the Petitioner filed Complaint before the District Forum.

10. Regarding maintainability of the Complaint, Learned Counsel for the Respondent contended that complicated questions are involved and the matter pertains to compliance of agreement and terms & conditions of the Insurance Policy, which are triable by a Civil Court. He also stated that Complainant/Respondent has not stated anywhere as to what complications are involved in this matter. Further, it has been held by this Commission in Harsolia Motors v. National Insurance Co. Ltd. I, (2005) CPJ 27 (NC) decided on 03.12.2004 that since an Insurance Policy is taken for reimbursement or for indemnity of the loss which may be suffered on account of insured perils, the services of the insurer cannot be said to have been hired or availed for a commercial purpose. This Commission does possess the requisite jurisdiction to entertain a Consumer Complaint wherever a defect or deficiency in the services rendered by an insurer is made out. In view of the above, the Complaint is held maintainable.

11. Main issue relates to the quantum of loss. Surveyor appointed by the Insurance Company assessed the loss to the tune of Rs.2,96,446.99 and the Complainant filed claim for Rs.7,60,000/-, on the basis of estimate given by Pink City Motors Pvt. Ltd. Surveyor was appointed by the Insurance Company, who visited and inspected the place of incident and thereafter gave his report. Report submitted by a Surveyor is an important piece of evidence and it has to be given due weight, though it is not

sacrosanct and can be ignored, provided there is cogent evidence otherwise. In the present case, the Complainant did not lead any evidence disproving the report submitted by the Surveyor of the Insurance Company. In the absence of any evidence to the contrary, the report submitted by the Surveyor of the Insurance Company is to be accepted. Whatever relief the Complainant was entitled, has already been given by the State Commission.

12. In view of the foregoing discussion, I am of the view that the State Commission had correctly relied on the report of the Surveyor appointed by the Insurance Company and allowed the claim to the tune of Rs.2,96,446.99. I do not find any illegality or irregularity in the impugned order warranting interference in exercise of revisional jurisdiction. Both Revision Petitions are hereby dismissed. .... C. VISWANATH PRESIDING MEMBER

CASE NO. 28
REVISION PETITION NO. 942 OF 2020

(Against the Order dated 12/02/2020 in Appeal No. 834/2018 of the State Commission Haryana)

ADAMA AGAN LIMITED & 2 ORS. ....Petitioner(s)

Versus

RAMESH & ANR. ....Respondent(s)

REVISION PETITION NO. 943 OF 2020

(Against the Order dated 12/02/2020 in Appeal No. 849/2018 of the State Commission Haryana)

ADAMA AGAN LIMITED & 2 ORS. ....Petitioner(s)

Versus

PARVESH & 2 ORS. ....Respondent(s)

BEFORE: HON'BLE MR. ANUP K THAKUR,PRESIDING MEMBER

For the Petitioner :

For the Petitioners : Mr. Satyam Bhatia, Advocate

For the Respondent :

Dated : 18 Jan 2021

ORDER

ANUP K. THAKUR

1. Under challenge in Revision Petition No. 942 of 2020 is the impugned order dated 12.02.2020 of the Haryana State Consumer Disputes Redressal Commission, Panchkula,(State Commission, hereafter), in F.A. No.834/2018.Vide this order, the State Commission had upheld the order dated 24.5.2018 of the District Consumer Disputes Redressal Forum, Rohtak (District Forum, hereafter). Under challenge in Revision Petition No. 943 of 2020 is the impugned order dated 12.02.2020 of the State Commission in F.A. No.849/2018 vide which it had upheld the order dated 24.5.2018 of the District Forum.

2. It is proposed to dispose off both these Revision Petitions by this common order.

3. Brief facts of the case in RP 942/2020 are that the respondent/complainant had sown sugarcane in one acre of land in village Baland, Tehsil and District Rohtak. He had purchased herbicides worth Rs.7,990/- vide receipt no.11460 dated 20.06.2016 from the petitioner no.1/OP1. It so happened that the crop which was otherwise doing well, as per the complaint, after spraying of herbicides, suffered severe damage. Upon informing the Ops, complainant received no response. The SDAO (sub divisional agriculture officer/office) was informed. Inspection of the affected crop was carried out and a report submitted.

4. A consumer complaint was then filed seeking compensation of Rs.1,60,000/- on account of crop damage, from the petitioners/OPs.

5. The complaint was resisted by the OPs. Grounds taken were that at the time of sale of the herbicide, the seal was intact. Further, this herbicide had been sold to various distributors/dealers and no other complaint from anywhere else had been received. Further, there had been non-compliance of Deputy Director's circular dated 03.01.2002 by the team which had assessed the loss: This had required that one representative of the agency concerned viz. Ops shall be a member of the inspecting team. It had been argued on behalf of the petitioners/OPs that this was not complied with and therefore, the report of the team finding crop loss could not be accepted.

6. The District Forum considered the arguments of the OPs and concluded that the fact that the circular of Deputy Director of Agriculture dated 3.1.2002 was not complied with while constituting the inspection team was a mere inadvertence and did not suggest any malafide intention. In any case, it was an irregularity and on this ground, equity and natural justice could not be denied to the complainant. So reasoning, it allowed the complaint to the extent of Rs.72,850/-, this being the loss on account of 235 quintals of sugarcane in one acre land @ Rs.310/- per quintal, with interest of 9% from the date of filing of the complaint i.e. 25.10.2016 till its realization. A cost of Rs.5,000/- was also awarded. In the appeal filed against this order of the District Forum, the reasoning and logic of the District Forum was upheld by the State Commission. Hence, this RP 942/2020 .

7. Learned counsel for the petitioners argued that to prove deficiency in service/defect in herbicides and the consequential damage to sugarcane crop, it was necessary to have included one member representative of the OPs in the inspection team. As much had been mandated vide a circular of the Deputy Director of Agriculture (supra). The fact that this was not done would make the inspection report liable to the rejected as illegal. He also argued that the inspection report dated 3.8.2016 had found 90% damage to the crop and had further found that upto 70% to 80% was due to the use of herbicides from it's "phytotoxicity effect". Learned counsel argued that it was difficult to take this report seriously as it comprised but a few handwritten lines to state what was found during the inspection.

8. After having heard the learned counsel and perused carefully the record, including the inspection report and the concurrent orders of the District Forum and the State Commission, I am of the considered view that no ground for revision of the State Commission's order is warranted, in the facts and circumstances of the case.

9. It is apt to reproduce the relevant portion of the order of the District Forum at this stage: "4. We have heard learned counsel for the parties and have gone through material aspects of the case very carefully. 5. The OPs have mainly relied Ex.R3 a circular of Deputy Director of Agriculture, Haryana, Panchkula dated 03.01.2002 regarding inspection of farmers fields on receipt of -2- complaint regarding sale of poor quality seeds (herbicides) to all Deputy Directors Agriculture to the effect that one representative of the agency concerned shall be a member besides other members and the OPs have demanded that since they were not notified by the Deputy Director (Agriculture, Rohtak) and did not make them a member of the inspection team constituted by him. The complainant cannot be punished as he did everything required under the procedure. The non inclusion of representative of the OP by the Deputy Director Agriculture as per circular Ex.3 is a mere irregularity. The members of the inspection team are all technical, qualified and independent person. The members of the committee gave an inspection report Ex.C7 approving the name of the complainant. If we concur with the OPs for rejecting the claim of the complainant for not adhering to the circular Ex.R3 in law and spirit by the Deputy Director Agriculture while constituting the inspection team, the order of the Deputy Director is a mere inadvertence and not with any malafide intention. If the complainant suffers due to this irregularity

and inadvertence on the part of the Deputy Director Agriculture, the same shall be a clog on equity and against all norms of natural justice. We also find support to our contention from case titled Kanta Kantha Rao Vs. Y. Surya Narayana (NCDRC), New Delhi cited in 2017(2)CPJ 549 . On the contrary the citation of Hon'ble NCDRC in Kuber Agro Corporationd & Ors. Vs. M/s. Nishant Trading Co cited in 2017(2)CPJ 8 is of no help to the OPs as acts were different in that case. As such the objections of the OPs are negated." (Ad verbatim per translated record)

10. Indeed, an internal circular of Deputy Director of Agriculture regarding composition of the inspection team is for the smooth functioning of the Department of Agriculture in its subordinate field offices for fulfilling it's role of assisting the farmers, including taking prompt action on any complaint such as the one under consideration in the instant case. To not have included a representative of the OPs was, at worst, an irregularity. It is not the case nor has it been so pleaded that there was any malafide on the part of the agriculture office or the inspection team. The fact of the matter is that there was a crop loss and the complainant farmer did therefore have to suffer this loss and the inspecting team found the loss to be largely due to the use of herbicides. That this report comprised a few hand written lines does not take away it's value: rural areas may not always have the facility of producing well crafted reports on letter heads and it must not be forgotten that these lines were penned by experienced field personnel.

11. It is apposite to also peruse the reasoning of the State Commission in para 13 of it's order: "13. Similarly, the other contention of learned counsel for appellants that Deputy Director did not comply with the instructions contained in circular/letter dated 03.01.2002 Ex.R-3 is not tenable in the eyes of law because due to non-compliance of any departmental instructions by the Deputy Director Agriculture is not sufficient to allow the farmer/complainant to suffer. More so, non compliance departmental instructions is only an irregularity but not an illegality. The authority titled 'Indian Farmers Fertilizers Vs. Shri Ram Swaroop (supra) relied upon by the learned counsel for the appellants is not relevant because facts and circumstances were different in that case. It was a case of defective seeds and not of defective herbicide medicines. In the case in hand, there is categorical observation of the inspecting team report Ex.C-8 dated 03.08.2016 that 90% loss to the crop was due to defective herbicide. Learned District Forum has rightly placed upon authority of Kanta Kantha Rao Vs. Y. Surya Narayana (NCDRC) New Delhi cited in 2017 (2) CPJ 549 . Similarly respondent -3- No.1- complainant could not be burdened for non-compliance of section 13 (1) (c) of the Act because he had left with no sample for getting the same tested or analyzed from an authorized laboratory. The appellants could have availed this opportunity on receiving the notice of the complaint but they did not do so for the reasons best known to them." (Ad verbatim per translated record)

12. It may be added that business entities viz. dealers, manufacturers of agri-inputs (seeds, herbicides) carry a special responsibility. They are expected to properly inform the farmer and follow up after sale, to ensure that the farmer has understood and is following all the instructions. In the instant case, the dealer ought not to have waited for an invitation to join the inspection team if it was already aware of the complaint through information furnished by the complainant. He should have been proactive rather than reactive. The same observation can also be made for the manufacturers of agri-inputs such as herbicides: their dealers should be properly trained to ensure that they see their job as not merely one of selling but as providing after sale service through regular follow up.

13. Finally, it is also well to note that the revisionary jurisdiction is limited to errors apparent as laid down by the Apex Court in the case of Mrs. Rubi (Chandra) Dutta Vs. M/s United India Insurance Co. Ltd., (2011) 11 SCC 269, relevant portion of which is reproduced below:- "8. Also, it is to be noted that the revisional powers of the National Commission are derived from Section 21 (b) of the Act, under which the said power can

be exercised only if there is some prima facie jurisdictional error appearing in the impugned order, and only then, may the same be set aside. In our considered opinion there was no jurisdictional error or miscarriage of justice, which could have warranted the National Commission to have taken a different view than what was taken by the two Forums. The decision of the National Commission rests not on the basis of some legal principle that was ignored by the Courts below, but on a different (and in our opinion, an erroneous) interpretation of the same set of facts. This is not the manner in which revisional powers should be invoked. In this view of the matter, we are of the considered opinion that the jurisdiction conferred on the National Commission under Section 21 (b) of the Act has been transgressed. It was not a case where such a view could have been taken by setting aside the concurrent findings of two fora.

14. In RP 943/2020 , the nature of the complaint is identical, the difference lying in two facts viz. area of crop was 3 acre and the claim allowed by the lower fora was Rs. 2,18,550/-.

15. In view of the discussion above, these Revision Petitions No. 942 & 943, both of 2020 , are dismissed, after consideration, at the stage of admission. No order as to costs.
.... ANUP K THAKUR PRESIDING MEMBER

CASE NO. 29
REVISION PETITION NO. 753 OF 2018

(Against the Order dated 07/12/2017 in Appeal No. 268/2014 of the State Commission Uttaranchal)
PUNJAB NATIONAL BANK Through Chief Manager, Sh. Pawan Kumar Koul,...........Petitioner(s)

Versus

DALJEET SINGH S/O. BALKAR SINGH,...........Respondent(s)
BEFORE: HON'BLE MRS. JUSTICE DEEPA SHARMA,PRESIDING MEMBER
For the Petitioner : Mr. Ajay Shanker, Advocate
For the Respondent : Mr. Avanish Kumar, Advocate
Dated : 19 Jan 2021

ORDER
JUSTICE DEEPA SHARMA, PRESIDING MEMBER

1. This revision petition under section 21 (b) of the Consumer Protection Act, 1986 (for short, "the Act") has been filed by the petitioner against the order dated 07.12.2017 of the Uttarakhand State Consumer Disputes Redressal Commission, Dehradun (for short, "the State Commission") in First Appeal no. 268 of 2014 of the petitioner wherein the order of the District Consumer Disputes Forum, Haridwar (for short, "the District Forum") dated 14.10.2014 in complaint no. 140 of 2014 was upheld.

2. The brief facts as stated by the complainant in his complaint are that on 17.10.2012, he had deposited a sum of Rs.5.00 lakh in his account against a duly executed receipt by the petitioner. He wanted to withdraw Rs.5000/- from this account on 25.10.2012 but he was informed that there is no sufficient balance in his account and was told that there was no entry made in his account regarding deposit of Rs.5.00 lacs. The complainant contended that this amounts to deficiency in service that despite deposit of money by him, money was not credited in his account and filed the complaint.

3. The petitioner contested the complaint and filed its written version. The plea taken by them was that deposit receipt was a fake and fabricated document. It was alleged that they had learnt that a bank official, namely, Sh. Ravinder Kumar committed forgery in the end of year 2012 and had issued a fake receipt under his signature and FIR had already been lodged against him with P.S. Kotwali, Laksar. It is submitted that there was no deficiency in service on their part and complaint was liable to be dismissed.

4. The parties led their evidence before the District Forum. After hearing the parties, the District Forum held as under: "There is a receipt of the respondent bank of Date

17.10.2012 by which the complainant had deposited Rs.5,00,000/- in the respondent bank. In this regard it is the statement of the respondent bank that the receipt of the complainant is fake and forged by conspiracy. In this regard it is also the statement of the respondent bank that his employee Ravindra making criminal relation with some consumers and outside people and making conspiracy prepared the fake receipts, the information of which has been given to the local police by the bank. In this way the respondent bank is considering that his employee had prepared the fake and conspired record by conspiracy. If the forgery is done by the bank employee then for that the complainant cannot be punished. The receipt present on the record is the indicative of this matter that the complainant had deposited Rs.5,00,000/- in the respondent bank. If its forgery is done by the employee of the bank then bank is responsible for that, the complainant cannot be punished for that. Thus, the complainant is entitled to get the amount of Rs.5,00,000/- and simultaneously the complainant is also appears to be entitled to get interest at the rate of 6% per annum on the deposit amount of Rs.5,00,000/- from the date of deposit date 17.10.2012 till the date of last payment to the complainant and accordingly this complaint of the complainant is entitled to be allowed."

5. This order was impugned by the petitioner by way of an appeal. The appeal was dismissed vide the impugned order and the plea of the petitioner that there was no deficiency in service on their part, since it was their employee who had committed fraud and other criminal offence and embezzled the amount, was rejected. The State Commission has held as under: "6. The bank has taken the stand that their employee has forged the receipt regarding deposit of the amount by the complainant and that their employee has committed fraud and has entered into illegal relations with certain customers of the bank and has embezzled the amount. If an employee of the bank has embezzled the amount of the customer, the bank being the employer, is also vicariously liable for the wrong committed by its employee. Since the bank itself has admitted that their employee has committed embezzlement and hence being the employer of the delinquent officer / employee of the bank, the bank is equally liable and responsible and the bank is liable to pay the amount to the complainant. We are not concerned with the fact as to whether the said deposit slip was forged by the delinquent officer of the bank in collusion with the complainant or not. The fact remains that the deposit slip has been issued to the complainant, but the amount mentioned therein was not credited to his account, thereby putting him to loss. 7. So far as deposit of the amount by the complainant in his account is concerned, the complainant has filed the original deposit slip before the District Forum, which also contains the signatures of the official concerned as well as seal of the bank. The fact that the bank itself has lodged an FIR against its employee, is sufficient to prove that their employee has embezzled the funds of the customers, in order to have wrongful gain and inspite of receiving the amount from the customer and issuing the deposit slip, did not make the entry of the said amount in their account. It is further pertinent to mention here that there is no cutting / overwriting in the said deposit slip, which rules out any malafide act on the part of the complainant."

6. This order is impugned before me. Similar contentions have been raised. It is contended that the criminal act of embezzlement i.e. issuing fake receipt without deposit of any money in the bank treasury, was done by its employee and hence it cannot be said that there was deficiency of service on the part of the petitioner and they are not liable. It is argued on behalf of the respondent that petitioner cannot escape from vicarious liability for the wrong of its employees.

7. I have heard the arguments and perused the relevant record. There is concurrent finding to the fact that a valid receipt had been issued by the employee of the petitioner. The petitioner has also admitted that person who had issued the receipt was its employee. The petitioner, therefore, is responsible for all acts of its employee and cannot shun its

responsibility if its employee had not performed its duty properly. There is concurrent finding of facts regarding deposit of the money by the complainant / respondent and this finding since is based on the documentary evidence, cannot be find fault with. Since employee of the petitioner did not make proper entries in the relevant register and did not credit the said money in the account of the respondent, the petitioner being an employer cannot escape its vicarious liability for the acts of its employees. It is apparent that similar revision petition relating to issuance of bank receipts on deposit by the account holder and thereafter not crediting the said amount in the account of the account holder by its employee had been dealt with by this Commission wherein this Commission in the matter of Punjab National Bank & Anr. Vs. Hari Ram Yadav in Revision Petition No. 1923 of 2015 decided on 12.08.2015 concluded that bank cannot escape its vicarious liability for the acts of its employees even if FIR for embezzlement, commission of fraud had been filed by the petitioner bank and this Commission had found the said revision petition frivolous and while dismissing the said revision petition, imposed a cost of Rs.10,000/-. Despite such finding of this Commission, the petitioner had endeavoured to file this frivolous revision petition. Therefore, while dismissing the present revision petition, I impose cost of Rs.20,000/- on the bank. This cost shall be paid by the petitioner bank within four weeks from the date of this order to the complainant by way of demand draft failing which complainant is free to file the execution petition for recovery and in that case, petitioner shall be liable to pay interest @ 6% on this amount from the date of filing of execution petition till its realization. Revision Petition stands disposed of . ...J DEEPA SHARMA PRESIDING MEMBER

<u>**CASE NO. 30**</u>
REVISION PETITION NO. 755 OF 2018

(Against the Order dated 07/12/2017 in Appeal No. 101/2015 of the State Commission Uttaranchal)
PUNJAB NATIONAL BANK Through Chief Manager, Sh. Pawan Kumar Koul,...........Petitioner(s)

Versus

MUNESH KUMAR S//O. SH. KHADAK SINGH,...........Respondent(s)
BEFORE: HON'BLE MRS. JUSTICE DEEPA SHARMA,PRESIDING MEMBER
For the Petitioner : Mr. Ajay Shanker, Advocate
For the Respondent : Mr. Avanish Kumar, Advocate
Dated : 19 Jan 2021

ORDER
JUSTICE DEEPA SHARMA, PRESIDING MEMBER

1. This revision petition under section 21 (b) of the Consumer Protection Act, 1986 (for short, 'the Act') has been filed by the petitioner against the order dated 07.12.2017 of the Uttarakhand State Consumer Disputes Redressal Commission, Dehradun (for short, the State Commission') in First Appeal no. 101 of 2015 of the petitioner wherein the order of the District Consumer Disputes Redressal Forum (for short, 'the District Forum') dated 01.05.2015 in complaint no. 330 of 2012 was upheld.

2. The brief facts as stated by the complainant in his complaint are that on 13.01.2012, he had deposited a sum of Rs.4,10,000/- in his account against a duly executed receipt by the petitioner. The complainant had further deposited a sum of Rs.3,00,000/- and Rs.5,00,000/- on 21.04.2012 and 10.07.2012 respectively against a duly executed receipt by the petitioner. However, the said amount of Rs.12,10,000/- was not shown deposited in his account. The complainant contacted the Branch Manager who told that the dealing

cashier / clerk has not shown the amount in his account. The complainant contended that this amounts to deficiency in service that despite deposit of money by him, money was not credited in his account and filed the complaint.

3. The petitioner contested the complaint and filed its written version. The plea taken by them was that complainant has not made the cashier a necessary party and that on complaint being made, the petitioner had lodged a criminal case against the bank official, namely, Sh. Rajendra. It is further contended that that there is no entry in the ledger of the bank regarding deposit of the amount by the complainant and that complainant has not deposited the amount with the cash counter of the bank. It was further contended that complainant was having some relation with delinquent officer of the bank and they have made some outside transaction in collusion. It is submitted that there was no deficiency in service on their part and complaint was liable to be dismissed.

4. The parties led their evidence before the District Forum. After hearing the parties, the District Forum held as under: "What the employee of the respondent bank do or what they enter in their authorized register or what they don't do, its responsibility is not of the complainant, because such record is out of reach of him. From the presented deposit and payment register by the respondent bank it is clear that any entry of depositing Rs.4,10,000/- on date 13.01.2012, Rs.3,00,000/- on Date 21.04.2012 and Rs.5,00,000/- on Date 10.07.2012 in the account of the complainant is not there, whereas the complainant had proved the fact of depositing of money Rs.4,10,000/-, Rs.3,00,000/- and Rs.5,00,000/- by presenting affidavit and copies of the deposit slips.

5. This order was impugned by the petitioner by way of an appeal. The appeal was dismissed vide the impugned order and the plea of the petitioner that there was no deficiency in service on their part, since it was their employee who had committed fraud and other criminal offence and embezzled the amount, was rejected. The State Commission has held as under: "7. If an employee of the bank has embezzled the amount of the customer, the bank being the employer, is also vicariously liable for the wrong committed by its employee. Since the bank itself has admitted that their employee has committed embezzlement and hence being the employer of the delinquent officer / employee of the bank, the bank is equally liable and responsible and the bank is liable to pay the amount to the complainant. We are not concerned with the fact as to whether the said deposit slips were forged by the delinquent officer of the bank in collusion with the complainant or not. The fact remains that the deposit slips have been issued to the complainant, but the amount mentioned therein was not credited to his account, thereby putting him to loss. 8. So far as deposit of the amount by the complainant in his account is concerned, the complainant has filed the copy of the deposit slips before the District Forum, which also contains the signatures of the official concerned as well as seal of the bank. The fact that the bank itself has lodged an FIR against its employee, is sufficient to prove that their employee has embezzled the funds of the customers, in order to have wrongful gain and inspite of receiving the amount from the customer and issuing the deposit slip, did not make the entry of the said amount in their account. It is further pertinent to mention here that there is no cutting / overwriting in the said deposit slips, which rules out any malafide act on the part of the complainant."

6. This order is impugned before me. Similar contentions have been raised. It is contended that the criminal act of embezzlement i.e. issuing fake receipt without deposit of any money in the bank treasury was done by its employee and hence it cannot be said that there was deficiency of service on the part of the petitioner and they are not liable. It is argued on behalf of the respondent that petitioner cannot escape from vicarious liability for the wrong of its employees.

7. I have heard the arguments and perused the relevant record. There is concurrent finding to the fact that a valid receipt had been issued by the employee of the petitioner. The

petitioner has also admitted that person who had issued the receipt was its employee. The petitioner, therefore, is responsible for all acts of its employee and cannot shun its responsibility if its employee had not performed its duty properly. There is concurrent finding of facts regarding deposit of the money by the complainant / respondent and this finding since is based on the documentary evidence, cannot be find fault with. Since employee of the petitioner did not make proper entries in the relevant register and did not credit the said money in the account of the respondent, the petitioner being an employer cannot escape its vicarious liability for the acts of its employees. It is apparent that similar revision petition relating to issuance of bank receipts on deposit by the account holder and thereafter not crediting the said amount in the account of the account holder by its employee had been dealt with by this Commission wherein this Commission in the matter of Punjab National Bank & Anr. Vs. Hari Ram Yadav in Revision Petition No. 1923 of 2015 decided on 12.08.2015 concluded that bank cannot escape its vicarious liability for the acts of its employees even if FIR for embezzlement, commission of fraud had been filed by the petitioner bank and this Commission had found the said revision petition frivolous and while dismissing the said revision petition, imposed a cost of Rs.10,000/-. Despite such finding of this Commission, the petitioner had endeavoured to file this frivolous revision petition. Therefore, while dismissing the present revision petition, I impose cost of Rs.20,000/- on the bank. This cost shall be paid by the petitioner bank within four weeks from the date of this order to the complainant by way of demand draft failing which complainant is free to file the execution petition for recovery and in that case, petitioner shall be liable to pay interest @ 6% on this amount from the date of filing of execution petition till its realization. Revision Petition stands disposed of . ...J DEEPA SHARMA PRESIDING MEMBER

CASE NO. 31
REVISION PETITION NO. 756 OF 2018

(Against the Order dated 07/12/2017 in Appeal No. 102/2015 of the State Commission Uttaranchal)
PUNJAB NATIONAL BANK Through Chief Manager, Sh. Pawan Kumar Koul, ...Petitioner(s)

Versus

SHIV KUMAR S/O. CHANDRAPAL SINGH...........Respondent(s)
BEFORE: HON'BLE MRS. JUSTICE DEEPA SHARMA,PRESIDING MEMBER
For the Petitioner : Mr. Ajay Shanker, Advocate
For the Respondent : Mr. Avanish Kumar, Advocate
Dated : 19 Jan 2021

ORDER
JUSTICE DEEPA SHARMA, PRESIDING MEMBER

1. This revision petition under section 21 (b) of the Consumer Protection Act, 1986 (for short, 'the Act') has been filed by the petitioner against the order dated 07.12.2017 of the Uttarakhand State Consumer Disputes Redressal Commission, Dehradun (for short, 'the State Commission') in First Appeal no. 102 of 2015 of the petitioner wherein the order of the District Consumer Disputes Redressal Forum, Haridwar (for short, 'the District Forum') dated 01.05.2015 in complaint no. 331 of 2012 was upheld.

2. The brief facts as stated by the complainant in his complaint are that on 23.06.2012, he had deposited a sum of Rs.4,00,000/- in his account against a duly executed receipt by the petitioner. However, the said amount of Rs.4,00,000/- was not shown deposited in his account. The complainant contacted the Branch Manager who told that the dealing cashier / clerk has not shown the amount in his account. The complainant contended that this amounts to deficiency in service that despite deposit of money by him, money was not credited in his account and filed the complaint.

99

3. The petitioner contested the complaint and filed its written version. The plea taken by them was that complainant has not made the cashier a necessary party and that on complaint being made, the petitioner had lodged a criminal case against the bank official, namely, Sh. Rajendra. It is further contended that that there is no entry in the ledger of the bank regarding deposit of the amount by the complainant and that complainant has not deposited the amount with the cash counter of the bank. It was further contended that complainant was having some relation with delinquent officer of the bank and they have made some outside transaction in collusion. It is submitted that there was no deficiency in service on their part and complaint was liable to be dismissed.

4. The parties led their evidence before the District Forum. After hearing the parties, the District Forum held as under: "What the employee of the respondent bank do or what they enter in their authorized register or what they don't do, its responsibility is not of the complainant, because such record is out of reach of him. From the presented deposit and payment register by the respondent bank it is clear that any entry of depositing Rs.4,00,000/- in the account of the complainant is not there on date 23.06.2012, whereas the complainant had proved the fact of depositing of money Rs.4,00,000/-, by presenting affidavit and copies of the deposit slip."

5. This order was impugned by the petitioner by way of an appeal. The appeal was dismissed vide the impugned order and the plea of the petitioner that there was no deficiency in service on their part, since it was their employee who had committed fraud and other criminal offence and embezzled the amount, was rejected. The State Commission has held as under: "7. If an employee of the bank has embezzled the amount of the customer, the bank being the employer, is also vicariously liable for the wrong committed by its employee. Since the bank itself has admitted that their employee has committed embezzlement and hence being the employer of the delinquent officer / employee of the bank, the bank is equally liable and responsible and the bank is liable to pay the amount to the complainant. We are not concerned with the fact as to whether the said deposit slip was forged by the delinquent officer of the bank in collusion with the complainant or not. The fact remains that the deposit slip has been issued to the complainant, but the amount mentioned therein was not credited to his account, thereby putting him to loss. 8. So far as deposit of the amount by the complainant in his account is concerned, the complainant has filed the copy of the deposit slip before the District Forum, which also contains the signatures of the official concerned as well as seal of the bank. The fact that the bank itself has lodged an FIR against its employee, is sufficient to prove that their employee has embezzled the funds of the customers, in order to have wrongful gain and inspite of receiving the amount from the customer and issuing the deposit slip, did not make the entry of the said amount in their account. It is further pertinent to mention here that there is no cutting / overwriting in the said deposit slip, which rules out any malafide act on the part of the complainant."

6. This order is impugned before me. Similar contentions have been raised. It is contended that the criminal act of embezzlement i.e. issuing fake receipt without deposit of any money in the bank treasury was done by its employee and hence it cannot be said that there was deficiency of service on the part of the petitioner and they are not liable. It is argued on behalf of the respondent that petitioner cannot escape from vicarious liability for the wrong of its employees.

7. I have heard the arguments and perused the relevant record. There is concurrent finding to the fact that a valid receipt had been issued by the employee of the petitioner. The petitioner has also admitted that person who had issued the receipt was its employee. The petitioner, therefore, is responsible for all acts of its employee and cannot shun its responsibility if its employee had not performed its duty properly. There is concurrent finding of facts regarding deposit of the money by the complainant / respondent and this

finding since is based on the documentary evidence, cannot be find fault with. Since employee of the petitioner did not make proper entries in the relevant register and did not credit the said money in the account of the respondent, the petitioner being an employer cannot escape its vicarious liability for the acts of its employees. It is apparent that similar revision petition relating to issuance of bank receipts on deposit by the account holder and thereafter not crediting the said amount in the account of the account holder by its employee had been dealt with by this Commission wherein this Commission in the matter of Punjab National Bank & Anr. Vs. Hari Ram Yadav in Revision Petition No. 1923 of 2015 decided on 12.08.2015 concluded that bank cannot escape its vicarious liability for the acts of its employees even if FIR for embezzlement, commission of fraud had been filed by the petitioner bank and this Commission had found the said revision petition frivolous and while dismissing the said revision petition, imposed a cost of Rs.10,000/-. Despite such finding of this Commission, the petitioner had endeavoured to file this frivolous revision petition. Therefore, while dismissing the present revision petition, I impose cost of Rs.20,000/- on the bank. This cost shall be paid by the petitioner bank within four weeks from the date of this order to the complainant by way of demand draft failing which complainant is free to file the execution petition for recovery and in that case, petitioner shall be liable to pay interest @ 6% on this amount from the date of filing of execution petition till its realization. Revision Petition stands disposed of . ...J DEEPA SHARMA PRESIDING MEMBER

CASE NO. 32
FIRST APPEAL NO. 300 OF 2013

(Against the Order dated 24/01/2013 in Complaint No. 70/2010 of the State Commission Maharashtra)

BUSHAN CHIMANLAL JAIN ....Appellant(s)

Versus

CITY & INDUSTRIAL DEVELOPMENT CORPORATION OF MAHARASHTRA LTD. (CIDCO LTD.) Corporation of Maharashtra Limited (Cidco Ltd.), " NIRMAL" ,

THE MANAGING DIRECTOR, CIDCO LTD., CIDCO BHAWAN,

THE MARKETING MANAGER-1, CIDCO LTD,

THE STATE OF MAHARASHTRA Through The Secretary, Urban Development Department,...........Respondent(s)

FIRST APPEAL NO. 301 OF 2013

(Against the Order dated 24/01/2013 in Complaint No. 71/2010 of the State Commission Maharashtra)

SANDEEP BHUSHAN JAIN Through its Constituted Attorney-Shri bhusan Chimanlal Jain,...........Appellant(s)

Versus

CITY & INDUSTRIAL DEVELOPMENT CORPORATION OF MAHARASHTRA LTD. (CIDCO LTD.) NIRMAL" ,

THE MANAGING DIRECTOR, CIDCO LTD., CIDCO BHAWAN,

THE MARKETING MANAGER-1, CIDCO LTD,

THE STATE OF MAHARASHTRA Through The Secretary, Urban Development Department...........Respondent(s)

FIRST APPEAL NO. 302 OF 2013

(Against the Order dated 24/01/2013 in Complaint No. 72/2010 of the State Commission Maharashtra)

VEENA BHUSHAN JAIN Through its Constituted Attorney-Shri bhusan Chimanlal Jain,...........Appellant(s)

Versus

CITY & INDUSTRIAL DEVELOPMENT CORPORATION OF MAHARASHTRA LTD. (CIDCO LTD.) NIRMAL" ,
THE MANAGING DIRECTOR, CIDCO LTD.,
THE MARKETING MANAGER-1, CIDCO LTD,
THE STATE OF MAHARASHTRA Through The Secretary, Urban Development Department,...........Respondent(s)

BEFORE: HON'BLE MR. JUSTICE R.K. AGRAWAL,PRESIDENT HON'BLE DR. S.M. KANTIKAR,MEMBER

For the Appellant :

For the Appellant : Mr. Bhushan Chimanlal Jain, In person (In FA No. 300 / 2013 and AR (in FA 301 & 302 / 2012)

For the Respondent :

For the Respondents : Mr. Ajit S. Bhasme, Advocate

Dated : 20 Jan 2021

ORDER

1. The challenge in these First Appeals, filed under Section 19 of the Consumer Protection Act, 1986 (hereinafter referred to as "the Act"), is to the Order dated 24.01.2013 in Complaint Case Nos. 70, 71 & 72 of 2010 passed by the Maharashtra State Consumer Disputes Redressal Commission (hereinafter to be referred to as "State Commission"), whereby the Complaints filed by the Complainants were dismissed with cost of 25,000/- to be paid to the Opposite Party No.1, "The City and Industrial Development Corporation of Maharashtra".

2. Since the facts and question of law involved in these Appeals are similar except for minor variations in the flat numbers and their sale consideration, these Appeals are being disposed of by this common Order. However, for the sake of convenience, First Appeal No. 300 of 2013 is treated as the lead case and the facts enumerated hereinafter are taken from Complaint No. 70 of 2010.

3. Briefly stated the facts as narrated in the Complaint are that the Opposite Party No. 1, namely, 'The City and Industrial Development Corporation of Maharashtra Ltd.' (hereinafter referred to as 'CIDCO') is a limited company duly registered under the Companies Act and engaged in development of new township at Navi Mumbai as a part of its housing Project; Opposite Party No. 2 is the Managing Director of CIDCO; Opposite Party No. 3 is the Marketing Manager-1 working with CIDCO and Opposite Party No. 4 is State of Maharashtra which is a formal party in the Complaint.The CIDCO proposed a housing Project under the name and style of "Seawoods Estate", Phase-II, Part - I&II" situated at Sector - 54, 56, 58, Nerul (West), Navi Mumbai. The Complainant by depositing a sum of 5,000/- towards Demand Registration Charges (DRC) booked his demand for an Apartment in the said Project with CIDCO on 19.11.2004.In the year 2007, the Complainant came to know about release of allotment of "Seawoods Estate Phase-II (Part-1)" to the registration holders.Since the Complainant was a registration holder, he applied for the allotment of apartment and deposited 6,00,000/- towards earnest money with CIDCO.CIDCO allotted Apartment No. 303, third floor in Building No. 52 [B-NL-SW2-52-303], admeasuring 1230.610 sq. ft. at 3,700/- per sq. ft. to the Complainant vide Allotment Letter dated 05.10.2007.According to Allotment Letter total sale consideration was 45,53,257/- and after adjusting the Demand Registration Charges and Earnest Money, the balance amount of 39,48,257/- was payable in four installments of 9,87,064/- each, scheduled to be paid on 04.01.2008, 04.04.2008, 04.07.2008 and 03.10.2008.The Complainant alleged that he had applied for Apartment solely in his name despite that CIDCO wrongly issued the Allotment Letter and the Permission Letter to mortgage the Apartment for obtaining housing loan, in joint names of Bushan Chimanlal Jain & Veena Bushan Jain. The Complainant sent letter dated 08.10.2007 to CIDCO and objected the same and brought the said lapses to their knowledge and requested to issue correct Allotment Letter. CIDCO vide letter

dated 31.12.2007 informed the Complainant that " your request for correcting the name in the allotment letter, NOC for loan and the payment has been considered and accordingly the necessary corrections have been made in our record. It is also stated that the said letter be treated as amendment to the original document already issued to him. The Complainant alleged that in the subject of the said letter CIDCO has mentioned Apartment No. B-NL-SW2-48-1303 instead of B-NL-SW2-52-303. The Complainant approached CIDCO Office in the middle of January 2008 to satisfy his doubts. On the advice and instruction of the Assistant Marketing Manager-1, CIDCO, the Complainant paid 200/- towards the administrative fees for the procurement of fresh allotment documents and pending receipt of earnest money deposited. The Complainant alleged that despite his repeated requests and depositing fees of 200/- to get the duplicate copy of amended Allotment Letter, the same was not issued by the CIDCO.It is alleged that CIDCO vide letter dated 05.05.2008 threatened him to cancel the allotment of Apartment and to forfeit the earnest money deposited and denied to deliver fresh, correct and authenticated allotment documents because of their computerized network server/system problem. In the year 2008, CIDCO had revised the rate of the apartments from 3,700/- to 7,500/- per sq. ft. The Complainant alleged that in order to have illegal monetary gain, CIDCO vide letter No. CIDCO/MM-1/SW2/2008/1241 dated 13 August th 2008, cancelled his allotment of apartment and forfeited the earnest money and registration charges. Alleging deficiency in service and unfair trade practice on the part of Opposite Party CIDCO, the Complainant filed a Consumer Complaint before the State Commission seeking following reliefs:- "A) That this Hon'ble Commission be pleased to issue the orders quashing & setting aside Opposite Party No. 3 fabricated, illegal & unauthorized apartment Allotment Cancellation Letter No. CIDCO/MM-1/SW2/2008/1241 dated 13/08/2008 received by the Complainant on 06.09.2008. B) That this Hon'ble Commission be pleased to direct the Opposite Party No. 2 & 3 to Either Revoke or Revive the Allotment of Apartment with original payment terms and conditions effective from the date of revival order with interest free waiver OR Else Compensate And Pay the Amount towards the costs for the Apartment Rate Difference as per the Present Market Value and the prevailing price per Sq. Ft. as on today, as detailed in para (12) on page No. (12) of this Complaint, alongwith the valued EMD amount and the registration charges now with interest, paid by the Complainant. C) That this Hon'ble Commission be pleased to direct the Opposite Parties jointly or severally to pay the costs of 6,00,000/- (Rupees Six Lacs Only) till date spent by this Complainant towards the Rents of the flats and the conveyance charges etc. due to their not giving Apartment Possession due to their severe documents defects. D) That this Hon'ble Commission be pleased to direct that the compensation by the Opposite Party must be given to the Complainant towards the Mental Torture and Harassment be compensated at 15,00,000/- (Rupees Fifteen Lacs Only). E) That this Hon'ble Commission be pleased to direct that the compensation by the Opposite Party must be given to the Complainant towards the Advocate fees be compensated at 25,000/- (Rupees Twenty Five Thousand only)."

4. The Opposite Party CIDCO contested the Complaint before the State Commission by filing Written Statement. In the Written Statement, they submitted that in reply to the letter dated 08.10.2007 regarding correction of name of allottee, they intimated to the Complainant vide letter dated 31.12.2007 that necessary corrections have been made in their record and letter dated 31.12.2007 be treated as amendment to the Original Allotment Letter issued to the Complainant. Despite that Complainant was requesting to issue Fresh Allotment Letter with malafide intentions and ulterior motive of delaying the payment of installments. They informed the Complainant that second fresh Allotment Letter could not be issued as the whole system of their Marketing Section run on SAP (Computerized Networking) and the dates of the installments are calculated automatically and not manually from the date of deposit of Earnest Money.They also

submitted that with the Allotment Letter, NOC to mortgage the Apartment for obtaining housing loan was also supplied with a list of 44 financial institutions/Banks. But the Complainant never approached to any of the 44 Financial Institutions/Banks for obtaining the Housing Loan for payment of installments.As per terms of the Allotment Letter, the Complainant was bound to make the payments of four installments on the dates specified in the Allotment Letter.However, the Complainant was also granted extension of time at his request to deposit the 1 installment upto 03.03.2008 st making him clear that if he failed to deposit the installment on or before 03.03.2008 his allotment would be cancelled as per terms and conditions of the Allotment Letter.Despite that Complainant failed to deposit not only the first installment, which was extended upto 03.03.2008 but next two installments also which were due on 04.04.2008 and 04.07.2008. The Complainant defaulted in making payment of three installments consecutively out of four installments, therefore, they had left with no alternative but to cancel the Allotment of the Complainant in terms of Condition No. 3 of the Allotment Letter.They submitted that there is no deficiency in service on their part and prayed that the Complaint be dismissed.

5. After hearing both the parties and on perusal of material on record, the State Commission dismissed the Complaints by observing as under:- " Prior to cancellation of the allotment after three consecutive defaults occurred in making payment as per schedule, supra, the CIDCO had also warned the Complainants of their defaults by their letter dated 09/04/2008 addressed to each one of the Complainants. They have invited attention of each one of the Complainants to Condition No.3 which speaks for power of CIDCO to cancel the allotment in case of default and also further invited their attention about further Clauses whereby the earnest amount deposited could be forfeited in case of cancellation. In spite of this the Complainants only preferred to engage themselves in exchange of correspondence. By their communication dated 05/05/2008 addressed to each of the Complainants, it was further brought to the notice of the Complainant by the CIDCO that their explanation for non-payment of the due installment was not satisfactory and they were expected to make the payment and it also mentioned to one time extension granted to pay the first installment to the Complainants which they failed to avail. In this background when by their letter dated 13/08/2008, the CIDCO cancelled the respective allotment of the Complainants they perhaps cannot be blamed and their action of cancellation of allotment cannot be held as arbitrary. Once cancellation of the allotment occurred, there is no subsisting relationship as a Consumer and service provider between the respective Complainants and CIDCO. Furthermore, since the cancellation of the respective allotment cannot be held arbitrary or capricious; no deficiency in service on the part of the CIDCO can be inferred. Under these circumstances, the Consumer Complaints are not maintainable and at the second instance, since no deficiency in service on the part of the CIDCO or its Managing Director or Marketing Manager-I could be inferred or established, the Complaints deserve to be dismissed. 15. Intention of the Complainants to gain unjust enrichment could be seen from the Complaints as well as from their letter dated 27/08/2008 whereby they air their intention to cash on the enhanced price of the apartment or houses by them since then prevailing rate was of 7,500/- per sq.ft. This is how they tried to claim more than 60 Lakhs from the CIDCO against their respective allotments. Thus, we find that the Complaints are filed with malafide intention and this would justify imposition of cost on the Complainants."

6. Aggrieved by the Order dated 21.01.2013 passed by the State Commission, the Appellants have filed the present Appeals before this Commission.

7. Mr. Bushan Chimanlal Jain, (Appellant in FA No. 300 / 2013 and Authorised Representative in FA No. 301 & 302 / 2013) submitted that they had deposited earnest money of 6 lakh in each case with CIDCO in the year 2007 and due to incorrect particular in Allotment Letter issued by CIDCO, they did not deposit the further

installments. Despite charging administrative charges for issuance of fresh document, CIDCO did not issue fresh Allotment Letter with correct particular but cancelled their allotment in order to gain more profit to sell their units at higher prices, which is a clear case of deficiency in service and Unfair Trade Practice on the part of CIDCO. It is also submitted that the Appellants have proved their bonafide by complying the directions given in Order 27.05.2013 passed by this Commission and deposited a sum of 40 lakh with this Commission. Due to stress, hypertension on need for house, one of the Appellants died during the proceedings. It is further submitted that due to Stay Order from this Commission, three flats, in question, are in locked condition for 13 years and certainly these flats were in highly depleted condition and cost of their maintenance may also be considered while deciding the matter. It is also submitted that the Society, in which these flats are located, is charging 7000/- per year for each flat towards society charges and CIDCO be directed to clear these outstanding charges. He also submitted that CIDCO be also directed to clear the outstanding bills of Electricity, Water and Municipality Tax arising during this period of 13 years. He prayed that the Order passed by the State Commission be set aside and their Appeals be allowed.

8. Per contra , Mr. Ajit S. Bhasme, learned Counsel appearing on behalf of the Respondents supported the order passed by the State Commission as according to him the State Commission had passed a well-reasoned order which is based on a correct and rightful appreciation of evidence and material available on record and does not call for any interference.

9. To test the bonafide of the Appellants, vide Order 27.05.2013 they were directed to deposit 13,33,333/- in each of the Complaints, totaling 40 lakh with this Commission and it was also made clear that " he shall have to pay the entire consideration amount with interest @12% from the date it became due till the date of payment."

10. During the proceedings in the Appeals, in compliance of directions given vide Order dated 14.11.2017, the Complainants sent comprehensive representation to the Managing Director, CIDCO highlighting their grievance and the injustice, allegedly meted out to them by CIDCO.The Managing Director, CIDCO vide letter No.CIDCO/MM(II)/Seawoods/2018/803 dated 19.01.2018 rejected their request for allotment of apartments.The relevant portion of letter dated 19.01.2018 reads as under:-
"However, despite time extension granted by CIDCO for payment of installments, all three allottees defaulted in making payment. As a result of which, Marketing Manager issued show cause notice to all three defaulters. After this, Marketing Manager forwarded proposal for cancellation of allotments to then Managing Director, who subsequently approved the cancellation of allotments as per office file noting of 26.04.2008. Therefore, all three allotments were cancelled by Marketing Manager as per letter issued on 13.08.2008. It is also seen from the file that, as per the order of State Information Commission, after hearing the Complaint of Mr. Bushan Chimanlal Jain, then Managing Director dismissed the request for correction of errors in letter of allotments, as these allotments were already cancelled. Also Hon. State Commission Disputes Redressal Commission, Maharashtra dismissed the said complaint filed by Mr. Bushan Chimanlal Jain and ordered the Complainants to pay Rupees 25,000/- as costs to CIDCO. After going through the representation and hearing given, I am of the opinion that the request of Mr. Bushan Chimanlal Jain on behalf of the three allottees for allotment of apartments deserves no consideration since, the allotments have already been cancelled. Hence, the request of Mr. Bushan Chimanlal Jain stands dismissed."

11. We have heard Mr. Bushan Chimanlal Jain, (Appellant in FA No. 300 / 2013 and Authorised Representative in FA No. 301 & 302 / 2013) and Mr. Ajit S. Bhasme, learned Counsel for CIDCO, perused the Impugned Order passed by the State Commission, the Complaint, the Written Statement as well as written submissions.

12. Undisputed facts of the case are that the Complainant had booked an Apartment with CIDCO in their Project, namely "Seawoods Estates", Phase II, Part I & II located at

Sectors 54, 56 and 58, Nerul (West), Navi Mumbai by paying Demand Registration Charges of 5,000/- on 19.11.2004. Complainant further deposited a sum 6,00,000/- with CIDCO towards Earnest Money on 04.10.2007. Vide Allotment Letter dated 05.10.2007, the Complainant was allotted Apartment No. B-NL-SW2-52-303 admeasuring 1230.610 sq. ft. @3,700/- sq. ft. for a total sale consideration of 45,53,257/- and after adjusting Demand Registration Charges and the Earnest Money totaling 6,05,000/-, the balance consideration payable by the Complainant was 39,48,257/-. The balance amount was to be paid in four equal quarterly installment of 9,87,064/- on 04.01.2008, 04.04.2008, 4.07.2008 and 03.10.2008. In terms of the Allotment Letter, the Complainant was also required to pay a sum of 61,835/- towards miscellaneous charges including parking charges of 61,835/-. Along with Allotment Letter, dated 5.10.2007, CIDCO has also issued a "No Objection Certificate" (for short "NOC") granting permission to mortgage the allotted Apartment for obtaining the housing loan either from Central Government, State Government, Employer of the Allottee or the 44 Financial Institutions mentioned in the Allotment Letter. However, in the Allotment Letter as well as NOC, the name of Complainant's wife, Mrs. Veena Bushan Jain, was wrongly mentioned by the CIDCO along with the name of Complainant as joint allottee though the Apartment was booked in his single name with single photograph. Considering that the said per se defective Allotment Letter and NOC would not be acceptable to the Financial Institutions for granting home loan to pay the installments of the balance consideration, the Complainant, vide letter dated 08.10.2007, made a request to the CIDCO to rectify the mistake and issue corrected Allotment Letter as well as NOC in his single name status as "Mr. Bushan Chimanlal Jain". He further requested to CIDCO to make the necessary changes in their Original Record and also to issue the Receipt for the payment of Earnest Money of 6,00,000/-. However, no action was taken by the CIDCO on the said letter for two and half months. As the next installment of the balance consideration was payable on 04.01.2008, the CIDCO, vide their letter dated 31.12.2007, informed the Complainant that the necessary corrections had been made in their record and the letter may be treated as amendment to the Original Documents issued to him. No fresh or rectified Allotment Letter and NOC were issued to the Complainant on his request which the Complainant strongly objected. It is also pertinent to mention here that in the subject of the said letter dated 31.12.2007, the Apartment allotted to the Complainant was wrongly mentioned as B-NL-SW2-48-1303 which was actually allotted to his wife, Mrs. Veena Bushan Jain. As the Allotment Letter, NOC and Letter dated 31.12.2007 were containing wrong information regarding allotment of Apartment to the Complainant and there was possibility of an objection on these title documents of the Property from the Financial Institutions in sanctioning home loan for payment of Balance Consideration of 39,48,257/-, the Complainant again approached the CIDCO for rectification of errors committed by them upon which he was advised to deposit a sum of 200/- towards administrative fees for procurement of fresh allotment documents and pending receipt of payment of Earnest Money. The Complainant immediately deposited a sum of 200/- along with Pay in Slip duly signed by an official of CIDCO on behalf of the Marketing Manager I. However, despite deposit of the fees of 200/-, the CIDCO did not bother to issue error free and authenticated Allotment documents to the Complainant which tantamount to deficiency in service on their part.

13. As the Complainant failed to deposit the amount of Ist Installment of balance Sale Consideration despite extension of time being granted upto 03.03.2008, the CIDCO vide letter dated 09.04.2008 threatened the Complainant to cancel the Allotment on the ground of default in payment. But, as a matter of fact, in the absence of a valid Allotment Letter, error free NOC for mortgaging the property in question and even amendment Letter dated 31.12.2007 having mentioned wrong number of the Apartment allotted to the Complainant as B-NL-SW2-48-1303 instead of B-NL-SW2-52-303, the

Complainant was not able to obtain loan from the Bank/Financial Institutions for payment of the balance Sale Consideration. We do not find any substance in the contentions of the CIDCO that the Complainant had not approached to any of the Banks/Financial Institutions mentioned in the Allotment Letter for obtaining the home loan while the "NOC" was already issued by the CIDCO to him along with Allotment Letter for mortgaging the allotted Apartment; the Complainant has miserably failed and neglected to pay the installments to the CIDCO in time and the Complainant was just taking an excuse for non-payment of the installments on the ground that as the Allotment documents were defective he could not take the home loan from the Bank/Financial Institutions. Except making the bald assertion, no cogent evidence has been led by the CIDCO that the Complainant had not approached any of the Banks/Financial Institutions mentioned in the Allotment Letter for obtaining the home loan and the Complainant was intentionally avoiding the payment of Installments. In our considered opinion, there is no reason to believe that having booked three apartments in the name of himself, his wife and son and paying a sum of 6,00,000/- each as Earnest Money, the Complainant was intentionally delaying the payment of installments. In fact, in his letter dated 21.04.2008 the Complainant has requested the CIDCO for extension of time to deposit the balance amount as because of unauthenticated and uncorrected Allotment documents, he could not apply for loan to the Financial Institutions.The relevant paragraph of the said letter is reproduced below:- "With reference to your above referred letter received by me only on 21.04.2008 at 1.30 P.M, and I am thankful for the same. In response and reply I once again (as repeatedly requested) request Hon'ble CIDCO Ltd. to provide me authenticated correct and error free (6 pages) allotment documents, correct and error free NOC for loans along with mandatory 6 months payment period extesion letter towards 6 months wasted period w.e.f. 08.10.2007, due to Hon'ble CIDCO Ltd. delayed functioning and negligence concerning above two most important matters, which till yesterday dated 20.04.2008 were not responded, which made me unsecured for allotted apartment documents and financial arrangements, thus making this term and request for 6 month payment extension period letter mandatory and essential for grant by Hon'ble CIDCO Ltd . Rest of explanations are detailed in this two page letter under reference along with another enclosed 3 page letter dated 21.04.2008. I eagerly wait for above important three document requirements with mandatory 6 months payment extension period for 6 valuable months wasted due to your departmental delayed services and negligence." (Emphasis supplied)

14. From a bare perusal of the afore-extracted para, it is crystal clear that because of non-issuance of corrected and error free Allotment Documents by the CIDCO despite the repeated requests and depositing the fee of 200/-, the Complainant was feeling unsecured about investment of his hard earned money and could not make financial arrangements for payment of balance Sale Consideration. Therefore, he sought extension of time to deposit the balance amount. It is pleaded by the CIDCO that had the Complainant approached any Bank/Financial Institution for availing of loan, the CIDCO was always in readiness to help Complainant in clarifying to the Bank/Financial Institution regarding correction and amendment made on 31.12.2007 in original allotment letter/mortgage NOC issued to the Complainant. It is very shocking and surprising that though the CIDCO has admitted a mistake done by them in the Allotment Letter and NOC but still they were not ready to issue a corrected Allotment and NOC to the Complainant for obtaining the Loan from the Financial Institutions. The Allotment Letter is a crucial property document for obtaining loan from the Bank or Financial Institution and if it contains any wrong or false information, the Financial Institutions may not accept it as a genuine document of property title and they may hesitate/decline to grant the loan against the said Property. Therefore, the Complainant was constantly insisting for issuance of correct Allotment Letter and NOC. The Complainant, on advice, had deposited a sum of 200/- towards administrative charges for issuance of

fresh allotment documents and pending receipt of payment of Earnest Money. It is not the case of the CIDCO that the amount of 200/- was deposited by the Complainant for some other purpose and not for issuance of fresh and amended Allotment documents. Once the said fees as advised, was deposited by the Complainant, the CIDCO was under an obligation either to issue the fresh Allotment Letter/NOC for mortgage of property or to refund the charged fees which has not been done in the present case for which also the CIDCO is liable to compensate the Complainants.

15. The defence taken by the CIDCO that the request for issuance of fresh Allotment documents could not be considered as the whole system of their Marketing Section run on SAP (Computerized Networking) and the dates of the installments are calculated automatically and not manually from the date of deposit of Earnest Money, does not hold any water. Even if, for the sake of arguments, it is presumed that the CIDCO was not in a position to issue afresh Allotment Letter and NOC for mortgage of property, at least a Certificate on their Letter-Head ought to have been issued by them to the effect that no third party interest has been created on the Apartment -10- allotted to the Complainant and his family Members and the three different Apartments have been allotted to the Complainants/Appellants in their individual names. Besides, on 08.10.2007, i.e. just after three days of issuance of the Allotment Letter dated 05.10.2007, the Complainant applied for issuance of a fresh, corrected and authenticated Allotment Letter/NOC. Had an immediate action on the request dated 08.10.2007 would have been taken by the CIDCO, the dispute with regard to the defective Allotment Letter/NOC would have been resolved immediately and Complainant would be in a position to apply for loan for payment of Balance Consideration. The most startling fact of the case is that in response to the request of the Complainant, the CIDCO had made the necessary correction in its Original Record and the same was conveyed to the Complainant vide letter dated 13.12.2007 but even the said letter was having wrong mentioning of the Apartment allotted to the Complainant as B-NL-SW2-48-1303 which was actually allotted to his wife, Mrs. Veena Bushan Jain. This shows the sheer careless and negligence on the part of CIDCO especially when they requested the Complainant to treat the said letter as amendment to the Original Documents already issued to him. The further tragedy of the case is that even the letter dated 31.12.2007 has been manipulated by the CIDCO in the record maintained by them. On the basis of the information received by the Complainant under the Right to Information Act, 2005, it was found that a set of three letters all dated 31.12.2007 was sent to the Complainant, his wife and son with outward reference numbers of CIDCO/MM-1/SE2/492, 493 ad 494. However, the same was replaced in the record of the CIDCO without the knowledge of the Complainant with different outward reference Nos. of CIDCO/MM-1/SE/538, 538 and 540. There was no dispatch entry on all these three letters. The most amazing fact is that all the three letters dated 31.12.2007 sent to the Bushan Chimanlal Jain, Sandeep Bushan Jain and Veena Bushan Jain were with respect to Apartment No. B-NL-SW2/48/1303 which was allotted only to Mrs. Veena Bushan Jain. But, the letters dated 31.12.2007 available in the record of CIDCO, were having different Apartment numbers in their subject with some corrections. The Complainant, after receiving the information under the Right to Information Act, 2005, came to know that there were some other omissions and manipulations by the CIDCO with regard to the Allotment documents available in their record which are also reflected in the order dated 09.07.2010 passed by the Ist Appellate Authority under the Right to Information Act, 2005. The relevant observations with regard to discrepancy in the record of the CIDCO are as under:- " It is rather disturbing to note that the Appellant further stated that again for the 2 time, certain corrections were made and corrigendum letters issued nd by then MM-I. However, the Appellants do not seem to have received these letters. On cross checking with the record of PIO/MMI, it is seen that such correction letters were issued, but the office copy bears the signatures of somebody other than the Appellants as a

token of receipt of such letters. Further discussions/dialogue with the Appellant reveals that even the correction letters subsequently issued were bearing the same dates (i.e. 31.12.2007) with different outward Nos. as 538, 539 and 540 whereas the earlier No. being 492 on the same date. Based on this contention of the Appellants, I had directed the PIO/MM-I to submit proof of their outward register. However, they have been unable to do so even after two complete working days. This again leads me to believe that the contention and the statements put forth by the Appellants must be true. In response to the above request, it is seen from the record that then PIO/MM-I has issued corrigendum letters to all the three allottees dated 31.12.2007 thereby rectifying the errors occurred. However, it was brought to the notice of the undersigned that even the corrigendum letters issued to rectify the mistakes were also erroneous i.e. by virtue of the fact that one and same flat has been allotted to all the three Appellants. The Appellant also contends that this error was brought to the notice of then MM-I and subordinate officers time and again. However, it seems the Appellants were made to run from pillar to post to get the rectification done. It is further disturbing to note that in spite of the Appellants proving the point and justifying the errors, which have taken place in the office of the MM-I, no efforts seem to have been taken either by the then MM-I and the staff below him or even the present MM-I and the staff posted under his now. Due to this, it is quite obvious that the grievance of the Appellant is genuine, because such mala-fide intentions/practices, disentitles their claim for the allotted flats and hence the Appellants obviously expect the case to be enquired in greater details and justice be granted to them by allotting fresh allotment letters. On further questioning the Appellants as to why they have not approached the Competent Authority of CIDO since the past nearly two and half years. To this they responded that they had met the then MD-Shri G.S. Gill, but unfortunately the MM-I and their staff mis-guided the MD by stating that the Appellant had filed a Writ Petition No.148/2009 and the same was dismissed by the Hon'ble High Court. In order to establish the authenticity of the court case, the Appellants have produced a copy of the order dated 10.09.09, perusal of which reveals that the Writ Petition is withdrawn by the Petitioners on the grounds of incomplete statements and documents available with them. In other words, the Hon'ble High Court has dismissed the case on their request, but not on merits. From all the above contention and facts put forth by the Appellants and proper perusal of the documents, it is prima-facie observed that the mistakes in the allotment letters issued on 05.10.2007 to these three Appellants remains to be rectified by the Marketing Mangers (ex and present), who have been handling the scheme right from the inception in the year 2007 and that too in spite of continuous and close follow up by the Appellants, for the reasons best known to the MMs themselves. Moreover, the fact that the PIO/MM-1 and their APIOs were not in a position to justify the various lapses which have occurred in the process of allotment procedures in these three cases leads me to believe that perhaps the errors have been continued intentionally and that to most probably with mala-fide intentions. However, if proven, this would amount to an offence which is beyond the scope of the RTI Act and as such the Appellants were advised to seek legal remedies at appropriate forum, if they so desire."

16. On the basis of the above observations, the State Information Commission, Maharashtra, Konkan Region, vide its order dated 21/10/2010 directed the State Government in the Urban Development Department to conduct an enquiry by Anti Correction Bureau or by an Independent Agency outside CIDCO into the Complaint filed by the Complainants.

17. From the foregoing discussions, it is amply clear that the CIDCO has failed to provide rectified and regularized afresh important property documents i.e. Allotment Letter without any ambiguity; correct and proper NOC to mortgage the Apartment and Earned Money paid Receipt despite the fact that the Registration, Consent and Allotment Applications were given strictly in individual names of the Bushan Chimanlal Jain, his wife, Veena Bushan Jain and his son, Sandeep Bushan Jain. By issuing the Allotment

Letters in multiple names and with reference to a single Apartment, the CIDCO itself has created a dispute on the ownership and possession right of the allotted Apartments to the Complainants/Appellant in these three Appeals. Without the rectified, regularized, correct and complete property/allotment documents in individual's name as applied for, the Complainants/Appellant were not able to arrange mortgage of Apartments so as to pay their balance Sale Consideration to CIDCO since the defective, wrong and incomplete Allotment documents cannot be accepted by the Financial Institutions as well as the buyer being matter of financial security and as such the Complainants/Appellants cannot be held liable for default in making the payment of installments. The Allotment Letters dated 5.10.2007, NOC for mortgage of Property and Letter dated 31.12.2007 being in big question mark and creating the confusion with regard to the title rights of the Apartments to be mortgaged by the Complainants/Appellants, they can be expected to pay the Balance Consideration until the dispute comes to an end. The Complainants have run post to pillar and had made all possible efforts to get the ill-defective allotment documents rectified so that they can obtain the home loan for payment of balance Sale Consideration. Under these circumstances, the CIDCO was not justified in cancelling the allotment of Apartments to the Complainants/Appellants and to forfeit the Earnest Money deposited by them. On the contrary, the CIDCO themselves had admitted their mistake by issuing the amendment letter dated 31.12.2007 and stating that they cannot issue afresh Allotment letter because of Computer Network System. There is a clear cut case of deficiency in service on the part of the CIDCO by not providing the correct, rectified and complete allotment documents to the Complainants/Appellant in the absence of which they could not obtain the home loan from the Bank/Financial Institutions to pay their balance amounts. A number of opportunities were provided to the CIDCO by the Court under the Right to Information Act, 2005 as well as this Commission to settle the dispute with the Appellants but because of adamant attitude of the official of the CIDCO, it lingers for a long period. The CIDCO cannot take the advantage of its own wrongs and blame the Complainant for not making the payment of the installment of balance consideration and as such the cancellation of the apartments by them was totally arbitrary and deserves to be quashed. We are of the considered opinion that the order passed by the State Commission dismissing all the complaints filed by the Complainants/Appellants, suffers from illegality as not based on the correct appreciation of the evidence available on record.

18. In the result, we allow all the three First Appeals filed by the Complainants, set aside the order passed by the State Commission and restore the Complaints. Accordingly, we direct the Opposite Party CIDCO to restore the cancelled Apartments in the individual names of Bushan Chimanlal Jain, Sandeep Bushan Jain and Veena Bushan Jain (now deceased and represented through legal heirs), as applied for in the Registration, Consent and Allotment Applications on the same terms and conditions of the Allotment Letter dated 5.10.2007. It is made clear here that this Commission vide Order dated 11.10.2013, had already directed the CIDCO to maintain status-quo with regard to nature, title and possession of the subject flats. Further, vide order, dated 27.05.2013 while directing the Complainants/Appellants in these Appeals, to deposit a sum of 13,33,333/- each to test their bona-fide, it was made clear to them that they have to pay the entire consideration amount with interest @ 12% p.a. from the date it became due till the date of payment. The Appellants had already complied with the said order. As such, in the spirit and letter of the Order dated 27.05.2013, we direct the Complainants/Appellants to pay the balance consideration minus the amount deposited with this Commission, with interest @ 12% p.a from the date it became due till the date of payment, within a period of 8 weeks from the date of receipt of a copy of this order and thereafter possession of the allotted Apartments shall be handed over to the Complainants by the CIDCO within two weeks. The amount deposited by the

Appellants with this Commission shall be released to the CIDCO along with interest accrued, if any. We are also of the view that the Complainants are entitled for some compensation on account of mental agony and harassment suffered by them during the last 13 years due to careless and negligent attitude of the CIDCO. Accordingly, we direct the CIDCO to pay an amount of 2,00,000/- each to the Complainants as lump sum compensation in addition to costs of pr oceedings quantified at 50,000/- each, within a period of 8 weeks from the date of receipt of a copy of this order. ....J R.K. AGRAWAL PRESIDENT .... DR. S.M. KANTIKAR MEMBER

<u>CASE NO. 33</u>
REVISION PETITION NO. 2192 OF 2014
(Against the Order dated 10/02/2014 in Appeal No. 2380/2012 of the State Commission Uttar Pradesh)
  PANKAJ KUMAR SHARMA S/O SH.OM PRAKASH SHARMA, 3 ....Petitioner(s)
Versus
GHAZIABAD DEVELOPMENT AUTHORITY VIKAS MARG, THROUGH ITS CHAIRMAN GHAZIABAD U.P ....Respondent(s)
BEFORE: HON'BLE MR. DINESH SINGH,PRESIDING MEMBER
For the Petitioner : Mr. Madhurendra Kumar, Advocate
For the Respondent : Mr. Shashank Shukla, Advocate with Mr. Shantanu Krishna, Advocate
Dated : 22 Jan 2021

ORDER
HON'BLE MR. DINESH SINGH, PRESIDING MEMBER
Taken up through video conferencing.

1. This Petition has been filed under Section 21(b) of The Consumer Protection Act, 1986 (the 'Act 1986') in challenge to the Order dated 10.02.2014 of The State Consumer Disputes Redressal Commission, Uttar Pradesh (the 'State Commission') in First Appeal No. 2380 of 2012 arising out of the Order dated 24.09.2012 in C.C. No. 66 of 10 of The District Consumer Disputes Redressal Forum, Ghaziabad (the 'District Forum'). The Petitioner, Mr. Pankaj Kumar Sharma, was the Complainant before the District Forum (the 'Complainant'). The Respondent, Ghaziabad Development Authority (GDA), was the Opposite Party before the District Forum (the 'GDA').

2. Arguments were heard from the learned Counsel on 07.01.2021. The material on record, including inter alia the Order dated 24.09.2012 of the District Forum, the impugned Order dated 10.02.2014 of the State Commission and the Petition, was perused.

3. The dispute relates to cancellation of allotment of a flat by the GDA on the Complainant failing to deposit the cost of the flat with the GDA.

4. The District Forum vide its Order dated 24.09.2012 allowed the Complaint. It directed the GDA to handover possession of the subject flat to the Complainant and to pay compensation of Rs. 5,000/- and cost of litigation of Rs. 2,000/-.

5. The State Commission vide its impugned Order of 10.02.2014 accepted the Appeal of the GDA. It set aside the Order dated 24.09.2012 of the District Forum. Consequently the Complaint stood dismissed.

6. It is admitted that no receipt(s) of depositing the cost of the subject flat with the GDA were produced by the Complainant in his evidence.

7. The GDA had not filed its Written Version before the District Forum. That being as it is, it was required of the District Forum to make fair appraisal of the evidence adduced by the Complainant, that the Complainant had in fact deposited the cost of the subject flat with the GDA. The District Forum erred in relying wholly and solely on the affirmation on affidavit made by the Complainant that he had deposited the cost of the subject flat with the GDA, overlooking that no evidence (in the form of receipts from the GDA, the Complainant's bank statements showing debit from his account and credit to the account

of the GDA, etc.) to establish that the Complainant had in fact deposited the cost of the flat with the GDA, had been proffered by the Complainant.

8. The State Commission has referred to the various letters written by the GDA asking the Complainant to deposit the cost of the subject flat, and to the GDA's unequivocal and explicit affirmation that the Complainant had in fact not made any deposit towards the cost of the subject flat. It has passed a reasoned order, determining that the Complainant had not made any deposit towards the flat.

9. The GDA is a government development authority. It functions is required and expected to function) as per its laid down administrative, financial and technical rules. In the ordinary wont it takes deposits through cheques, drafts, electronically. Its accounts are subject to audit.

10. The Complainant failed to furnish any receipt or any bank statement etc. in support of his affirmation of having made deposit for the subject flat with the GDA. The GDA made its affirmation on the basis of its official record. The Complainant also failed to show any infarction of a financial or administrative norm, or that the GDA adopted any unlawful or corrupt etc. practice in his case.

11. As such the critique made by the State Commission cannot be faulted. The Revision Petition preferred by the Complainant before this Commission fails. The State Commission's Order of 10.02.2014 is confirmed. The Complaint stands dismissed.

12. A copy each of this Order be sent by the Registry to both sides within three days of its pronouncement. .... DINESH SINGH PRESIDING MEMBER

<u>**CASE NO. 34**</u>
CONSUMER CASE NO. 886 OF 2020
M/S. FREIGHT SYSTEM (INDIA) PRIVATE LIMITED ....Complainant(s)
Versus
OMKAR REALTORS & DEVELOPERS PRIVATE LIMITED & ANR. ....Opp.Party(s)
BEFORE: HON'BLE MR. DINESH SINGH,PRESIDING MEMBER
For the Complainant : Mr. Vivek Kohli, Sr. Advocate with Ms. Bharti Chawla, Advocate
For the Opp.Party :
Dated : 25 Jan 2021

ORDER
HON'BLE MR. DINESH SINGH, PRESIDING MEMBER
Taken up through video conferencing.

1. This Complaint has been filed by M/s Freight System (India) Private Limited (the 'Complainant Co.') under Section 58(1)(a) read with Section 59 of The Consumer Protection Act, 2019 (the 'Act 2019').

2. Mr. Vivek Kohli, learned senior Counsel for the Complainant Co. was heard on admission on 20.01.2021. The record was perused. The Complaint contains allegations against the Opposite Party No. 1, Omkar Realtors and Developers Private Limited, the builder / developer (the 'Builder Co.') and the Opposite Party No. 2, The Summit Business Park Cooperative Society Limited, the maintenance agency (the 'Maintenance Society').

3. The subject matter of the Complaint is 11 units, together admeasuring 17,203 sq. ft., comprising the entire Mezzanine Floor of Summit Business Bay Andheri, purchased by the Complainant Co. from the Builder Co. for a total consideration of Rs. 17,95,30,000/-
.

4. On the preliminary issue of whether the Complainant Co. is a 'consumer' under the Act 2019, learned senior Counsel submitted that the said 11 units have been purchased by the Complainant Co. for its office. He argued that the Complainant Co.'s office has no direct and close nexus with its profit generating activity, the dominant purpose of purchasing space for its office in the business park is not linked to its commercial

activity. In support of his argument he principally relied on Hon'ble Supreme Court's judgment dated 14.11.2019 in Lilavati Kirtilal Mehta Medical Trust vs. Unique Shanti Developers & Ors. IV (2019) CPJ 65 (SC) and on this Commission's Order dated 08.07.2016 in Crompton Greaves Limited & Anr. vs. Daimler Chrysler India Private Limited & Ors. (Consumer Case No. 51 of 2006) . Learned senior Counsel submitted that the Complainant Co. is a 'consumer' under Section 2(7)(ii) of the Act 2019.

5. Section 2(7) of the Act 2019 is first reproduced for ready convenience. Section 2(7): "consumer" means any person who— (i) buys any goods for a consideration which has been paid or promised or partly paid and partly promised, or under any system of deferred payment and includes any user of such goods other than the person who buys such goods for consideration paid or promised or partly paid or partly promised, or under any system of deferred payment, when such use is made with the approval of such person, but does not include a person who obtains such goods for resale or for any commercial purpose; or (ii) hires or avails of any service for a consideration which has been paid or promised or partly paid and partly prom-ised, or under any system of deferred payment and includes any beneficiary of such service other than the person who 'hires or avails of the services for consideration paid or promised, or partly paid and partly promised, or under any system of deferred payment, when such services are availed of with the approval of the first mentioned person, but does not include a person who avails of such service for any commercial purpose; Explanation .— For the purposes of this clause,- (a) the expression "commercial purpose" does not include use by a person of goods bought and used by him exclusively for the purposes of earning his livelihood, by means of self-employment; -2- (b) the expressions "buys any goods" and "hires or avails any services" includes offline or online transactions through electronic means or by teleshopping or direct selling or multi-level marketing;

6. A company is included in the definition of 'person' contained in Section 2(31), it is not per se precluded from being 'consumer', provided, if, for a particular purpose, it meets the requirements of 'consumer' as defined in Section 2(7) of the Act 2019. 'housing construction' falls under 'service' in Section 2(42). Sub-section (ii) of Section 2 (7) specifically stipulates "but does not include a person who avails of such service for any commercial purpose".

7. On the face of it itself: [a] 'housing construction' under the definition of 'service' in Section 2(42) cannot be construed to include construction of a commercial complex for commercial activity; and [b] commercial space in a commercial complex for an office of a company engaged in a business to generate profit is for 'commercial purpose'.

8. Explanation (a) to Section 2 (7), that "the expression "commercial purpose" does not include use by a person of goods bought and used by him exclusively for the purpose of earning his livelihood, by means of self-employment.", provides an exception for 'goods', not for 'service'. Even if a simile with 'goods' is conjectured, "exclusively for the purpose of earning his livelihood" has to be adjudged rationally and logically with the due understanding and significance of "exclusively" and "livelihood" and "self-employment". Reasonable and logical interpretation has to be kept limited and confined to reason and logic, not hypothesized towards anyhow allowing anyone in.

9. A plain reading of Section 2(7)(ii) and Section 2(42) of the Act 2019 makes it clear that the Complainant Co., which has purchased commercial space for its office in a commercial complex, is not a 'consumer' under the Act 2019.

10. Denial to avail additional remedy in consumer protection fora to a 'person' who is not a 'consumer' does not take away or affect his right to agitate his case in an appropriate forum / court as per the law. Conversely, the availability of additional remedy in consumer protection fora does not take away the option of a 'consumer' to agitate his case in any other appropriate forum / court. As such, if, for a particular purpose, a company does not meet the ingredients of 'consumer' under the Act 2019, it will not be left remediless, it can avail of remedies available under other existing laws.

11. Whether, for a particular purpose, a company is a 'consumer', has principally to be determined by examining the facts and specificities of the case. This has been settled by Hon'ble Supreme Court in the Lilavati Kirtilal Mehta Medical Trust case, wherein the Hon'ble Court has held that: 7. To summarize from the above discussion, though a straight-jacket formula cannot be adopted in every case , the following broad principles can be culled out for determining whether an activity or transaction is 'for a commercial purpose': (i) The question of whether a transaction is for a commercial purpose would depend upon the facts and circumstances of each case. However, ordinarily, 'commercial purpose' is understood to include manufacturing/industrial activity or business-to-business transactions between commercial entities. (ii) The purchase of the good or service should have a close and direct nexus with a profit-generating activity. (iii) The identity of the person making the purchase or the value of the transaction is not conclusive to the question of whether it is for a commercial purpose. It has to be seen whether the dominant intention or dominant purpose for the transaction was to facilitate some kind of profit generation for the purchaser and/or their beneficiary. (iv) If it is found that the dominant purpose behind purchasing the good or service was for the personal use and consumption of the purchaser and/or their beneficiary, or is otherwise not linked to any commercial activity, the question of whether such a purchase was for the purpose of 'generating livelihood by means of self-employment' need not be looked into. (emphasis supplied) The Hon'ble Court has also laid-down 'broad principles', including the yardsticks of 'close and direct nexus' and 'dominant purpose'. The summarization made by Hon'ble Supreme Court in the Lilavati Kirtilal Mehta Medical Trust case has to be rationally and logically adopted, with the due understanding and significance of "a straight-jacket formula cannot be adopted in every case" and "broad principles" and "The question of whether a transaction is for a commercial purpose would depend upon the facts and circumstances of each case" and "close and direct nexus" and "The identity of the person making the purchase or the value of the transaction is not conclusive to the question of whether it is for a commercial purpose." and "dominant purpose". If, for a particular purpose, a company wants to enter the consumer protection fora, whether or not it is a 'consumer' has to be (reasonably and logically) adjudged in the given facts and specificities of each case ("a straight-jacket formula cannot be adopted in every case" ; "The question of whether a transaction is for a commercial purpose would depend upon the facts and circumstances of each case"). "The identity of the person making the purchase is not conclusive to the question of whether it is for a commercial purpose." also implicitly conveys that the distinctive difference between the each of the juridical persons with the each of the other has also to be appreciated. A company is differently placed from a trust, and moreso a medical trust. The tests of 'close and direct nexus' and 'dominant purpose' for a company have to be adopted inter alia keeping in mind that a company is distinctively different from a medical trust providing hostel facilities to nurses working in its hospital, as in the Lilavati Kirtilal Mehta Medical Trust case. The tests of 'close and direct nexus' and 'dominant purpose' cannot be mechanically extrapolated to every juridical person without keeping in mind that every juridical person is distinctively different from the each of the other.

12. The question here relates to purchase of commercial space in a commercial complex, in its own name, as its, the company's, property, its immovable capital assets. Human resource is an integral part of the operating requirements of a company, it is an indispensable part of its operating requirements, without which it cannot undertake its profit-generating activity. Capital expenditure for its human resource decidedly has a 'close and direct nexus' with a company's profit generating activity, the 'dominant purpose' is decidedly linked to its commercial activity. To view the capital expenditure on human resource in isolation or opacity to its profit–generating activity, as to anyhow enable a company to fall in the definition of 'consumer', is per se illogical and incorrect,

and it defeats the purpose for which "but does not include a person who avails of such service for any commercial purpose." has been specifically provided in Sub-section (ii) of Section 2(7).

13. It has also to be noted that a company creating immovable capital assets in the form of lands and buildings, in its own name, for its office, is differently placed from a company buying a car, in its own name, 'solely or principally' for the personal use of its Directors or employees. A car is not an immovable capital asset in the nature of lands and buildings. The two cannot be equated, drawing a simile is non sequitur. Thus, creation of immovable capital assets in the form of lands and buildings is materially different from the question which was answered as below by a bench comprising three members of this Commission in the Crompton Greaves Limited case. 11. For the reasons stated hereinabove, the issue referred to the larger Bench is answered as follows: (a) if a car or any other goods are obtained or any services are hired or availed by a company for the use/personal use of its directors or employees, such a transaction does not amount to purchase of goods or hiring or availing of services for a commercial purpose, irrespective of whether the goods or services are used solely for the personal purposes of the directors or employees of the company or they are used primarily for the use of the directors or employees of the company and incidentally for the purposes of the company. (b) The purchase of a car or any other goods or hiring or availing of services by a company for the purposes of the company amount to purchase for a commercial purpose, even if such a car or other goods or such services are incidentally used by the directors or employees of the company for their personal purposes.

14. The question at hand, in respect of a company purchasing commercial space for its office in a commercial complex, is also materially different from a company indemnifying its raw materials, goods in process, finished goods, plant and machinery, lands and buildings, etc., by taking insurance. In such case, the purpose is indemnification against perils, nothing per se to do 'closely and directly' with its profit-generating activity, the 'dominant purpose' is not linked with its commercial activity, as such the company straightaway falls within the meaning of 'consumer' in accordance with Section 2(7), without necessitating a detailed exposition.

15. It may be added for completeness that the lands and buildings of a company, its property, its immovable capital assets, should ordinarily not be viewed in isolation of its objects as given in its Memorandum (Section 4(1)(c) of The Companies Act, 2013). A company formed with charitable objects, etc. (Section 8 of The Companies Act, 2013), which has in its objects the promotion of commerce, art, science, sports, education, research, social welfare, religion, charity, protection of environment, or any such other object, and intends to apply its profits, if any, or other income in promoting its objects, and intends to prohibit the payment of any dividend to its members, is differently placed from a company formed with the sole intention of earning profit. Learned senior Counsel submitted that the Complainant Co. is not a company formed with charitable objects, etc.

16. The Complainant Co.'s case, that it is a 'consumer', fails on its facts and on the law. It may however also be observed here that anyhow allowing anyone into consumer protection fora has adverse ramifications, including inter alia : [a] evasion of court fee in civil courts; and [b] eroding into the time and resources of consumer protection fora, which could otherwise be better devoted to the ordinary general consumers, who straightaway fall, ex facie , in the definition of 'consumer' (without having to write a treatise to enable their anyhow entry into the fora).

17. To conclude: [a] the Complainant Co. does not fall in the definition of 'consumer' contained in Section 2(7) of the Act 2019; and [b] it does not get benefit from the Lilavati Kirtilal Mehta Medical Trust case and the Crompton Greaves Limited case.

18. The Complaint is dismissed as not maintainable before this Commission.

19. It is made explicit that the merit of the dispute between the opposing sides has not been entered into. The Complainant Co. is free to agitate its case in any appropriate forum / court as per the law.

20. The Registry is requested to send a copy each of this Order to the Complainant Co. and to its learned Counsel within three days of its pronouncement. .... DINESH SINGH PRESIDING MEMBER

CASE NO. 35
FIRST APPEAL NO. 842 OF 2020

(Against the Order dated 31/10/2019 in Complaint No. 47/2015 of the State Commission Orissa)

VARUN ENGINEERS ....Appellant(s)

Versus

M/S. RSB TRANSMISSION INDIA LTD. ....Respondent(s)

BEFORE: HON'BLE MRS. JUSTICE DEEPA SHARMA,PRESIDING MEMBER

For the Appellant : Mr. R. Santhaan Krishnan, Advocate

For the Respondent :

Dated : 25 Jan 2021

ORDER
JUSTICE DEEPA SHARMA (ORAL) THROUGH VIDEO CONFERENCING

1. The present Appeal, under Section ---51(1) of the Consumer Protection Act, 2019 (for short "the Act") has been filed by the Appellant against the order dated -----31.10.2019 of the State Consumer Disputes Redressal Commission, Orissa (for short "the State Commission") in Complaint No.47 of 2015 whereby the Complaint of the Respondent was allowed.

2. Learned Counsel for the Appellant, who was the Opposite Party in the complaint, has contended that the impugned order suffers with illegality as the State Commission has not exercised its jurisdiction correctly since it has nowhere discussed whether the Consumer Complaint was maintainable and it did not have the jurisdiction to entertain the Complaint and the correct forum for raising the dispute was the civil court since the dispute has arisen from the contractual relationship between the parties. It is argued that the Appellant had filed the written version but since it was filed beyond the statutory period of limitation provided under the Act, the same was not taken on record and therefore, there was no defence of the Appellant and hence, the impugned order was passed, believing the one sided testimony of the Complainant.

3. I have heard the learned Counsel for the Appellant at length and perused the file.

4. The brief facts of the case are that the Complainant being Director of the Company named as M/s RSB Transmission India Ltd. had ordered on 19.04.2021 one 5MT Crane for raw material handling and one 10MT Crane for liquid metal transportation with the Appellant. The case of the Complainant was that the Appellant did not supply the 5MT Crane and did not install the 10MT Crane due to which he had suffered loss and was not able to start the production unit for sophisticated cast components. He had also contended that he had paid an advance of 50,01,458/-in total on different dates and also paid a sum of 1,80,000/- towards transportation cost as well as 10,000/- for payment to be made to service engineers of the Appellant for supply of the Cranes. Despite repeated communications, the Appellant failed to do the needful as per the agreement. Hence, the Complaint.

5. Notice of the Complaint was duly served and the Appellant had attended the trial but did not file the written version within the time and their right to file the written version was closed. This order was not challenged by the Appellant before any appropriate forum and the said order had attained its finality. The Complainant filed his evidence by way of affidavit and other documents. Relying on the evidence of the Complainant, the State Commission made the following observations: "5. On perusal of documents it is clear

116

that complainant had placed one Capital Purchase Order to O.P. for supply of 05T & 10T DG EOT Crane Cabin Operated, Remote & Pendent Operated DSL System & LT Rails for value of 43,64,000/-. O.P. acknowledged and requested for advance payment which was made as per payment details at page 36 of complaint petition. Complainant paid 51,91,458/-. O.P. supplied one Crane which is valued for 21,82,616/-. Letter dated 18.10.2014 of complainant to O.P. reveals that complainant requested O.P. for installation of Crane. As O.P. did not respond, complainant served legal notice dated 29.06.2015 to O.P. and thereafter filed the complaint on 28.08.2015 before this Commission. 6. From the above, it is clear that there is deficiency in service on the part of O.P. for non installation of the Crane supplied and non supply of another Crane as per the order placed by complainant, which has caused mental agony and financial loss. 7. In view of the above we are of the considered opinion that O.P. is liable to compensate the loss suffered by complainant. O.P. is also liable to pay the balance amount of 28,18,842/- to complainant along with 12% interest. 8. In the result complaint is allowed directing O.P. to pay 28,18,842/- along with 12% interest per annum from the date of filing complain till realisation."

6. Even at the time when the matter was listed for final arguments and final arguments were being heard, none had argued on behalf of the Appellant before the State Commission since none had attended the proceedings before the State Commission on that date.

7. This order is impugned before me by the Appellant on the ground that the State Commission has acted beyond its jurisdiction because it is not a consumer dispute and the Complainant could have filed only a suit before the civil court and therefore, the impugned order is liable to be set aside.

8. This argument has no merit since Section 2(6) of the Act defines the Consumer Complaint and also defines deficiency in service. (6) "complaint" means any allegation in writing, made by a complainant for obtaining any relief provided by or under this Act, that— (i) an unfair contract or unfair trade practice or a restrictive trade practice has been adopted by any trader or service provider; (ii) the goods bought by him or agreed to be bought by him suffer from one or more defects; (iii) the services hired or availed of or agreed to be hired or availed of by him suffer from any deficiency; (iv) a trader or a service provider, as the case may be, has charged for the goods or for the services mentioned in the complaint, a price in excess of the price— (a) fixed by or under any law for the time being in force; or (b) displayed on the goods or any package containing such goods; or (c) displayed on the price list exhibited by him by or under any law for the time being in force; or (d) agreed between the parties; (v) the goods, which are hazardous to life and safety when used, are being offered for sale to the public— (a) in contravention of standards relating to safety of such goods as required to be complied with, by or under any law for the time being in force; (b) where the trader knows that the goods so offered are unsafe to the public; (vi) the services which are hazardous or likely to be hazardous to life and safety of the public when used, are being offered by a person who provides any service and who knows it to be injurious to life and safety; (vii) a claim for product liability action lies against the product manufacturer, product seller or product service provider, as the case may be;"

9. From the definitions, it is apparent that deficiency in service can arise only when there is a contract between the parties to provide such services. Non-supply of purchased goods is a deficiency in service under the Consumer Protection Act, 2019. Therefore, the argument of learned Counsel that since the dispute relates to a civil contract, the jurisdiction exclusively lies with the civil court, has no merit. Under the Consumer Protection Act, the State Commission had the jurisdiction to deal with the dispute raised by the Complainant before it. Thus, the impugned order does not suffer with any illegality on this account.

10. From the perusal of record, it is apparent that the State Commission while passing the impugned order had relied on the material evidence before it. No defence has been raised by the Appellant before the State Commission. The State Commission order is based on the evidences before it and it cannot be said that the order of the State Commission is perverse. 10. I found no illegality or infirmity or perversity in the impugned order. The present Appeal has no merit and the same is dismissed in limine.

11. Copy of this order be sent to the State Commission as well as to the Complainant.
.......................J DEEPA SHARMA PRESIDING MEMBER

<u>**CASE NO. 36**</u>
REVISION PETITION NO. 3715 OF 2017

(Against the Order dated 07/11/2017 in Appeal No. 278/2017 of the State Commission Telangana)

M/S. SAI PRIYA ESTATES REP. BY ITS MANAGING PARTNER, MR. N. RAMA MOHAN REDDY S/O. N. BAL REDDY,...........Petitioner(s)

Versus

VVL SUJATHA D/O. LT. SRI V. LAKSHMI NARAYANA, ...Respondent(s)

BEFORE: HON'BLE MR. JUSTICE R.K. AGRAWAL,PRESIDENT HON'BLE DR. S.M. KANTIKAR,MEMBER

For the Petitioner :
For the Petitioner : Mr. J. Krishna Dev, Advocate
For the Respondent : For the Respondent : In Person
 Dated : 25 Jan 2021

ORDER

1. The present Revision Petition u/s 21 (b) of the Consumer Protection Act, 1986 (for short, "the Act") has been filed by the Opposite Party, M/s. Sai Priya Estate, against the order, dated 07.11.2017 passed by the State Consumer Disputes Redressal Commission, Telangana (for short, "the State Commission") whereby the First Appeal No. 278 of 2017 preferred by them u/s 27A of the Act has been dismissed.

2. The District Consumer Disputes Redressal Forum III, Hyderabad (for short, "the District Forum") has allowed the Consumer Complaint Case No. 1026 of 2007 filed by the Respondent/Complainant with the following directions:- "1. The Complainant is directed to deposit a sum of Rs.6,00,000/- (Rupees six Lakh only) from out of Caution Deposit amount of Rs.12,00,000/- to the credit of this C.C. on or before 28.12.2009 and further directed the Complainant to pay -1- the remaining balance of the Caution Deposit amount of Rs.6,00,000/- (Rupees six lakh only) at the time of handing over the flats i.e. 45% share by the Opposite Party to her. 2. The Opposite Party upon deposit of Rs.6,00,000/- representing Caution Deposit amount by the Complainant to the credit of this C.C. is directed to construct the pending works and complete the construction of the building complex within 4 months commencing from 29.12.2009 and after completion of the building, both of them have to execute the Memorandum of Understanding (MOU) on selection of flats between the Complainant and the Opposite party in the ration of 45% and 55% respectively as per Clause 3 of the Development Agreement dated 01.06.2003. 3. The Opposite Party is further directed to deposit the rent @ Rs.7,000/- (Rupees seven thousand only) per month to the credit of this C.C. from March, 2006 till December, 2009 and continue to deposit the rent at the rate every month till the construction of the building is completed. 4. The Opposite Party is not entitled to recover the amount of Rs.50,00,000/- (Rupees five lakh only) which is said to have been lent to the Complainant, as it is outside the purview of the Ex.A1 Development Agreement dated 01.06.2003. The Opposite Party is so advised is entitled to seek his redressal through proper Forum for recovery of the amount from the Complainant. 5. In so far as, the amount of Rs.10,000/- (Rupees ten thousand only) to be payable by the Opposite Party during the period of construction of the building is

concerned, no finding can be given as the Complainant did not ask that relief. However, the Complainant admitted that the Opposite Party paid Rs.10,000/- (Rupees ten thousand only) till March, 2006 can be amicably settled at the time of execution of Memorandum of Understanding (MOU) after completion of the entire construction of the building.'" In view of the reasons stated on the point No. 1 to 5 and also taking into the total facts and circumstances of case, there are some latches on the part of the Complainant as well as Opposite Party in completion of the construction of the building and further in order to maintain harmonious relationship between the parties in future so as to reach the finality of the lis inter-se, we are of the view that there is no need to award any compensation to the Complainant. However, the Complainant is entitled to a sum of Rs.3,000/- (Rupees three thousand only) towards costs and the rest of the claims claimed by the Complainant is dismissed. The above order is to be complied with as per direction given supra.'"""

3. The Petitioner/Opposite Party as well as the Respondent/Complainant challenged the Order dated 09.12.2009 passed by the District Forum in C.C. No.1026/2007, before the State Commission. First Appeal No. 208 of 2010 was filed by the Opposite Party and the First Appeal No. 316 of 2010 was filed by the Complainant. State Commission after a detailed discussion on record, disposed of both the appeals by giving following directions: - " (1) That the tenant by name Sri Brij Gopal be made as a proforma O.P. No.2 in C.C. 1026/2007 by amending the cause title. So also in the appeals which are to be carried out by the parties. (2) That the OP/Builder shall demolish the old structure in South-East corner of schedule property and proceed with the construction by completion of 10% work and deliver 45% share of flats to the complainant within three months of the demolition of the old structure. (3) That the OP/Builder is permitted to take the help of Police in case he was resisted either by Brij Gopal or his representative from demolishing the old structure. He may apply to the Registry for issuing a requisition to the concerned police for demolition of the old structure and complete the remaining work as directed. (4) That the complainant is entitled for rent @ Rs.7,000/- for the period from 21.7.2005 to 19.10.2006 only. Rent due and payable to be worked out from the amount already withdrawn by the complainant. (5) That the complainant shall return half of refundable deposit of Rs.6 Lakhs on delivery of 45% share of her flats."

4. Aggrieved by the said order of the State Commission, both the parties filed separate Revision Petitions before this Commission which were dismissed vide Order dated 20.04.2020 and as such the Order of the State Commission attained finality.

5. The proceedings u/s 27 of the Act were initiated against the Petitioner/Opposite Party and the Petitioner was sentenced to two years imprisonment and fine of 10,000/- in default to suffer 3 months imprisonment. An Appeal was preferred u/s 27A of the Act which was dismissed by the State Commission by the impugned Order dated 07.11.2017.

6. Without going into the merits of the case, we may mention that the Hon'ble Supreme Court in the case of Karnataka Housing Board Vs. K.A. Nagamani – (2019) 6 SCC 424 has held that no Revision Petition against the order passed in Appeal filed U/s 27A of the Act, is maintainable before this Commission inasmuch as the original complaint is not pending. Relevant paragraphs of the said judgment are reproduced below:- "6.2. The exercise of revisional jurisdiction Under Section 21(b) by the National Commission is limited to a consumer dispute which has been filed before the State Commission. The jurisdiction Under Section 21(b) of the 1986 Act can be exercised by the National Commission only in case of a "consumer dispute" filed before the State Commission. The National Commission in exercise of its supervisory jurisdiction Under Section 21(b) is concerned about the correctness or otherwise of the orders passed by the State Commission in a "consumer dispute"." 7.1 The revisional jurisdiction conferred on the National Commission u/s 21(b) is with respect to a pending or disposed of "consumer dispute" before the State Commission. "7.2. Section 25 of the 1986 Act, provides for the

enforcement of Orders passed by the District Forum, State Commission or National Commission. Section 25(3) states: 25. Enforcement of orders of the District Forum, the State Commission or the National Commission. (3) Where any amount is due from any person under an order made by a District Forum, State Commission or the National Commission, as the case may be, the person entitled to the amount may make an application to the District Forum, the State Commission or the National Commission, as the case may be, and such District Forum or the State Commission or the National Commission may issue a certificate for the said amount to the Collector of the district (by whatever name called) and the Collector shall proceed to recover the amount in the same manner as arrears of land revenue. An Order passed for enforcement, would not be an order in the 'consumer dispute' since it stands finally decided by the appellate forum, which has conclusively determined the rights and obligations of the parties. 7.3. The nature of execution proceedings is materially different from the nature of proceedings for adjudication of a consumer complaint. Execution proceedings are independent proceedings. Orders passed for enforcement of the final order in the Consumer dispute, cannot be construed to be orders passed in the 'Consumer Dispute'." XXXXXXXXX "7.7. We affirm the view taken by the Full Bench of the Andhra Pradesh High Court and Patna High Court. Execution proceedings even though they are proceedings in a suit, cannot be considered to be a continuation of the original suit. Execution proceedings are separate and independent proceedings for execution of the decree. The merits of the claim or dispute, cannot be considered during execution proceedings. They are independent proceedings initiated by the decree holder to enforce the decree passed in the substantive dispute. 7.8. There is no remedy provided Under Section 21 to file a Revision Petition against an Order passed in appeal by the State Commission in execution proceedings. Section 21(b) does not provide for filing of a Revision Petition before the National Commission against an Order passed by the State Commission in execution proceedings. 7.9. In the present case, the National Commission committed a jurisdictional error by entertaining the Revision Petition Under Section 21(b) filed by the Appellant-Board against an appeal filed before the State Commission, in Execution proceedings." (Emphasis supplied)

7. The Hon'ble Supreme Court has referred to and followed its earlier judgement in the case of Karnataka Housing Board (Supra) in Civil Appeal Nos. 1213-1215 of 2017 – M/s. Ambience Infrastructure Private Limited Vs. Ambience Island Apartment Owners and Ors . – decided on 28.08.2020. For ready reference, the paragraph 8 of the aforesaid judgment is reproduced below:- In a recent judgment in Karnataka Housing Board Vs. K.A. Nagamani – (2019) 6 SCC 424, this Court made a distinction between execution proceedings and original proceedings and held that the former are separate and independent. In our view, having regard to Section 23 of the Consumer Protection Act, 1986, an appeal will not lie to this Court against an order which has been passed in the course of execution proceedings. The appeals are hence dismissed as not being maintainable.

8. Respectfully following the law laid down in aforesaid judgments of the Hon'ble Supreme Court, as the National Commission has no jurisdiction to entertain any Revision u/s 21 (b) of the Act against an order passed by the State Commission u/s 27A of the Act in execution proceedings, we dismiss the present Revision Petition as not maintainable, leaving it open to the Petitioner to seek appropriate remedy in accordance with the law. ....J R.K. AGRAWAL PRESIDENT .... DR. S.M. KANTIKAR MEMBER

<u>CASE NO. 37</u>
CONSUMER CASE NO. 2778 OF 2018

MOKUL SHRIRAM EPC JV ....Complainant(s)

Versus

120

EXPORT CREDIT GUARANTEE CORPORATION OF INDIA LTD. ....Opp.Party(s)

BEFORE: HON'BLE MR. JUSTICE R.K. AGRAWAL,PRESIDENT HON'BLE DR. S.M. KANTIKAR,MEMBER

For the Complainant :

For the Complainant Company : Mr. Devesh Tripathi, Advocate Mr. Mohd. Faraz Anees, Advocate

For the Opp.Party :

For the Opposite Party : Mr. Bharat Sangal, Sr. Advocate Mr. R.R. Kumar, Advocate Ms. Babita, Advocate

Dated : 27 Jan 2021

ORDER

R. K. AGRAWAL, J., PRESIDENT

1. The present Consumer Complaint has been filed under Section 21(a)(i) of the Consumer Protection Act, 1986 (hereinafter referred to as the Act) by Mokul Shriram EPC JV (hereinafter referred to as the Complainant Company) against Export Credit Guarantee Corporation of India Limited (hereinafter referred to as the Opposite Party ECGC).

2. Brief facts as narrated in the Consumer Complaint are that the Complainant Company, Mokul Shriram EPC JV, which is an unincorporated Joint Venture between Shriram EPC Limited and Mokul Infrastructure Pvt. Ltd., was awarded a Contract, i.e. Contract No. 708 dated 22.12.2011, by the Government of Basra (hereinafter referred to as the "GoB") in Iraq for construction of Rain Water Drainage, Heavy Sewerage and Municipal Road System.The value of the Project was Iraqi Dinar 275,566,491,217 equivalent to 11,99,94,98,834/- (at an exchange rate of 1 INR = 22.964 IQD).The said Project was to be completed within 1095 days from the date on which the Letter of Credit was established by GoB in favour of the Complainant Company.The Complainant Company obtained two Specific Contract (L/C Comprehensive Risks) Policies, i.e., Policy No. 1421 / 12 dated 13.09.2012 for covering the 90% of the LC portion in which liability of the Opposite Party ECGC was upto 534.58 Crore and Policy No. 1422 / 12 dated 13.09.2012 for covering the 90% of the Non-LC portion in which liability of the Opposite Party ECGC was upto 437.38 Crore, by paying a sum of 10,38,03,912/- towards Premium to Opposite Party ECGC.The Policies were valid till 01.05.2015 + 12 months maintenance period.The relevant extracts regarding risk of the Policies reads as follows :- " Relevant Extracts from ECGC Policy 1421 / 12 (ii) Failure of the opening bank to pay the Exporter within four months after due date of payment the gross invoice value of goods delivered to and accepted by the buyer; or (vi) the occurrence of war, hostilities, civil war, rebellion, revolution, insurrection or other disturbance in the buyer's country; or (viii) The cancellation, in circumstances outside the control of the exporter and/or the buyer of a previously issued and currently valid authority to import the goods; or (xi) any other cause not being inherent in the nature of the goods and not being within the control of the Exporter and / or of the buyer which arises from events occurring outside India; or" Relevant Extracts from ECGC Policy 1422 / 12 (ii) Failure of the buyer to pay the Exporter within four months after due date of payment the gross invoice value of goods delivered to and accepted by the buyer; or (iii) the failure or refusal on the part of the buyer, to accept goods which have already been exported from Indian, where any such failure or refusal is not excused by and does not arise from or in connection with any breach of conditions or warranty on the part of the Exporter or from any other cause within his control and provided also that the Corporation is satisfied that no good purpose would be served by the institution of legal proceedings against the buyer in respect of his said failure or refusal, or (vi) the occurrence of war, hostilities, civil war, rebellion, revolution, insurrection or other disturbance in the buyer's country; or (viii) The cancellation, in circumstances outside the control of the exporter and/or the buyer of a previously issued and currently valid authority to import the goods; or (xi) any other cause not being inherent in the nature of

121

the goods and not being within the control of the Exporter and / or of the buyer which arises from events occurring outside India; or (xii) the failure or refusal on the part of the buyer to fulfill the terms of the contact, such failure or refusal not arising from any breach of contract or Warranty on the part of the Exporter nor from 'any cause within the control of the Exporter, provided that the buyer is an overseas government or performance of the contract is guaranteed by an overseas government and the Corporation further elects in writing that this sub-clause shall apply either unconditionally or upon such conditions as the corporation shall think fit."

3. By an Amendment dated 27.11.2012 in the Contract, LC cover was enhanced from 55% to 100% of the value of the Contract.By another Amendment dated 12.02.2013, the payment terms were further amended and the commencement date was set to 02.05.2013.As per terms of the Contract, the Complainant Company established Advance Bank Guarantee (ABG) and Performance Bank Guarantee (PBG) in favour of GoB.Despite that GoB did not release any advance / mobilization money in favour of the Complainant Company.The Contract was converted into USD and value was reset at USD 236,326,321.79.The Complainant Company raised two Invoices, i.e., MSJV/ADV/001/2013-2014 dated 18.12.2013 for USD 23,632,632 andSEPC / EXP / 001 /2013-14 dated 11.01.2014 for USD 341,114.00 on the GoB for the work done under the Contract but GoB without any justification suspended payments under the irrevocable LC opened in favour of the Complainant Company.Vide letter dated 20.02.2014, GoB informed the Complainant Company that the work assigned vide Contract dated 22.12.2011 was being withdrawn due to alleged lack of completion.It is alleged that there was no alleged shortcoming on their part but the Contract was withdrawn owing to inter-party political rivalry by the GoB.It was submitted that GoB withdrawn the Contract within 53 days of establishment of the LC and all the payments under the Contract were suspended, its Securities / Guarantees were forfeited and receivable were also frozen despite blacklisting it.

4. The Complainant Company approached the Hon'ble Madras High Court and filed Civil Suit No. 133 / 2014 and vide Order dated 25.02.2014 obtained an interim injunction against their Banker, i.e., Axis Bank, Chennai from encashing or releasing any monies from the ABG and PBG.

5. The Complainant Company also moved the Baghdad Court in Iraq and filed matter No. 73 / B / 2014.By Order dated 07.04.2014 a 'non-disposal' mark (injunction) over the PBG issued by Byblos Bank restraining it from paying any monies to GoB.

6. The Complainant Company raised two invoices on the GoB for work done being Invoices No. MSJV / COMM / 001 / 2014 – 15 dated 12.06.2014 for USD 596,189 and MSJV / COMM / 002 / 2014-15 dated 12.06.2014 for USD 3,781,221.The GoB had rejected the payment for the said Invoices and requested Trade Bank of Iraq to return the documents.

7. Aggrieved by the decision of GoB to withdraw the Contract, the Complainant Company also filed cases before the First Insurance Court of Commercial, Basra in Iraq, which vide Order dated 09.11.2014 directed the GoB to withdraw the work withdrawal order dated 20.02.2012 and enable the Complainant Company to perform their obligation under the Contract.In Appeal, the Appellate Court vide Order dated 01.03.2015 rejected the Claim of Complainant Company. The Complainant Company challenged the Order dated 01.03.2015 before the Federal Court of Cassation but the Order dated 01.03.2015 was upheld. The Complainant Company filed Rectification / Correction which was also dismissed by Judgment dated 15.06.2015.

8. Since the risk was covered under the Policies issued by Opposite Party ECGC, the Complainant Company preferred claim in prescribed form with the Opposite Party ECGC vide letters dated 19.08.2015 and 27.08.2015.Requisite information alongwith various clarifications sought by the Opposite Party ECGC were duly provided by the Complainant Company.Despite that the Opposite Party ECGC, arbitrarily without any

legitimate ground, vide letter dated 19.09.2016 rejected the Insurance Claim of the Complainant Company.Feeling aggrieved, the Complainant Company filed Representation on 13.10.2016 before Apex Customer Grievance Committee of the Opposite Party ECGC. The Apex Customer Grievance Committee of the Opposite Party ECGC vide letter dated 08.02.2017 rejected their Representation.Alleging deficiency in Service and Unfair Trade Practice on the part of the Opposite Party ECGC, present Complaint has been filed seeking the following reliefs:- "(a) The Hon'ble Commission may be pleased to hold that the services rendered by the Opposite Party are deficient in nature and for such deficiencies the Opposite Party be directed to pay to the Complainant Company an amount of 440.50 Crores (as detailed in Para 49), (i.e., Amount claimed under the Policies 265.01 Crore, Interest on the amount, i.e., 174.99 Crore, and Compensation for losses suffered by Complainant Company 50,00,000/-) (b) This Hon'ble Commission may be pleased to award all costs, litigation expenses etc. in favour of the Complainant Company.; (c) This Hon'ble Commission may be pleased to award, any other appropriate relief, which the Hon'ble Commission may deem fit and proper in the circumstances of the case."

9. Upon Notice, the Opposite Party ECGC contested the Complaint and filed its Written Statement.In the Written Statement, the Opposite Party submitted that the Complainant Company was involved in various litigations with GoB, Byblos Bank at Iraq, The Trade Bank of Iraq and Axis Bank, Chennai before the Courts of London, Iraq and Chennai and have relied upon selective Proceedings of these Courts.The Complaint is bad for non-joinder of necessary Parties as the Complainant Company had not made them Parties in the present matter. The litigation are pending in the Courts before London, Iraq and Chennai and Complainant Company should also file the final Order / decree for justification of its contentions, in the absence of which the Complaint is premature.The Opposite Party ECGC further submitted that the Complainant Company has not come before this Commission with clean hands and concealed the material facts to the effect that they had not disclosed the warning letters issued by GoB and without receiving Operational Advance from GoB it started the Work, which is a clear violation of Clause 2 of the Policy.The Complainant Company entered into a Settlement Agreement with GoB and assigned its remaining work to an Irani sub-contractor without written approval from Opposite Party ECGC, which is a clear violation of the Provisions of Clause 13(b) read with Clause 19 of the Policies. The Opposite Party ECGC submitted that the Complainant Company has raised claim for 328.82 Crore for following five bills:- Claim Bill/Invoice Particulars under the service contract Amount (in Crores) 1 Bill dated 11.01.2014 – Towards alleged non-payment for supply of pipes 1.74 2 Bill dated 12.06.2014 – Towards alleged non-payment for payment of Designs 19.26 Bill dated 12.06.2014 – Towards alleged non-payment for site survey (No Invoice) – Towards alleged expense incurred w.e.f. portion of the work carried out by Complainant Company under the Service Contract 104.78 5 (No Invoice) – Towards alleged Losses due to alleged refusal and failure on part of GoB 200.00 TOTAL 328.82

10. Out of above Bills/Invoice for Claim No. 2 & 3 had been raised by the Complainant Company on GoB after termination of the Service Contract by GoB on 20.02.2014, whereas no invoice has been raised by the Complainant Company on GoB for Claim No. 4 & 5. The Complainant Company is not entitled for these Claims as the Claims qua the GoB under the Contract are not only pre-mature but vexatious, disputed, imaginary and inflated. They also submitted that in terms of Clause (xii) read with Proviso (d) of the Risk Insured, the Claim is not admissible. The Complainant Company has not disclosed the material facts, therefore, as per terms of the Policies, the Claim was not payable. They further submitted that the Complainant Company had violated the terms and conditions of the Policies, therefore, their Claims were rejected. The Opposite Party ECGC further submitted that there is no deficiency in service on their part and prayed that the Consumer Complaint be dismissed with Costs. We have heard Mr. Devesh

Tripathi, learned Counsel for the Complainant Company, Mr. Bharat Sangal, learned Senior Counsel for the Opposite Party ECGC and perused the material available on record. Mr. Devesh Tripathi, learned Counsel appearing for the Complainant Company submitted that the Contract was unilaterally withdrawn by GoB on 20.02.2014 due to inter-party political rivalry despite no fault on their part.After a long litigation, finally the Apex Court of Iraq held that the Contract was terminated due to Force Majeure with no fault of the Complainant Company and the Complainant Company should be compensated for the work done after assessment by an Expert.The GoB proposed a settlement which they accepted in order to limit the loss.As far as the warning letters issued by GoB are concerned, it was submitted that the said letters were replied to and after satisfying with the replies / clarifications, GoB never acted upon the said letters.They started the work without receiving any advance from GoB because they had tight deadline to complete the work.He further submitted that they had raised two invoices dated 18.12.2013 and 11.01.2014 before withdrawal of Contract and two invoices both dated 12.06.2014 after withdrawal of Contract but these invoices pertained to the period when work was done before the Contract was withdrawn.He further submitted that the Proceedings before London Courts were pertained to guaranteeing and counter guaranteeing obligations between the Banks involved in the transactions in which neither the Complainant Company nor GoB was Party.As far as the Proceedings before Madras High Court are concerned, these proceedings were regarding encashment of Performance and Advance Bank Guarantee and since the said Contract has already been reinstated and the matter settled, therefore, the question of discussing all above-said proceedings in the instant case before this Commission did not arise.He further submitted that despite having received hefty amount towards premium of the Policies, the Opposite Party ECGC having knowledge of all the facts, in a malafide manner, rejected the Complainant Company's legitimate claim, which is clear case of gross deficiency in service on their part and prayed that their Complaint be allowed and the reliefs as sought in the Complaint be awarded.

11. Mr. Bharat Sangal, learned Senior Counsel appearing for the Opposite Party ECGC submitted the Claim of the Complainant Company falls under Exclusion Clause of the Policies as the Contract of the Complainant Company was withdrawn by the GoB due to breach of contract by the Complainant Company and their payment was refused by GoB, therefore, risk is not covered under clause (xii) and proviso (d) of "Risk Insured" Clause of the Policies.He further submitted that in terms of Clause 22 and 23 of the Policies, the Complainant Company was under obligation to perform and follow the terms and conditions of the Policies, which it failed to do and it had also violated various terms of the Policies, therefore, their claim was rightly rejected.The Complainant Company without getting prior written approval from the opposite Party ECGC, assigned their contract to sub-Contractor, which is a clear violation of Clause 19 of the Policies on their part.The Complainant Company did not disclose the material facts, i.e., warning letters issued by GoB and without receiving Operational Advance from GoB, it started the Work, which is a clear violation of Clause 2 of the Policies. He further submitted that the Complainant Company without obtaining any prior written approval from them, entered into Settlement Agreement with the GoB, therefore, the Opposite Party ECGC is not liable to pay the loss in terms of Clause 13(b) of the Policies.He relied upon various Judgments passed by the Hon'ble Supreme Court especially in "Oriental Insurance Co. Ltd. vs. Sony Cheriyan" [(1999) 6 SCC 451] and "BHS Industries vs. Export Credit Guarantee Corporation Ltd. & Anr." [(2015) 9 SCC 414] in support of his contentions.He further submitted that the Insurance is a Contract which is based on utmost good faith and the insured cannot claim more than that what is covered under the Policy and the Insured has to act strictly in accordance with the statutory limitations or terms of the policy.He further submitted that there is no

deficiency in service on their part and prayed that the Consumer Complain be dismissed with costs.

12. We have given our thoughtful consideration to the various pleas raised by the learned Counsel for the Parties and have perused the averments made in the Complaint, Written Version as also the documents filed by the respective Parties.

13. In order to decide the issue raised in the present Complaint we deem it appropriate to reproduce the relevant clauses of the ECGC Policy No. 1421 / 2012.The relevant extract regarding the risks of the Policy has already been reproduced in Para 2 of this order and is not being reproduced here again.The Clause (xii) of the Risk Insured alongwith clause (d) of the proviso which provides that the Corporation shall not be liable for loss in certain circumstances, is reproduced as follows:- "(xii) The Failure or refusal on the part of the buyer to fulfill the terms of the Contract, such failure or refusal not arising from any breach of Contract or Warranty on the part of the Exporter nor from 'any cause within the control of the Exporter, provided that the buyer is an overseas government or performance of the contract is guaranteed by an overseas government and the Corporation further elects in writing that this sub-clause shall apply either unconditionally or upon such conditions as Corporation shall think fit. (d) which arises due to the failure or refusal on the part of the buyer to accept the goods and/or due to the claim of the buyer that he is justified in withholding payment of the contract price or the gross invoice value of the said goods or any part thereof by reason of any payment, credit set-off or counter-claim and/or due to his claim that for any other lawful reason he is excused from performing his obligations under the contract, unless, except where the Corporation agrees in writing to the contrary, the Exporter has for the amount of his loss obtained by legal proceedings in a competent court of law in the country of the buyer a final judgment enforceable against him."

14. Clauses 2,13(a) and (b), 19, 22 and 23 of the Policy are reproduced as follows:- "2. Disclosure of facts : Without prejudice to any rule, or law it is declared that this policy is given on condition that the Exporter has at the date of issue of the policy disclosed and will at all time during the operation of this policy promptly disclose all facts in any way affecting the risk insured. 13. Limitation of Liability : The Corporation shall not be liable for loss – (a) In respect of the contract or any shipment made or to be made thereunder if all or any part of the contract price or gross invoice value of any shipment receivable by the Exporter has been assigned without the prior approval in writing of the Corporation; or (b) In respect of a debt as to which the Exporter has extended the period for payment, or has accepted a composition arrangement with the buyer or entered into any settlement with the buyer without the prior approval in writing of the Corporation; 19. Assignment – This policy, or any amount payable hereunder is assignable only with the previous approval in writing of the Corporation. 22. Observance of conditions : The due performance and observance of each of the terms and conditions contained herein or in the Proposal or Declaration shall be a condition precedent to any liability of the Corporation hereunder and to the enforcement thereof by the Exporter. 23. Failure to comply with conditions : No failure by the Exporter to comply with the terms and conditions of the Policy shall be deemed to have been waived, excused or accepted by the Corporation unless the same is expressly so waived, excused or accepted by the Corporation in writing."

15. From the conjoint reading of the aforesaid Clauses, we find that in the Specific Contract (L/C Comprehensive Risks) Policies, i.e., Policy No. 1421 / 12 and Policy No. 1422 / 12 both dated 13.09.2012, the Complainant Company had been covered in the widest term of risk by the Opposite Party ECGC.Further, the Complainant Company had disclosed all the facts required under Clause 2 of the said Policy and had also informed the Opposite Party ECGC regarding the settlement which is proposed to be entered into by it with the other Party, viz., GoB as required under Clause 13(b) and it had observed each of the terms and conditions as contained in the Policy.Moreover, the Complainant

Company is limiting its claim under the aforementioned two Policies by reducing the liability of the Opposite Party ECGC by the amount which has already been received by it from the GoB.Earlier, the Complainant Company had made a claim of 328.82 Crores which had been reduced to 265.01 Crores.It is also not in dispute that the Complainant Company in terms of the two Policies had been updating the Opposite Party ECGC regarding all the developments concerning Contract dated 22.12.2011 from time to time and disclosing all relevant facts of work withdrawal decision, non-payment of any monies by GoB and the suspension of the payments under the irrevocable LC by the Trade Bank of Iraq.Further, the Working Group of this Project consisting of the representatives from the RBI, ECGC, EXIM Bank, Axis Bank and Orient Bank of Commerce were duly kept apprised from time to time, of all the adverse and unfortunate developments emanating in the wake of suspension of the LC and the work withdrawal decision. Further, the Opposite Party ECGC was also informed of all the litigations pertaining to the Contract and also the arrangements contemplated in the Subcontract Agreement dated 20.05.2018.Thus, the stand taken by the Opposite Party ECGC is contrary to the terms and conditions of the Policies as we find that the Complainant Company had complied with all the terms and conditions and their claim, therefore, should not have been rejected.

16. In view of the foregoing discussions, we are of the considered opinion that the Consumer Complaint is liable to be allowed as the Complainant Company is entitled for 265.01 Crore towards the claim made under the aforementioned two Policies, i.e., Policy No. 1421 / 12 and Policy No. 1422 / 12.It is also entitled for compensation in the form of simple interest @10% p.a. from 19.09.2016 (when the claim was rejected by the Opposite Party ECGC) till the date of actual payment.

17. Accordingly, we direct the Opposite Party ECGC to pay a sum of 265.01 Crore (Rupees Two Hundred Sixty Five Crores and One Lakh only) alongwith compensation in the form of simple interest @10% p.a. w.e.f. 19.09.2016 till the date of realization to the Complainant Company within a period of three months from today failing which the Opposite Party ECGC will be liable to pay compensation in the form of simple interest @12% p.a..The Opposite Party ECGC shall also pay costs of litigation, which we assess at 5 lakh, to the Complainant Company.

18. The Consumer Complaint is allowed. ....J R.K. AGRAWAL PRESIDENT .... DR. S.M. KANTIKAR MEMBER

<u>CASE NO. 38</u>
FIRST APPEAL NO. 690 OF 2020

(Against the Order dated 07/03/2018 in Complaint No. 336/2016 of the State Commission Punjab)

GOLDEN   GREEN   TOWERS   LIMITED   LIABILITY   PARTNERSHIP   (LLP) ....Appellant(s)

Versus

VARUN SALWAN & 3 ORS. ....Respondent(s)

BEFORE: HON'BLE MRS. JUSTICE DEEPA SHARMA,PRESIDING MEMBER

For the Appellant : MR. AMIT KOHAR

For the Respondent :

Dated : 27 Jan 2021

ORDER
JUSTICE DEEPA SHARMA
(ORAL) THROUGH VIDEO CONFERENCING

1. The present Appeal, under Section ---51(1) of the Consumer Protection Act, 2019 (for short "the Act"), has been filed by Golden Green Towers Limited Liability Partnership who was Opposite Party No.3 in the Complaint filed by the Respondent No.1, against

the order dated 07.03.2018 of the State Consumer Disputes Redressal Commission, Punjab (for short "the State Commission")

2. Since the present Appeal is delayed by 881 days, an application IA No.6239 of 2020 seeking condonation of delay has been filed. Arguments have been heard on this application. IA 6239 of 2020 (condonation of delay)

3. Learned Counsel for the Appellant has submitted that there is no delay in filing the present Appeal and the application has been moved only on technical grounds. It is submitted that as soon as they received the certified copy of the impugned order, within 30 days the present Appeal has been filed. It is argued by the learned Counsel for the appellant that the Appellant had duly participated in the trial before the State Commission and his Counsel had also addressed the final arguments on 26.02.2018 and thereafter the matter was reserved and the final order was pronounced on 07.03.2018. He has submitted that the copy of the impugned order was never served upon the Appellant and the Appellant learnt of the passing of the impugned order only on 11.08.2020 when his house was raided in the execution petition filed by the Complainant. It is submitted that immediately, the Appellant obtained the certified copy and within 30 days, filed the present Appeal. Hence, there is no delay. Reliance is placed on "State (NCT of Delhi) vs. Ahmed Jaan, 2008 (14) SCC 582", "Housing Board, Haryana vs. Housing Board Colony Welfare Association And Others, 1996 AIR (SC) 92", "R. B. Ramlingam vs. R. B. Bhveshwari, 2009 (1) SCC 689"and "Rita Kesh vs. Biswanath Singha, 2018 (3) CPJ 599 (NC)".

4. I have heard the arguments and have perused the relevant record.

5. The present Appeal is barred by limitation since it has been filed after a delay of 881 days of the passing of the impugned order dated 07.03.2018. It is admitted by the learned Counsel that the Appellant had participated in the trial and his Counsel had also addressed the arguments on 08.02.2018 when the matter was reserved. On enquiry, the learned Counsel has submitted that during the pendency of the proceedings before the State Commission, the Appellant had changed its address and admits that the change of address was not brought to the notice of the State Commission and to the Complainant. The State Commission apparently had the address of the Appellant on which it was served of the Complaint. There is no contention in the application that the copy of the impugned order was not sent by the State Commission to the Appellant at the address which was available with the State Commission. Further it is argued by learned Counsel that the Appellant had informed his counsel about the change of address but somehow the Counsel had not brought this fact to the knowledge of the State Commission. On enquiry, the learned Counsel has submitted that the address of the appellant was changed on 09.03.2016. It is strange that although the Appellant had changed its address on 09.03.2016 and continued participating in the proceedings till the time matter was reserved on 26.02.2018, i.e., for two years he made no efforts to bring on the record of the State Commission its changed address. It was the duty of the parties to ensure that his Counsel brings on record all the facts which are relevant. The parties cannot take the benefit of its own wrong. They have to act diligently and if they continue to sleep over their duties they cannot be allowed subsequently to take advantage of their own wrong. The Appellant had failed to discharge the obligatory duty which is casted upon him to ensure that his Counsel brings to the notice of the State Commission the changed address and the changed circumstances. He must have been aware that his Counsel has not done so because had his Counsel moved an appropriate application to bring on record the changed address of the Appellant, his Counsel must have got the affidavit singed by him. When he was aware that no such affidavit has been obtained by his Counsel for almost two years, he was aware that his Counsel had not brought to the notice of the State Commission the changed address and changed circumstances. It is nothing but a deliberate act on the part of the Appellant to conceal the material facts and material circumstances from the notice of the Complainant and the State Commission.

The cases relied upon by the learned Counsel have no relevance on the facts and circumstances of the present case. The findings in those cases are given entirely on different set of facts and circumstances. The Hon'ble Supreme Court has been dealing time and again on this aspect of condonation of delay. It is a settled proposition of law that condonation of delay is not a matter of right and sufficient causes/reasons which prevented a person from filing the Revision Petition/Appeal within the period of limitation are required to be shown. It has been so held by Hon'ble Supreme Court in "Ram Lal and Ors. vs. Rewa Coalfields Limited, AIR 1962 Supreme Court 361" as under: "12. It is, however, necessary to emphasize that even after sufficient cause has been shown a party is not entitled to the condonation of delay in question as a matter of right. The proof of a sufficient cause is a discretionary jurisdiction vested in the Court by S.5. If sufficient cause is not proved nothing further has to be done; the application for condonation has to be dismissed on that ground alone. If sufficient cause is shown then the Court has to enquire whether in its discretion it should condone the delay. This aspect of the matter naturally introduces the consideration of all relevant facts and it is at this stage that diligence of the party or its bona fides may fall for consideration; but the scope of the enquiry while exercising the discretionary power after sufficient cause is shown would naturally be limited only to such facts as the Court may regard as relevant."

6. The Hon'ble Supreme Court has also held in the case of "R. B. Ramlingam vs. R. B. Bhavaneshwari, I (2009) (2) CLJ (SC) 24" that true guide to judge whether the delay is reasonable or sufficient is to see whether the Petitioner has acted with reasonable diligence. The Hon'ble Apex Court has held as under: "5. We hold that in each and every case the Court has to examine whether delay in filing the special appeal leave petitions stands properly explained. This is the basic test which needs to be applied. The true guide is whether the petitioner has acted with reasonable diligence in the prosecution of his appeal/petition."

7. The Hon'ble Supreme Court has further cautioned this Commission in "Anshul Aggarwal vs. New Okhla Industrial Development Authority, (2011) 14 SCC 578," that while dealing with the applications for condonation of delay under the Consumer Protection Act, 1986 the special nature of period of limitation provided therein has to be kept in mind. It has been so held: "5. It is also apposite to observe that while deciding an application filed in such cases for condonation of delay, the Court has to keep in mind that the special period of limitation has been prescribed under the Consumer Protection Act, 1986 for filing appeals and revisions in consumer matters and the object of expeditious adjudication of the consumer disputes will get defeated if this court was to entertain highly belated petitions filed against the orders of the consumer Fora."

8. In view of the above, I found that the Appellant has failed to reasonably explain the delay. The application for condonation of delay has no merit and the same is dismissed. Appeal No.690 of 2020 Since the Appeal is barred by limitation, the same is dismissed in limine. Copy of this order be sent to the State Commission and to the Complainant. ....J DEEPA SHARMA PRESIDING MEMBER

CASE NO. 39
REVISION PETITION NO. 1098 OF 2020

(Against the Order dated 13/10/2020 in Appeal No. 446/2019 of the State Commission Rajasthan)

ORIENTAL INSURANCE COMPANY LIMITED ....Petitioner(s)

Versus

MADHU KHANDELWAL ....Respondent(s)
BEFORE: HON'BLE MRS. JUSTICE DEEPA SHARMA,PRESIDING MEMBER
For the Petitioner : MR. SUBODH KUMAR JHA
For the Respondent :

Dated : 27 Jan 2021

ORDER
JUSTICE DEEPA SHARMA
(ORAL) THROUGH VIDEO CONFERENCING

1. The present Revision Petition, under Section 58 (1) (b) of the Consumer Protection Act, 2019 (for short "the Act"), has been filed against the order dated 13.10.2020 of the State Consumer Disputes Redressal Commission, Rajasthan (for short "the State Commission") allowing the Appeal No.446 of 2019 of the Respondent/Complainant. The said Appeal was filed by the Complainant against the order dated 23.04.2019 of the District Consumer Disputes Redressal Forum, Jaipur-IV (for short "the District Forum") dismissing her Complaint No.893 of 2017.

2. It is argued by the learned Counsel for the Petitioner that the Fora below have reached to a wrong conclusion that the deceased/insured had not committed suicide while their investigation report clearly shows that he had committed suicide. It is further argued that the insured had not taken the bridge for crossing the railway line and by crossing the railway line he had put his life to danger and therefore, he is not entitled for the benefit under the Consumer Protection Act.

3. The brief admitted facts of the case are that the insured Sh.Kailash Kumar Khandelwal, husband of the Complainant took an insurance policy and during the validity of the insurance policy, he died while crossing a railway line track as he was ran over by the train. A police report was lodged. Investigation was done by the police. The police filed its investigation report whereby it concluded that the death was due to accident on the railway track. The police had also concluded that many people used to cross the railway line from that place and for that purpose, cement walls had been raised on both sides of the railway track by the Railway but the miscreants of the area had broken the walls and people instead of using the bridge used to cross the railway line from that place. The statement of the wife of the insured/deceased was that on the date of the incident, she learnt that there was accident and two persons had died on the railway track. The statement of the Complainant as well as the report of the police concludes that the deceased had died due to accident on the railway track. The stand of the Insurance Company is that it was a suicide and for that purpose they have relied on their investigation report by investigator/surveyor who has opined that the death could be due to suicide. No facts which could put light on the motive on the part of the deceased to commit suicide were neither investigated nor placed on record.

4. It is evident that the findings of the Foras below are based on evidences on record.

5. It is settled proposition of law that this Commission in exercise of its revisional jurisdiction cannot re-assess or re-appreciate the evidences on record and substitute the findings of the Fora below by its own conclusion on facts, moreso when there are concurrent findings on the facts. The limited jurisdiction which this Commission has is to judge whether the findings are perverse or whether the Fora below have exceeded its jurisdiction or have not acted within its jurisdiction. The Hon'ble Supreme Court in a number of cases including "Rubi (Chandra) Dutta Vs. United India Insurance Co. Ltd. – (2011) 11 SCC 269" has held as under: "23. Also, it is to be noted that the revisional powers of the National Commission are derived from Section 21 (b) of the Act, under which the said power can be exercised only if there is some prima facie jurisdictional error appearing in the impugned order, and only then, may the same be set aside. In our considered opinion there was no jurisdictional error or miscarriage of justice, which could have warranted the National Commission to have taken a different view than what was taken by the two Forums. The decision of the National Commission rests not on the basis of some legal principle that was ignored by the Courts below, but on a different (and in our opinion, an erroneous) interpretation of the same set of facts. This is not the manner in which revisional powers should be invoked. In this view of the matter, we are of the considered opinion that the jurisdiction conferred on the National Commission

under Section 21 (b) of the Act has been transgressed. It was not a case where such a view could have been taken by setting aside the concurrent findings of two Fora".

6. Again in "Lourdes Society Snehanjali Girls Hostel and Ors. Vs. H&R Johnson (India) Ltd. and others, (2016) 8 Supreme Court Cases 286," the Hon'ble Supreme Court has reiterated the same principle and has held as under: "17. The National Commission has to exercise the jurisdiction vested in it only if the State Commission or the District Forum has either failed to exercise their jurisdiction or exercised when the same was not vested in them or exceeded their jurisdiction by acting illegally or with material irregularity. In the instant case, the National Commission has certainly exceeded its jurisdiction by setting aside the concurrent finding of fact recorded in the order passed by the State Commission which is based upon valid and cogent reasons."

7. In T. Ramalingeswara Rao (Dead) Through L.Rs. and Ors. Vs. N.Madhava Rao and Ors. decided on 05.04.2019 passed in Civil Appeal No. 3408 of 2019, the Hon'ble Supreme Court has held as under: "12. When the two Courts below have recorded concurrent findings of fact against the Plaintiffs, which are based on appreciation of facts and evidence, in our view, such findings being concurrent in nature are binding on the High court. It is only when such findings are found to be against any provision of law or against the pleading or evidence or are found to be perverse, a case for interference may call for by the High Court in its second appellate jurisdiction."

8. It is apparent that the Foras below have relied on the testimonies on record. Learned Counsel for the Petitioner has failed to point out that the findings of the Fora below are perverse or without jurisdiction. I found no illegality or infirmity in the impugned order. The present Revision Petition has no merit and the same is dismissed in limine.

9. Copy of this order be sent to the Fora below and to the Complainant. ....J
DEEPA SHARMA PRESIDING MEMBER

CASE NO. 40
REVISION PETITION NO. 1134 OF 2020

(Against the Order dated 07/08/2020 in Appeal No. 245/2020 of the State Commission Rajasthan)
MOHAN LAL MEENA ....Petitioner(s)
Versus
UNITED INDIA INSURANCE COMPANY LTD. & ANR. ....Respondent(s)
BEFORE: HON'BLE MR. ANUP K THAKUR,PRESIDING MEMBER
For the Petitioner : Mr. Aditya Jain, Advocate
For the Respondent :
Dated : 27 Jan 2021

ORDER
ANUP K.THAKUR, PRESIDING MEMBER
(ORAL)

1. Heard learned counsel for the petitioner / complainant. This revision petition challenges the order dated 07.8.2020 of the State Commission, Jaipur, Rajasthan vide which the appeal against the order of the District Forum, Jaipur dated 11.2.2020, had been dismissed. In turn, the District Forum had also, vide its order dated 11.2.2020, dismissed the consumer complaint.

2. Very briefly, the facts are that the petitioner / complainant had taken an insurance policy for his car RJ 14 CC 3823, from the respondent insurance company, for the period 09.10.2011 to 08.10.2012. On 01.10.2012, the car suffered an accident and was taken for repairs to Respondent No.2- M/s. P.L. Hyundai, Jaipur. The complainant paid the bill raised for repairs of Rs.1,51,905/- through cheque No.023532 dated 12.12.2012 on ICICI Bank and thereafter, filed an insurance claim before the Respondent No.1/OP-1-

United India Insurance Company Limited. Opposite Party No.1, however, reimbursed an amount of Rs.84,400/- only to the complainant. As the complainant had spent Rs.1,51,905/-, he filed a consumer complaint before the District Forum, seeking the balance amount from OP-1/.

3. The District Forum reasoned that after a final payment based on the surveyor's report has been made by the insurance company and the same has also been received, without any protest at that time, it could not be said that there was any deficiency in service on the part of the insurance company. The Forum had relied on the principle enunciated in two decisions: (i) the case of the National Insurance Company Limited Vs. Kuka Rice and General Mills, 1(2008) CPJ 338 (Haryana Commission) and (ii) Shiv Vilas Resorts Private Limited Vs. United Insurance Company Limited & Anr. 1(2012) CPJ 184 (NC) for arriving at its decision.

4. An appeal, FA/245/2020 was filed before the State Commission. Finding no error in the order of the District Forum, the State Commission dismissed the appeal at the stage of admission. Operative portion of the State Commission's order is reproduced as under: " The car of the appellant which was insured from 09.10.2011 to 08.10.2012 got accidented on 01.10.2012. P.L. Motors repaired the car, the expenses occurred was Rs.1,51,905/-, Surveyor was appointed, surveyor assessed the loss of Rs.84,400 and it was paid to appellant. Surveyor is an independent person, the Report of the surveyor cannot be set aside unless otherwise charged with. Learned District forum has dismissed the complaint, there is no error in it. Resultantly, the appeal is liable to be dismissed at Admission stage. And is accordingly, dismissed."

5. Hence this revision petition. The learned counsel for the petitioner/ complainant has argued that it would be noted that the District Forum had relied on two judgments, one of the State Commission and the other of the National Commission, who had taken the view that since full and final settlement had been made by the insurance company and the same had been received without protest, there was no case for any further clam by the complainant. The learned counsel stressed that in both the judgments it was clearly indicated that full and final payment had been made. However, there was no such indication in the settlement offered and accepted by the petitioner/complainant. In the instant case, learned counsel argued that there is no such averment in the Disbursement Voucher of the insurance company. As such, the complainant was within its right to file a claim for the balance amount of the expenses incurred by the complainant for repair of his car. This claim, counsel argued, was based on bills and these bills had been submitted to the insurance company, as also to the surveyor engaged, for assessing the cost of repairs.

6. It would be seen that the ground taken by the learned counsel for the petitioner is that merely because "full and final settlement" had not been mentioned in the Disbursement Voucher, the complainant was therefore, free to file a complaint for the balance amount. This however, is no reason why such a complaint for the balance amount has to be also accepted. Report of the surveyor, who was entrusted the task of assessing the damage and arriving at an estimate of cost of repairs, is an important document and cannot be simply brushed aside, without cogent reasons. The fact that the surveyor had a copy of the claim and the bills along with the claim before it made its estimate of repairs clearly shows that these had been considered by the surveyor while preparing its report. It is after such consideration that the surveyor recommended an amount of Rs.84,400/-. This amount was then disbursed by the opposite party No.1, insurance company.

7. I can find no error apparent, of either law or fact, in the impugned order, warranting revisionary interference. Accordingly, this revision petition, being devoid of any merit, is dismissed at the stage of Admission. .... ANUP K THAKUR PRESIDING MEMBER

<u>**CASE NO.41**</u>

REVISION PETITION NO. 696 OF 2015

(Against the Order dated 17/10/2014 in Appeal No. 483/2012 of the State Commission Tamil Nadu)

S. MANIKANNAN S/O SEENIVASAGAM,...........Petitioner(s)

Versus

DR. T. PANDIARAJ & ANR. SONOLOGIST & RADIOLOGIST,

DR. G. RAJKUMAR, RADIOLOGIST, VIKRAM SCEN & DIGNOSTICS CENTRE,...........Respondent(s)

BEFORE: HON'BLE MR. JUSTICE R.K. AGRAWAL,PRESIDENT HON'BLE DR. S.M. KANTIKAR,MEMBER

For the Petitioner :

For the Respondent :

Dated : 27 Jan 2021

ORDER

Appeared at the time of arguments through Video Conferencing

For Petitioner : Mr. P. V. Yogeswaran, Advocate

For Respondent No. 1 : NEMO

For Respondent No. 2 : Mr. Vikas Mehta, Advocate Mr. Adith Nair, Advocate

Pronounced on: 27 January 2021

ORDER

PER DR. S. M. KANTIKAR, MEMBER

1. The present Revision Petition has been filed under Section 19 of the Consumer Protection Act, 1986 against the Order dated 17.10.2014 passed by the Tamil Nadu State Consumer Disputes Redressal Commission (hereinafter referred to as the "State Commission") in F.A. No. 483/2012 wherein the State Commission dismissed the Appeal filed by the Complainant and upheld the Order passed by the District Consumer Disputes Redressal Forum, Theni in C.C. No. 82 of 2010 (hereinafter referred to as the "District Forum") wherein the Complaint was dismissed.

2. Briefly stated, the facts of the case are that the Complainant S. Manikannan (hereinafter referred to as the 'patient') consulted a physician – Dr. Muthuramalingam on 05.06.2007 for stomach pain for which he was advised to take abdomen scan. The abdominal ultrasound (USG) was performed by Dr. T. Pandiaraj, Radiologist (hereinafter referred to as the "Opposite Party No. 1"), who reported it as retro-cecal appendicitis. However, the Physician was not satisfied with the said report, and again advised to repeat the USG with the Opposite Party No. 1. On 07.06.2007, USG scan was repeated and reported as being suggestive of 'appendicitis'. The Physician, being not satisfied with the USG findings, referred the patient to Dr. Sakthivel, the Surgeon for further treatment. On 07.06.2007, after examination, Dr. Sakthivel advised another USG from Dr. G. Rajkumar at Vikram Scan & Diagnostic Centre (hereinafter referred to as the "Opposite Party No. 2") and the report suggested possibility of "sub-hepatic appendicitis". Based on the reports, the patient was operated by Dr. Sakthivel on 08.06.2007 and suspected tuberculosis in the abdomen and biopsy of Omentum was taken for Histopathological examination (HPE). The HPE revealed "no evidence of tuberculosis or malignancy and it was fibrosis with chronic non-specific infection". The Surgeon Dr. Sakthivel told that it was the infection in the large intestine causing the pain and the same was removed by surgery. The Complainant, however, alleged that it was a failure on the part of the Opposite Parties Nos. 1 and 2, who negligently gave wrong report of appendicitis and because that he had to undergo unnecessary operation. The operation could have been avoided and the pain could have been cured by medicines only. Due to unnecessary operation Complainant suffered physically, financially and he could not carry out his work efficiently. Being aggrieved, Complainant filed a Complaint before the District Forum, Theni and claimed compensation to the tune of Rs. 10 lakh.

3. The District Forum dismissed the Complaint by holding that the scan reports of the Opposite Parties Nos. 1 and 2 were only suggestive in nature and not confirmatory. Aggrieved by the said Order, the Complainant filed an Appeal before the State Commission, Madurai which was dismissed on the ground that the Complainant failed to prove by expert opinion or medical literature any negligence. Being aggrieved, the Complainant filed the instant Revision Petition.

4. We have heard the arguments from the learned Counsel for the parties. Perused the entire material on record including USG reports dated 05.06.2007 and 07.06.2007 done by different Radiologists.

5. We note, admittedly, the Complainant consulted one Dr. Muthuramalingam, the Physician for his severe abdominal pain. After examination the Physician advised few investigations including USG san. The USG scans were performed by two Radiologist on consecutive days and reported it as "Appendicitis". We have carefully perused the USG scan reports. The initial 1 st USG done by the Opposite Party No. 1, reported as "retrocecal appendicitis". The USG scan was repeated by the Opposite Party No. 1 again on 07.06.2007 and it revealed 'Appendicitis'. The report is reproduced as below: 7.6.07: Repeat Scan Shows In the right iliac fossa, a short narrow segment of bowel shows thick edematous wall with aperistalisis. Could be Inflammed appendix. Tenderness present over that region. Other abdominal organs are Sonographically normal. Findings are suggestive of Appendicitis . The Physician was not satisfied with both the reports, and he referred the patient to the Surgeon, Dr. Sakthivel, who after examination sought another USG from other Radiologist Dr. Rajkumar at Vikram Scan & Diagnostic Centre. The USG scan is reported as below: IMPRESSION: There is evidence of localized non peristaltic thickened bowel loop [wall thickening measures 7.2 mm] with peri lesional fluid collection around 5 ml [1.9 x 4.2 x 1.1 cm] seen in the Right lumbar region, close to the anterior abdominal wall. Suggest the possibility of Sub hepatic appendicitis .

6. Dr. Sakthivel on the basis of the patient's clinical symptoms & signs and both the USG reports; made the provisional diagnosis of Acute appendicitis, Ureteric colic and Acute cholecystitis. He operated the patient on 8.6.2007 and found intraoperatively the infected bowel loops and Omentum. He removed the infected material and took Omental biopsy, sent for HPE study. According to the Surgeon, it was a case of Omental infection causing the pain to the patient.

7. As per the standard text books on Surgery any abdominal pain several reasons to be considered. If the clinical signs and investigations (Lab & Radiology) are not leading to definite diagnosis, in that case, opening of the abdomen (laparotomy – exploration) is necessary to find out the cause of pain. The HPE report and the prescription issued by the Surgeon, Dr. Sakthivel confirms that the continuous abdominal pain to the patient was due to Omental and Intestinal infection. The prescription is reproduced as below: DR K.R. SAKTHIVEL M.S. PHONE 254045 (GENERAL SURGEON) Date:- 07.05.2008 Mani Kannan 32 Years, Male DOA: 05.06.2007 DOO: 08.06.2007 DOD: 20.06.2007 Terminal ileum Caecum ascending color inflamed & friable appendix normal. Greater omentum caseous material gangrenous, right side cake like patch attached to anterior abdominal wall and terminal ileam .no ascites, nodes, nodules. Greater omentum exceed & sent for HPE. ATT given for months. Post-OP-uneventful. KULASEKAR CLINIC 588, MADURAI ROAD, THENI- 625 531.

8. On consideration of the treatment and the sequence of events and from careful perusal of the prescription above, it is pertinent to note that the appendix was friable, the loops of intestine were inflamed, Caseous and gangrenous Omental tissue; thus, emergency operation was needed. In our considered view the operation was necessary to save the life of patient. Thus, the allegation of the Complainant that the operation was unnecessarily performed is not sustainable. Abdomen is a 'Pandora's box'. Many times the appendicular pain gives symptoms of referred pain. Though both the Radiologists

(Opposite Party No.1 and 2) reported it as Appendicitis; it was to be correlated clinically. Thus the treating surgeon's clinical assessment with relevant laboratory investigations should be given more credence. The Doctor will choose line of treatment and in the instant case the Surgeon performed exploratory laparotomy (operation) and found inflamed organs as a cause for pain and treated thereafter. In our view, the act of Surgeon was as per standard of practice. The Radiologists - Opposite Parties Nos. 1 and 2 have given their opinion of USG study been indicative and not confirmatory; it should not be construed as a wrong report. We have to consider the operation was imminent the instant case, it was diagnosed operatively and patient got cure.

9. Based on the discussion above, we find the Order of the State Commission to be well-appraised and well-reasoned. The State Commission concurred with the findings of the District Forum. Within the meaning and scope of section 21(b), we find no grave error in appreciating the evidence by the two fora below. And, on the face of it, we find no jurisdictional error, or a legal principle ignored, or miscarriage of justice. The Revision Petition, being without any merit, is dismissed. There shall be no Order as to costs.
.....................J R.K. AGRAWAL PRESIDENT .... DR. S.M. KANTIKAR MEMBER

CASE NO.42
CONSUMER CASE NO. 205 OF 2012

M/S. MAURIA UDYOG LIMITED...........Complainant(s)

Versus

UNITED INDIA INSURANCE COMPANY LTD. & 2 ORS. through its divisional Manager Divisional
UNITE INDIA INSURANCE CO. LTD. THROUGH ITS DEPUTY GENERAL MANAGER,
UNITED INDIA INSURANCE CO. LTD. THROUGH ITS CHAIMAN-CUM-MANAGING DIRECTOR...........Opp.Party(s)
BEFORE: HON'BLE MR. ANUP K THAKUR,PRESIDING MEMBER
For the Complainant :
For the Complainant : Mr. Joy Basu, Sr. Advocate with Mr. T.S. Ahuja, Advocate
For the Opp.Party :
For the Opposite Parties : Mr.Amit Kr. Singh, Advocate
Dated : 28 Jan 2021

ORDER
Anup K. Thakur

1. By this order it is proposed to decide C.C. No.205 of 2012 and C.C. No.206 of 2012. In C.C. No.205 of 2012, the complainant is M/s. Mauria Udyog Ltd. and in C.C. No.206 of 2012, the -1- complainant is M/s. Jotindra Steel & Tubes Limited. Both had purchased marine cargo specific voyage insurance policy from United India Insurance Co. Ltd., Noida (OP-1 henceforth) and facts in both are almost identical.

2. Arguments were heard on 25.11.2020. Facts were taken from CC 206 of 2012.

3. Learned Sr. Counsel for the complainant briefly narrated the facts. On 04.06.2010, a Marine Cargo Specific Voyage Policy No.221800/21/10/01/00000043 (policy hereafter) was taken by the complainant from OP1 (Annexure-1). This policy, for voyage from Jingtang, China to Kandla Port, Gujrat, covered a consignment of H.R. Steel Coils with the sum insured at Rs.10,31,93,25/-. Premium paid was Rs.22,764/-. Details such as Invoice, Container Details, Vessel name etc., were not shown initially in the policy; instead, the relevant box for these details carried the remark "To be declared" . Subsequently, these details were submitted to OP1 and were duly endorsed in the policy on 20.07.2010 (Annexure-4). Learned counsel explained that the initial policy read with this endorsement made the whole policy of insurance.

4. Per the plaint, on 18.7.2010 , the marine vessel, Khallijia-3 (M.V. hereafter),at 20:45 hours, experienced ingress of water below the water line, which caused damage to cargo. Since there were other cargoes also on the M.V., general average principle became applicable. So, a Salvor, M/s. Smith Singapore Pvt. Ltd., was appointed who, in turn, appointed another company to procure guarantees from the affected parties i.e. owner of the M.V. and owners of their respective cargoes. OP provided a guarantee on behalf of the complainant on 10.8.2010 (Annexure-8). This guarantee was however recalled by the OP on 12.8.2010 (Annexure-9). Learned counsel submitted that in the recall letter, OP had taken the ground that the M.V. classification was not as required under the 'Institute Classification Clause' of the policy and resultantly, it was constrained to withdraw the 'average guarantee' given to the Adjusters.

5. Counsel referred to complainant's letter to the OP dated 15.6.2010 (Ann.-2) whereby all relevant details of the shipment, including the name of the M.V., MV Khalijia 3 V.10086, had been furnished. Again, vide letter dated 7.7.2010 (Ann. 3), the complainant had, in continuation of letter dated 15.6.2010 , enclosed invoice number, packing list, copy of bill of lading to the OP. On this basis, OP had duly endorsed the policy (Ann.-4).

6. Learned counsel then drew attention to the policy schedule (Ann.-1), specifically to the box describing the "Terms of Insurance Cover: As per the following Clauses" , and thereunder, to clause no. 8 viz. "Institute Classification Clause with deletion of held cover provision" . He pointed out that the first 7 clauses – Important Notice, Institute Radio-Active Contamination Exclusion Clause, Institute Replacement Clause, Institute War Clauses (Cargo), Institute Strike Clauses (Cargo), Strike, Riots & Civil Commotion Clause and Cargo ISM endorsement were all elaborated in the body of the policy. Not so, however, the clause "Institute Classification Clause with deletion of held cover provision" (supra). His argument therefore was that this clause was never meant to be operationalized at any point of time else it would have also found elaboration in the body of the policy. He then argued that it was this clause which was the basis for repudiation of the insurance claim. He submitted that except for this, the policy covered the voyage from Jingtag, China to Kandla Port, Gujarat, India, " ON WAREHOUSE TO WAREHOUSE BASIS" , and thus clearly covered the incident which took place in Mumbai, enroute to Kandla and warehouse.

7. He further submitted that despite intimation of 15.6.2010 (supra) having been stamp receipted by the OP's office, OP had denied having received the same. Counsel submitted that this could not be. He drew attention to complainant's further intimation dated 7.7.2010 (Ann.-3) whose receipt was acknowledged by the OP: this too had a similar stamp of the OP company, without any initial. Counsel argued that both these letters had therefore been similarly received by the OP1 and accepting receipt of one and denying receipt of other was not understood. His argument was that in both these letters, the name and number of the M.V. was mentioned, and thus, there was no question that the name of the vessel had been declared to the OP and that the OP was aware of it. To therefore deny knowledge of the M.V.'s classification on 12.8.2010 and withdraw the guarantee(supra) was unwarranted. Learned counsel then explained in some detail the events following the incident resulting in damage to the vessel and loss to the cargo. He explained that as per international practice, a salvor was appointed who, in turn, appointed the average adjuster who then wrote to the owners of the M.V. and the cargoes to provide guarantees in order to cover all expenses incurred by the salvor on prorata basis. This being so, the complainant had approached the OP, the insurer, to provide a guarantee to M/s. Richards Hogg Lindley (Hellas) Ltd., the average adjuster appointed by the M/s. Smit Singapore Pvt. Ltd., salvor. The complainant provided a counter guarantee to the OP for this purpose and the OP then provided the said guarantee on 10.08.2010 (Ann. 8). In this guarantee, the name of the vessel was duly mentioned, clearly showing therefore that the OP was always in the know of the M.V.

carrying the cargoes. Counsel argued that it has to be presumed that the OP had provided guarantee only after being satisfied with the classification and condition of the M.V.. It was therefore strange that the OP, after only 2 days, vide letter dated 12.8.2010, withdrew the guarantee from the adjuster (Ann. 9). He argued that this withdrawal of guarantee and repudiation of the claim was untenable as the OP could not deny its liability: the insurance policy was fully operational at the time of the incident, and all details necessary for the voyage including the name of the vessel, was in the knowledge of the OP. He further argued that OP's repudiation was inexplicable: what could have transpired between 10.8.2010 , the date OP extended guarantee to the adjuster and 12.8.2010 when the OP withdrew this guarantee? Still further, he submitted that a perusal of this letter dated 12.8.2010 (supra) would show that it was cryptic and bereft of any detail. OP's contention that the M.V. Khalijia did not possess the classification required under the Institute Classification Clause of the policy was unacceptable as this clause was neither reproduced in this letter nor had been elaborated in the policy, as explained earlier. Since no clear reasons were given for repudiation in this letter of 12.8.2010, learned counsel argued that this by itself was also a deficiency in service. He then submitted that the M.V. was registered in the International Register of Shipping and had an interim certificate of classification issued on 2.6.2010 which was valid till November 2010 . He cemented this argument by further submitting that it was not as if it was the complainant's responsibility alone to have ascertained the classification of the M.V., it being the case that it was only one of the cargo owners on this vessel and could not be expected to know the vessel's status etc. since the import was on CIF basis. So, the complainant was not privy to the classification of the vessel and also not responsible for the correct classification. OP, the insurer, also had a responsibility to check all this before extending the guarantee to the adjustor.

8. Learned counsel then drew attention to complainant's reply dated 17.8.2010 (Ann. 10) to the OP's letter of repudiation dated 12.8.2010 (Ann.9): it had been contended by the complainant that the OP remained fully responsible for all the losses covered under the policy as the cargo was fully insured by a named vessel in good faith; that the policy was issued on 4.6.2010 and OP was subsequently informed about the particulars of shipment with vessel name, value and quantity -3- details which were duly endorsed on the policy. OP replied to this vide its letter dated 3.9.2010: It denied receipt of letter dated 15.6.2010 and held that " the vessel did not qualify for cover in terms of the Classification Clause as it was found not to have held classification by any entity contemplated by the said clause" . Learned counsel argued that even in this reply, there was no reproduction of the classification clause being relied upon by the OP (Ann.-11).

9. Learned counsel then referred to an internal circular of the OP viz. HO:MC:Cir:30:2013 dated 30.04.2013, obtained by the complainant through RTI. This circular had made it obligatory upon OP's offices issuing marine insurance policies to first verify the vessel particulars; if the vessel was not classed as per recognized classification society, no cover was to be granted i.e. NO CLASS, NO COVER. Counsel argued that it seems to be the case that OP had failed to carry out this due diligence. In such a case, however OP ought to have refunded the premium and cancelled the policy. Instead, it has repudiated the insurance claim. Counsel further argued that nowhere in the pleadings or in the various documents on record is the institute classification clause mentioned and that it has been mentioned for the first time in the synopsis of arguments filed in the proceedings. This was not acceptable, argued the counsel. Without this, the OP's case fails completely.

10. Summing up, the learned counsel reiterated that the institute classification clause and the factum of M.V. being not classified under this cannot be considered as a ground for repudiation by the OP because this clause does not form part of the policy nor has it been explained in the repudiation letter of 12.8.2010 nor does it form part of the

documents on record. Second, it is not the case that the M.V. was not a registered vessel; it was registered in the International Shipping Register.

11. Towards evidence supporting the consumer complaint, learned counsel pointed to affidavit by way of evidence of Shri V.K. Sureka, Chairman of the complainant company, affidavit of Shri Gopal Gupta, Manager of Import & Export and A.R. of the complainant company, and affidavits of Shri Sandeep Sharma and Shri Dinesh Sharma, Field Boys employed with the complainant company for delivery of letters etc. In particular, he emphasized the affidavit of Shri Sandeep Sharma: It has been stated that he had delivered various letters to OP-1's office, including on 15.6.2010, and that these had been received by the officials and acknowledged by affixing seal on the duplicate copy.

12. Finally, learned counsel invoked some citations in support of his arguments. In the case of Saurashtra Chemicals Ltd. Vs. National Insurance Co. Ltd. decided on 13.12.2019 , the Apex Court had held that "It is a settled position that an insurance company cannot travel beyond the grounds mentioned in the letter of repudiation." He submitted that the only issue in the letter of repudiation of 12.8. 2010 was to do with the classification of the M.V.. And he had already shown that the M.V. was indeed classified though with another society and not IACS which the OP was insisting upon. In the case of Modern Insulators Ltd. Vs. Oriental Insurance Company Ltd. 2000 (2) SCC 734 , it was held that "Exclusion clauses which are not explained to the insured, are not binding to the insured and are required to be ignored." This would apply to the " Institute Classification Clause with deletion of held cover provision" which was never made clear to the complainant, as argued by the counsel. In the case, National Insurance Co. Ltd. Vs. Sh. D.P. Jain , it was held by the National Commission in its order dated 15.05.2007 that "In our view, the unexplained or unnoticed exclusion would not be binding to the insured." In UII vs MKJ Coproration, the Apex Court had held that "An insurer cannot reply on and the insured is not bound by, a clause that the insurer should have but did not incorporate into the policy." Learned counsel argued that in the case in hand, the Institute Classification Clause was unexplained, vague, non-specific and ambiguous and thus, the insured complainant was not bound by it and the OP could not take advantage of it.

13. Learned counsel for the OP also began his submissions by referring to the policy (Annexure-1) to submit that it was not in doubt at all that the following had been clearly mentioned under Terms of Insurance Cover viz. "Institute Classification Clause with deletion of held cover provision" . He then argued that nowhere in the initial complaint of the complainant filed in March 2016 was there any whisper of this policy not having been supplied to the complainant for the complainant to claim that it was not aware of this clause, especially because the complainant company was a regular importer and should have known better. If the insured had any doubt about this clause, it could have asked the OP. Merely advancing rhetorical arguments was of no avail as it would not make the claim admissible under the policy.

14. Referring to the internal circular of the OP argued by the counsel for the complainant (Ex-CW 1), he argued that this circular was dated 30.4.2013 and had referred to another circular dated 24.1.2012 . None of these were available when the M.V. was insured and suffered damage in 2010. It is obvious that the OP following instances such as the one in hand, learnt this lesson and issued these circulars qua exercising care about the classification of M.V. before issuing insurance coverage. Be that as it may, counsel argued that these circulars could not have retrospective effect and therefore this argument of the complainant fails. Referring to learned counsel for the complainant's argument qua the policy wherein it had drawn attention to clause 4.1 which had mentioned that "In no case shall this insurance cover loss damage or expense arising from unseaworthiness of vessel or craft, unfitness of vessel craft conveyance container or liftvan for the safe carriage of the subject matter insured, where the assured or their servants are privy to such unseaworthiness or unfitness, at the time the subject matter

insured is loaded therein. ", Counsel submitted that this exclusion clause was in respect of "Institute War Clauses (Cargo)" and had no applicability to the present complaint.

15. Regarding letter dated 15.6.2010 (supra) claiming intimation of M.V.'s particulars, Counsel submitted that OP had denied receipt of this unequivocally. He further argued that even if, for the sake of argument, it's receipt were to be acknowledged, it would be seen that this letter had only mentioned the M.V.'s name, not it's classification. This would be a violation of good faith. As for endorsement on the insurance policy on 20.7.2010 , counsel submitted that this was on the basis of the letter dated 7.7.2010. He further pointed out that the endorsement clearly mentioned that "All other terms and conditions were unaltered." Thus, the original policy condition qua vessel classification remained as intended.

16. He then referred to the report of the D.G. Shipping mentioned in the surveyor's report which had listed as many as 37 deficiencies in the vessel. His argument was that there was little doubt that the M.V. was an old, substandard vessel, not worthy of being insured.

17. Referring to the surveyor's report, pages 6 and 7 thereof, he pointed out that it was clear that the loss to the cargo was on account of the poor condition of the vessel and that the collision on 7.8.2010 , after the incident of ingress of water on on 18.7.2010 , was again due to steering failure of the M.V.. The surveyor report had also mentioned that the loss to the cargo was on account of ingress of sea water and not due to the accident. Further, this report also mentioned that the cargo on the M.V. had already been sold on the high seas; if so, in any case, the counsel argued, there was no loss to the complainant and so the question of any claim did not arise.

18. Referring to the average guarantee extended by the OP to the adjuster, he drew attention to letter of Richards Hogg Lindley dated 18.7.2010 to the complainant to make the point that the amount of security sought was to the tune of US$ 600,000 (Rs. 2.74 crore at Rs. 45.73 per US $) whereas the claim of the complainant was for a loss of Rs.4.41 crore, questioning therefore as to how this was justifiable.

19. Finally, he argued that it has to be understood that the purpose of classification of M.V. is to ensure that it is safe and seaworthy and therefore insurable. This basic principle was incorporated in the insurance policy which was given to the complainant on good faith. This basic ingrdient having been violated, the OP was justified in repudiating the claim. Learned counsel further mentioned that strictly speaking, in fact, there was no repudiation of the claim but only a withdrawal of guarantee that had been extended on behalf of the complainant wherein the grounds for so doing were explained.

20. In a short rebuttal, learned counsel for the complainant made the following points: i. Terms and conditions of the insurance policy are available in the public domain; the policy issued had eight sub clauses, of which 7 had been explained in the body of the policy and only one, "Institute Classification Clause with deletion of held cover provision" had not been explained. If so, OP could only rely upon the first 7 clauses. ii. OP's argument that clause 4.1 under Exclusions under "Institute War clauses(Cargo)" did not apply to the case in hand as there was no war, was not quite correct because on the right hand side, it had been described as "Unseaworthiness And Unfitness Exclusion Clause", i.e. a general clause with general applicability. iii. Reference the internal circular of 2012 referring to the circular of 2010 (supra), he clarified that in fact both related to a memo of 2001and therefore both were clarificatory in nature; he argued that they had applicability to the instant case. iv. Regarding the endorsement of the insurance policy incorporating the insurance details furnished by the complainant, counsel argued that this endorsement is not disputed in any away, and the only submission here was that the complainant had merely filled up the blank box of the initial policy that had been issued. v. As far as M.V. being old and unfit leading to the repudiation made on 12.8.2010 , he argued that clearly the OP's counsel's argument was that the vessel had not been classified as per OP's classification, and that as argued earlier, the vessel was

registered and classified elsewhere. vi. Regarding further argument of the OP that the surveyor's report has mentioned that the damage to the cargo was not because of collision was immaterial as this ground had not been taken in the letter of repudiation. vii. As for the amount of insurance claim, the policy was for total sum insured of Rs.10.31 crore and the estimated gross expenses due to the incident had been estimated to be Rs.5.81 crore by the surveyor.

DISCUSSION AND ORDER

21. It is clear from the detailed arguments articulated on behalf of the parties that the facts of the case viz. the policy (4.6.2010), the endorsement (20.7.2010), the incident of water ingress(18.7.2010) and collision with another vessel subsequently (7.8.2010), the granting of average guarantee (10.8.2010) and it's withdrawal (12.8.2010) are not in dispute. What is in dispute is whether the OP had committed any deficiency in service by withdrawing the guarantee and impliedly, denying the insurance claim on the ground that the M.V. was not a classified M.V., and did not satisfy the condition mentioned in the policy viz. the "Institute Classification Clause with deletion of held cover provision" . It is this issue that has to be decided in this consumer complaint, first and foremost. Main argument of the complainant is that if this was the case, it was not known to the complainant: As far as the complainant was concerned, it had acted in good faith, had furnished all relevant information on which basis, the insurance policy had also been duly endorsed, and that for the OP to take this plea now was not tenable.

22. Both parties have claimed that they had acted in good faith. OP's case is that it depended entirely on the information furnished by the insured to issue the policy and when it came to know that the M.V. was not a classified M.V., it immediately withdrew the guarantee it had extended to the adjusters and informed the complainant. Complainant, on the other hand, has argued that it supplied information on the M.V. when it came to it's knowledge, as early as 15.6.2010 , and that, in as much as it was only one of the importers of cargo, on CIF basis, it had no means of knowing the classification of the vessel any sooner. Further, it was not it's responsibility alone to have ascertained the classification of the M.V. and the implied seaworthiness or otherwise. OP too could have and should have ascertained the M.V.'s classification status, as per it's own internal circulars. That the OP singularly failed to do so was a deficiency in service and the complainant should not have to suffer repudiation of it's genuine claim on this account.

23. Indeed, insurance contract is a contract of utmost good faith, as laid down by the Hon'ble Apex Court. This is a basic, well established, well understood principle of insurance law. What has to be decided in the case in hand is whether this principle of good faith was violated. It is very clear, from a reading of the surveyor's report and other documents, that the M.V. was old and that at the time of it's engagement in the instant case, it was not classed with any approved society under International Association of Classification Societies (IACS). First para under "CLASSIFICATION OF THE VESSEL M.V. KHALIJIA-3" reads as below: "The Vessel M.V. Khalijia-3 was found classed with LRS till 09/10/07 (A member of IACS) and thereafter, she was found classed with non approved Classification Society-International Register of Shipping." This finding of the surveyor has not been disputed. Indeed, complainant's argument has remained confined to claiming that it was not as if the vessel was not classified at all; rather, it was listed in the International Register of Shipping. OP has, on the other hand, firmly held that the vessel was not classified as required by the policy clause "Institute Classification Clause with deletion of held cover provision" . Indisputably therefore, it can be safely concluded that as per OP's policy clause, the vessel was not worthy of being insured. Yet, it was. The next question therefore is that if so, should the OP have insured the complainant's cargo, without full knowledge of the vessel and its classification? A related question is whether the OP should then have conducted due diligence on the vessel as soon as it came to know it's name which, as

per the complainant, was furnished vide letter dated 15.6.2010 , and was certainly known to the OP by letter dated 7.7.2010 , received by the OP on 20.7.2010, delivered by the insurance broker, M/s SREI Insurance Private Broking Ltd.. 24. After having considered the rival arguments, the record, the surveyor's report, it is my considered view that the complainant has failed to establish it's case. It was the complainant, the importer, who had purchased the insurance cover. It was therefore reasonable that it had to be vigilant about all the conditions of taking insurance cover. It is also reasonable, as argued by the counsel for the OP, that the complainant, a regular importer, ought to have known the terms and conditions accompanying a Marine Cargo Specific Voyage Policy. It argued that it was importing on a CIF basis and that it's own consignment would be on a vessel carrying other consignments also and therefore it had no means of knowing, at the time it took the policy (4.6.2010), any particulars about the vessel. This is reasonable and fair. However, what is not reasonable is the further argument of the complainant that since the import was on CIF basis, it's responsibility ended with this declaration and that it was for the OP to do the necessary due diligence on the classification of the vessel. It was the complainant whose cargo was to be insured against all risks associated with the marine voyage. It was therefore for the complainant to have ensured full compliance of all the policy conditions, in it's own interest. Merely a cover note, with details of vessel and voyage left blank, on "To Be Declared" basis, from the OP-insurance company, could not have meant that the complainant could then have assumed the contract of insurance as complete and taken no further steps other than a mere communication of details of the shipment, including the vessel's name, to the OP. The insurance policy conditions should have been known to the complainant and taking the plea that it was not it's responsibility alone, is unacceptable. It ought to have insisted with the exporter or to whoever was the contracting party to make sure that the vessel for voyage satisfy the policy condition of suitable classification. There is no averment on this aspect in the complaint or in the arguments. The only argument appears to be that it was for the OP to have done due diligence before issuing the policy in the first instance and before making the endorsement in the policy subsequently.

24. On the other hand, it was not unreasonable for the OP insurance company to proceed on good faith and issue the insurance policy, in the hope that all terms and conditions would be complied with, if and when a claim were to be filed. If OP were to find subsequently, at any stage, that the M.V. did not satisfy the classification criteria, it would indeed have no option but to hold the complainant to be non-compliant with the policy condition(s) and deny the claim. In the instant case, it is this perspective which explains the revealed facts. OP displayed the good faith in issuing the insurance policy, leaving the box in the policy schedule blank. It did so because it would have had no good reason not to do so. Even though the voyage particulars were not known, they would be known later. So, the policy could be issued, for a voyage yet to be undertaken, on the understanding that the details would be furnished and that the policy conditions set out clearly in the policy schedule would be fulfilled. So, when details of the specific voyage were furnished by the complainant, these details were duly endorsed on the policy. This again was an act of good faith, and for the same reasons. After all, the complainant would have satisfied itself that the vessel met the classification condition clearly set out in the policy, there being no reason why it would not do so. When the incident of water ingress happened (18.7.2010), upon a request to provide guarantee to the average adjuster, OP did so (10.8.2010). This again was an act of good faith. When however it learnt that the M.V. did not satisfy the classification criteria, it immediately withdrew the guarantee as well as intimated the complainant that it was doing so (12.8.2010). It is apt to reproduce OP's letter of 12.8.2010 at this stage: -8- "We send herewith a copy of the letter given to the Average Adjusters on the subject. We understand from the Surveyors that the vessel MV Khalijia 3 did not possess classification as required under the Institute classification Clause of the policy.

Accordingly, we are constrained to inform you that in terms of the policy conditions, prima-facie, we as insurers would not be liable for loss or expenses in respect of the subject cargo, and hence have been constrained to withdraw the Average Guarantee given to the Adjusters."

25. The above letter clearly reveals that the OPs were surprised when they found, from the surveyor, that M.V. Khalijia 3 did not possess classification as required under the Institute Clause of the policy. Further, in such a situation, they, prima-facie, felt that they would not be liable for the loss and therefore withdrew average guarantee given to the adjusters. This letter answers the question that was put during the arguments by the learned counsel for the complainant: It was mentioned that between issuing letter of guarantee on 10.8.2010 and withdrawal of the guarantee on 12.8.2010, it was not understood what had transpired, leading OPs to deny their insurance liability. The answer lies in the OP's interaction with surveyors of the case. In fact, the OPs were, vide this letter of 12.8.2010, alerting the complainants of the possibility of not being in a position to entertain the claim on account of the loss while immediately withdrawing their guarantee; arguably, not having done so could have led to a further valid argument that the OP did not withdraw the guarantee as soon as it came to know. Indeed, in a contract of utmost good faith, the only proper and defensible course of action is to act as soon as any violation of any kind comes to notice.

26. The principle of utmost good faith, in the instant case, favours the OP strongly. It was the complainant's responsibility, first and foremost, to have kept the OP fully apprised of the classification status of the M.V. as soon as it came to know. As argued by the counsel for the OP, too much cannot be made of the letter of 15.6.2010 which the OP denies having received. Indeed, even if OP had received the letter earlier, it may not have materially had any effect on it's action of endorsement which was carried out in good faith. The letter only mentioned the vessel's name and nothing more. The complainant should have done more than this and apprised the OP about the vessel's seaworthiness. Of course, this could have been done only if the complainant had first made the effort to find out. It failed to do so. It has only itself to blame. It cannot foist it's own negligence on to the OP by arguing that it was not it's responsibility alone. Even if this averment is conceded, it has still to be said that the complainant failed to carry out what was also very much it's own responsibility. By failing to do so, and by then advancing arguments such as have been e.g. not the complainant's responsibility alone, OP cannot deny receipt of letter dated 15.6.2010 , complainant not made aware of the policy condition qua classification properly enough, cannot absolve the complainant. Finally, the underlying factum in the case is that the M.V. was not at all compliant with the policy condition of classification per " Institute Classification Clause with deletion of held cover provision." In the face of this basis, fundamental fact, this consumer complaint cannot sustain.

27. Facts in CC 205/2012 are almost identical, the only difference being in the value of the cargo and the loss claimed.

28. In view of the discussion above, both consumer complaints, CC/206/2012 and CC/205/2012, are dismissed. In the facts of the case, there shall be no order as to costs.

.... ANUP K THAKUR PRESIDING MEMBER

CASE NO.43

CONSUMER CASE NO. 206 OF 2012

M/S. JOTINDRA STEEL & TUBES LIMITED through its divisional Manager Divisional office...........Complainant(s)

Versus

UNITED INDIA INSURANCE COMPANY LTD. & 2 ORS. through its divisional Manager Divisional.

UNITED INDIA INSURANCE CO. LTD THROUGH ITS DEPUTY GENERAL MANAGER,

UNITED INDIA INSURANCE CO. LTD. THROUGH ITS CHAIMAN-CUM-MANAGING DIRECTOR...........Opp.Party(s)

BEFORE: HON'BLE MR. ANUP K THAKUR,PRESIDING MEMBER

For the Complainant :

For the Complainant : Mr. Joy Basu, Sr. Advocate with Mr. T.S. Ahuja, Advocate

For the Opp.Party :

For the Opposite Parties : Mr.Amit Kr. Singh, Advocate

Dated : 28 Jan 2021

ORDER

Anup K. Thakur

1. By this order it is proposed to decide C.C. No.205 of 2012 and C.C. No.206 of 2012. In C.C. No.205 of 2012, the complainant is M/s. Mauria Udyog Ltd. and in C.C. No.206 of 2012, the complainant is M/s. Jotindra Steel & Tubes Limited. Both had purchased marine cargo specific voyage insurance policy from United India Insurance Co. Ltd., Noida (OP-1 henceforth) and facts in both are almost identical.

2. Arguments were heard on 25.11.2020. Facts were taken from CC 206 of 2012.

3. Learned Sr. Counsel for the complainant briefly narrated the facts. On 04.06.2010, a Marine Cargo Specific Voyage Policy No.221800/21/10/01/00000043 (policy hereafter) was taken by the complainant from OP1 (Annexure-1). This policy, for voyage from Jingtang, China to Kandla Port, Gujrat, covered a consignment of H.R. Steel Coils with the sum insured at Rs.10,31,93,25/-. Premium paid was Rs.22,764/-. Details such as Invoice, Container Details, Vessel name etc., were not shown initially in the policy; instead, the relevant box for these details carried the remark "To be declared" . Subsequently, these details were submitted to OP1 and were duly endorsed in the policy on 20.07.2010 (Annexure-4). Learned counsel explained that the initial policy read with this endorsement made the whole policy of insurance.

4. Per the plaint, on 18.7.2010 , the marine vessel, Khallijia-3 (M.V. hereafter),at 20:45 hours, experienced ingress of water below the water line, which caused damage to cargo. Since there were other cargoes also on the M.V., general average principle became applicable. So, a Salvor, M/s. Smith Singapore Pvt. Ltd., was appointed who, in turn, appointed another company to procure guarantees from the affected parties i.e. owner of the M.V. and owners of their respective cargoes. OP provided a guarantee on behalf of the complainant on 10.8.2010 (Annexure-8). This guarantee was however recalled by the OP on 12.8.2010 (Annexure-9). Learned counsel submitted that in the recall letter, OP had taken the ground that the M.V. classification was not as required under the 'Institute Classification Clause' of the policy and resultantly, it was constrained to withdraw the 'average guarantee' given to the Adjusters.

5. Counsel referred to complainant's letter to the OP dated 15.6.2010 (Ann.-2) whereby all relevant details of the shipment, including the name of the M.V., MV Khalijia 3 V.10086, had been furnished. Again, vide letter dated 7.7.2010 (Ann. 3), the complainant had, in continuation of letter dated 15.6.2010 , enclosed invoice number, packing list, copy of bill of lading to the OP. On this basis, OP had duly endorsed the policy (Ann.-4).

6. Learned counsel then drew attention to the policy schedule (Ann.-1), specifically to the box describing the "Terms of Insurance Cover: As per the following Clauses" , and thereunder, to clause no. 8 viz. "Institute Classification Clause with deletion of held cover provision" . He pointed out that the first 7 clauses – Important Notice, Institute Radio-Active Contamination Exclusion Clause, Institute Replacement Clause, Institute

142

War Clauses (Cargo), Institute Strike Clauses (Cargo), Strike, Riots & Civil Commotion Clause and Cargo ISM endorsement were all elaborated in the body of the policy. Not so, however, the clause "Institute Classification Clause with deletion of held cover provision" (supra). His argument therefore was that this clause was never meant to be operationalized at any point of time else it would have also found elaboration in the body of the policy. He then argued that it was this clause which was the basis for repudiation of the insurance claim. He submitted that except for this, the policy covered the voyage from Jingtag, China to Kandla Port, Gujarat, India, " ON WAREHOUSE TO WAREHOUSE BASIS" , and thus clearly covered the incident which took place in Mumbai, enroute to Kandla and warehouse.

7. He further submitted that despite intimation of 15.6.2010 (supra) having been stamp receipted by the OP's office, OP had denied having received the same. Counsel submitted that this could not be. He drew attention to complainant's further intimation dated 7.7.2010 (Ann.-3) whose receipt was acknowledged by the OP: this too had a similar stamp of the OP company, without any initial. Counsel argued that both these letters had therefore been similarly received by the OP1 and accepting receipt of one and denying receipt of other was not understood. His argument was that in both these letters, the name and number of the M.V. was mentioned, and thus, there was no question that the name of the vessel had been declared to the OP and that the OP was aware of it. To therefore deny knowledge of the M.V.'s classification on 12.8.2010 and withdraw the guarantee(supra) was unwarranted. Learned counsel then explained in some detail the events following the incident resulting in damage to the vessel and loss to the cargo. He explained that as per international practice, a salvor was appointed who, in turn, appointed the average adjuster who then wrote to the owners of the M.V. and the cargoes to provide guarantees in order to cover all expenses incurred by the salvor on prorata basis. This being so, the complainant had approached the OP, the insurer, to provide a guarantee to M/s. Richards Hogg Lindley (Hellas) Ltd., the average adjuster appointed by the M/s. Smit Singapore Pvt. Ltd., salvor. The complainant provided a counter guarantee to the OP for this purpose and the OP then provided the said guarantee on 10.08.2010 (Ann. 8). In this guarantee, the name of the vessel was duly mentioned, clearly showing therefore that the OP was always in the know of the M.V. carrying the cargoes. Counsel argued that it has to be presumed that the OP had provided guarantee only after being satisfied with the classification and condition of the M.V.. It was therefore strange that the OP, after only 2 days, vide letter dated 12.8.2010, withdrew the guarantee from the adjuster (Ann. 9). He argued that this withdrawal of guarantee and repudiation of the claim was untenable as the OP could not deny its liability: the insurance policy was fully operational at the time of the incident, and all details necessary for the voyage including the name of the vessel, was in the knowledge of the OP. He further argued that OP's repudiation was inexplicable: what could have transpired between 10.8.2010 , the date OP extended guarantee to the adjuster and 12.8.2010 when the OP withdrew this guarantee? Still further, he submitted that a perusal of this letter dated 12.8.2010 (supra) would show that it was cryptic and bereft of any detail. OP's contention that the M.V. Khalijia did not possess the classification required under the Institute Classification Clause of the policy was unacceptable as this clause was neither reproduced in this letter nor had been elaborated in the policy, as explained earlier. Since no clear reasons were given for repudiation in this letter of 12.8.2010, learned counsel argued that this by itself was also a deficiency in service. He then submitted that the M.V. was registered in the International Register of Shipping and had an interim certificate of classification issued on 2.6.2010 which was valid till November 2010 . He cemented this argument by further submitting that it was not as if it was the complainant's responsibility alone to have ascertained the classification of the M.V., it being the case that it was only one of the cargo owners on this vessel and could not be expected to know the vessel's status etc. since the import was on CIF basis. So,

the complainant was not privy to the classification of the vessel and also not responsible for the correct classification. OP, the insurer, also had a responsibility to check all this before extending the guarantee to the adjustor.

8. Learned counsel then drew attention to complainant's reply dated 17.8.2010 (Ann. 10) to the OP's letter of repudiation dated 12.8.2010 (Ann.9): it had been contended by the complainant that the OP remained fully responsible for all the losses covered under the policy as the cargo was fully insured by a named vessel in good faith; that the policy was issued on 4.6.2010 and OP was subsequently informed about the particulars of shipment with vessel name, value and quantity details which were duly endorsed on the policy. OP replied to this vide its letter dated 3.9.2010: It denied receipt of letter dated 15.6.2010 and held that " the vessel did not qualify for cover in terms of the Classification Clause as it was found not to have held classification by any entity contemplated by the said clause" . Learned counsel argued that even in this reply, there was no reproduction of the classification clause being relied upon by the OP (Ann.-11).

9. Learned counsel then referred to an internal circular of the OP viz. HO:MC:Cir:30:2013 dated 30.04.2013, obtained by the complainant through RTI. This circular had made it obligatory upon OP's offices issuing marine insurance policies to first verify the vessel particulars; if the vessel was not classed as per recognized classification society, no cover was to be granted i.e. NO CLASS, NO COVER. Counsel argued that it seems to be the case that OP had failed to carry out this due diligence. In such a case, however OP ought to have refunded the premium and cancelled the policy. Instead, it has repudiated the insurance claim. Counsel further argued that nowhere in the pleadings or in the various documents on record is the institute classification clause mentioned and that it has been mentioned for the first time in the synopsis of arguments filed in the proceedings. This was not acceptable, argued the counsel. Without this, the OP's case fails completely.

10. Summing up, the learned counsel reiterated that the institute classification clause and the factum of M.V. being not classified under this cannot be considered as a ground for repudiation by the OP because this clause does not form part of the policy nor has it been explained in the repudiation letter of 12.8.2010 nor does it form part of the documents on record. Second, it is not the case that the M.V. was not a registered vessel; it was registered in the International Shipping Register.

11. Towards evidence supporting the consumer complaint, learned counsel pointed to affidavit by way of evidence of Shri V.K. Sureka, Chairman of the complainant company, affidavit of Shri Gopal Gupta, Manager of Import & Export and A.R. of the complainant company, and affidavits of Shri Sandeep Sharma and Shri Dinesh Sharma, Field Boys employed with the complainant company for delivery of letters etc. In particular, he emphasized the affidavit of Shri Sandeep Sharma: It has been stated that he had delivered various letters to OP-1's office, including on 15.6.2010, and that these had been received by the officials and acknowledged by affixing seal on the duplicate copy.

12. Finally, learned counsel invoked some citations in support of his arguments. In the case of Saurashtra Chemicals Ltd. Vs. National Insurance Co. Ltd. decided on 13.12.2019 , the Apex Court had held that "It is a settled position that an insurance company cannot travel beyond the grounds mentioned in the letter of repudiation." He submitted that the only issue in the letter of repudiation of 12.8. 2010 was to do with the classification of the M.V.. And he had already shown that the M.V. was indeed classified though with another society and not IACS which the OP was insisting upon. In the case of Modern Insulators Ltd. Vs. Oriental Insurance Company Ltd. 2000 (2) SCC 734 , it was held that "Exclusion clauses which are not explained to the insured, are not binding to the insured and are required to be ignored." This would apply to the " Institute Classification Clause with deletion of held cover provision" which was never made clear to the complainant, as argued by the counsel. In the case, National Insurance Co. Ltd. Vs. Sh. D.P. Jain , it

was held by the National Commission in its order dated 15.05.2007 that "In our view, the unexplained or unnoticed exclusion would not be binding to the insured." In UII vs MKJ Coproration, the Apex Court had held that "An insurer cannot reply on and the insured is not bound by, a clause that the insurer should have but did not incorporate into the policy." Learned counsel argued that in the case in hand, the Institute Classification Clause was unexplained, vague, non-specific and ambiguous and thus, the insured complainant was not bound by it and the OP could not take advantage of it.

13. Learned counsel for the OP also began his submissions by referring to the policy (Annexure-1) to submit that it was not in doubt at all that the following had been clearly mentioned under Terms of Insurance Cover viz. "Institute Classification Clause with deletion of held cover provision" . He then argued that nowhere in the initial complaint of the complainant filed in March 2016 was there any whisper of this policy not having been supplied to the complainant for the complainant to claim that it was not aware of this clause, especially because the complainant company was a regular importer and should have known better. If the insured had any doubt about this clause, it could have asked the OP. Merely advancing rhetorical arguments was of no avail as it would not make the claim admissible under the policy.

14. Referring to the internal circular of the OP argued by the counsel for the complainant (Ex-CW 1), he argued that this circular was dated 30.4.2013 and had referred to another circular dated 24.1.2012 . None of these were available when the M.V. was insured and suffered damage in 2010. It is obvious that the OP following instances such as the one in hand, learnt this lesson and issued these circulars qua exercising care about the classification of M.V. before issuing insurance coverage. Be that as it may, counsel argued that these circulars could not have retrospective effect and therefore this argument of the complainant fails. Referring to learned counsel for the complainant's argument qua the policy wherein it had drawn attention to clause 4.1 which had mentioned that "In no case shall this insurance cover loss damage or expense arising from unseaworthiness of vessel or craft, unfitness of vessel craft conveyance container or liftvan for the safe carriage of the subject matter insured, where the assured or their servants are privy to such unseaworthiness or unfitness, at the time the subject matter insured is loaded therein. ", Counsel submitted that this exclusion clause was in respect of "Institute War Clauses (Cargo)" and had no applicability to the present complaint.

15. Regarding letter dated 15.6.2010 (supra) claiming intimation of M.V.'s particulars, Counsel submitted that OP had denied receipt of this unequivocally. He further argued that even if, for the sake of argument, it's receipt were to be acknowledged, it would be seen that this letter had only mentioned the M.V.'s name, not it's classification. This would be a violation of good faith. As for endorsement on the insurance policy on 20.7.2010 , counsel submitted that this was on the basis of the letter dated 7.7.2010. He further pointed out that the endorsement clearly mentioned that "All other terms and conditions were unaltered." Thus, the original policy condition qua vessel classification remained as intended.

16. He then referred to the report of the D.G. Shipping mentioned in the surveyor's report which had listed as many as 37 deficiencies in the vessel. His argument was that there was little doubt that the M.V. was an old, substandard vessel, not worthy of being insured.

17. Referring to the surveyor's report, pages 6 and 7 thereof, he pointed out that it was clear that the loss to the cargo was on account of the poor condition of the vessel and that the collision on 7.8.2010 , after the incident of ingress of water on on 18.7.2010 , was again due to steering failure of the M.V.. The surveyor report had also mentioned that the loss to the cargo was on account of ingress of sea water and not due to the accident. Further, this report also mentioned that the cargo on the M.V. had already been sold on the high seas; if so, in any case, the counsel argued, there was no loss to the complainant and so the question of any claim did not arise.

18. Referring to the average guarantee extended by the OP to the adjuster, he drew attention to letter of Richards Hogg Lindley dated 18.7.2010 to the complainant to make the point that the amount of security sought was to the tune of US\$ 600,000 (Rs. 2.74 crore at Rs. 45.73 per US \$) whereas the claim of the complainant was for a loss of Rs.4.41 crore, questioning therefore as to how this was justifiable.

19. Finally, he argued that it has to be understood that the purpose of classification of M.V. is to ensure that it is safe and seaworthy and therefore insurable. This basic principle was incorporated in the insurance policy which was given to the complainant on good faith. This basic ingrdient having been violated, the OP was justified in repudiating the claim. Learned counsel further mentioned that strictly speaking, in fact, there was no repudiation of the claim but only a withdrawal of guarantee that had been extended on behalf of the complainant wherein the grounds for so doing were explained.

20. In a short rebuttal, learned counsel for the complainant made the following points: i. Terms and conditions of the insurance policy are available in the public domain; the policy issued had eight sub clauses, of which 7 had been explained in the body of the policy and only one, "Institute Classification Clause with deletion of held cover provision" had not been explained. If so, OP could only rely upon the first 7 clauses. ii. OP's argument that clause 4.1 under Exclusions under "Institute War clauses(Cargo)" did not apply to the case in hand as there was no war, was not quite correct because on the right hand side, it had been described as "Unseaworthiness And Unfitness Exclusion Clause", i.e. a general clause with general applicability. iii. Reference the internal circular of 2012 referring to the circular of 2010 (supra), he clarified that in fact both related to a memo of 2001and therefore both were clarificatory in nature; he argued that they had applicability to the instant case. iv. Regarding the endorsement of the insurance policy incorporating the insurance details furnished by the complainant, counsel argued that this endorsement is not disputed in any away, and the only submission here was that the complainant had merely filled up the blank box of the initial policy that had been issued. v. As far as M.V. being old and unfit leading to the repudiation made on 12.8.2010 , he argued that clearly the OP's counsel's argument was that the vessel had not been classified as per OP's classification, and that as argued earlier, the vessel was registered and classified elsewhere. vi. Regarding further argument of the OP that the surveyor's report has mentioned that the damage to the cargo was not because of collision was immaterial as this ground had not been taken in the letter of repudiation. vii. As for the amount of insurance claim, the policy was for total sum insured of Rs.10.31 crore and the estimated gross expenses due to the incident had been estimated to be Rs.5.81 crore by the surveyor.

DISCUSSION AND ORDER

21. It is clear from the detailed arguments articulated on behalf of the parties that the facts of the case viz. the policy (4.6.2010), the endorsement (20.7.2010), the incident of water ingress(18.7.2010) and collision with another vessel subsequently (7.8.2010), the granting of average guarantee (10.8.2010) and it's withdrawal (12.8.2010) are not in dispute. What is in dispute is whether the OP had committed any deficiency in service by withdrawing the guarantee and impliedly, denying the insurance claim on the ground that the M.V. was not a classified M.V., and did not satisfy the condition mentioned in the policy viz. the "Institute Classification Clause with deletion of held cover provision" . It is this issue that has to be decided in this consumer complaint, first and foremost. Main argument of the complainant is that if this was the case, it was not known to the complainant: As far as the complainant was concerned, it had acted in good faith, had furnished all relevant information on which basis, the insurance policy had also been duly endorsed, and that for the OP to take this plea now was not tenable.

22. Both parties have claimed that they had acted in good faith. OP's case is that it depended entirely on the information furnished by the insured to issue the policy and when it came to know that the M.V. was not a classified M.V., it immediately withdrew the guarantee it had extended to the adjusters and informed the complainant. Complainant, on the other hand, has argued that it supplied information on the M.V. when it came to it's knowledge, as early as 15.6.2010 , and that, in as much as it was only one of the importers of cargo, on CIF basis, it had no means of knowing the classification of the vessel any sooner. Further, it was not it's responsibility alone to have ascertained the classification of the M.V. and the implied seaworthiness or otherwise. OP too could have and should have ascertained the M.V.'s classification status, as per it's own internal circulars. That the OP singularly failed to do so was a deficiency in service and the complainant should not have to suffer repudiation of it's genuine claim on this account.

23. Indeed, insurance contract is a contract of utmost good faith, as laid down by the Hon'ble Apex Court. This is a basic, well established, well understood principle of insurance law. What has to be decided in the case in hand is whether this principle of good faith was violated. It is very clear, from a reading of the surveyor's report and other documents, that the M.V. was old and that at the time of it's engagement in the instant case, it was not classed with any approved society under International Association of Classification Societies (IACS). First para under "CLASSIFICATION OF THE VESSEL M.V. KHALIJIA-3" reads as below: "The Vessel M.V. Khalijia-3 was found classed with LRS till 09/10/07 (A member of IACS) and thereafter, she was found classed with non approved Classification Society-International Register of Shipping." This finding of the surveyor has not been disputed. Indeed, complainant's argument has remained confined to claiming that it was not as if the vessel was not classified at all; rather, it was listed in the International Register of Shipping. OP has, on the other hand, firmly held that the vessel was not classified as required by the policy clause "Institute Classification Clause with deletion of held cover provision" . Indisputably therefore, it can be safely concluded that as per OP's policy clause, the vessel was not worthy of being insured. Yet, it was. The next question therefore is that if so, should the OP have insured the complainant's cargo, without full knowledge of the vessel and its classification? A related question is whether the OP should then have conducted due diligence on the vessel as soon as it came to know it's name which, as per the complainant, was furnished vide letter dated 15.6.2010 , and was certainly known to the OP by letter dated 7.7.2010 , received by the OP on 20.7.2010, delivered by the insurance broker, M/s SREI Insurance Private Broking Ltd..

24. After having considered the rival arguments, the record, the surveyor's report, it is my considered view that the complainant has failed to establish it's case. It was the complainant, the importer, who had purchased the insurance cover. It was therefore reasonable that it had to be vigilant about all the conditions of taking insurance cover. It is also reasonable, as argued by the counsel for the OP, that the complainant, a regular importer, ought to have known the terms and conditions accompanying a Marine Cargo Specific Voyage Policy. It argued that it was importing on a CIF basis and that it's own consignment would be on a vessel carrying other consignments also and therefore it had no means of knowing, at the time it took the policy (4.6.2010), any particulars about the vessel. This is reasonable and fair. However, what is not reasonable is the further argument of the complainant that since the import was on CIF basis, it's responsibility ended with this declaration and that it was for the OP to do the necessary due diligence on the classification of the vessel. It was the complainant whose cargo was to be insured against all risks associated with the marine voyage. It was therefore for the complainant to have ensured full compliance of all the policy conditions, in it's own interest. Merely a cover note, with details of vessel and voyage left blank, on "To Be Declared" basis, from the OP-insurance company, could not have meant that the complainant could then

have assumed the contract of insurance as complete and taken no further steps other than a mere communication of details of the shipment, including the vessel's name, to the OP. The insurance policy conditions should have been known to the complainant and taking the plea that it was not it's responsibility alone, is unacceptable. It ought to have insisted with the exporter or to whoever was the contracting party to make sure that the vessel for voyage satisfy the policy condition of suitable classification. There is no averment on this aspect in the complaint or in the arguments. The only argument appears to be that it was for the OP to have done due diligence before issuing the policy in the first instance and before making the endorsement in the policy subsequently.

25. On the other hand, it was not unreasonable for the OP insurance company to proceed on good faith and issue the insurance policy, in the hope that all terms and conditions would be complied with, if and when a claim were to be filed. If OP were to find subsequently, at any stage, that the M.V. did not satisfy the classification criteria, it would indeed have no option but to hold the complainant to be non-compliant with the policy condition(s) and deny the claim. In the instant case, it is this perspective which explains the revealed facts. OP displayed the good faith in issuing the insurance policy, leaving the box in the policy schedule blank. It did so because it would have had no good reason not to do so. Even though the voyage particulars were not known, they would be known later. So, the policy could be issued, for a voyage yet to be undertaken, on the understanding that the details would be furnished and that the policy conditions set out clearly in the policy schedule would be fulfilled. So, when details of the specific voyage were furnished by the complainant, these details were duly endorsed on the policy. This again was an act of good faith, and for the same reasons. After all, the complainant would have satisfied itself that the vessel met the classification condition clearly set out in the policy, there being no reason why it would not do so. When the incident of water ingress happened (18.7.2010), upon a request to provide guarantee to the average adjuster, OP did so (10.8.2010). This again was an act of good faith. When however it learnt that the M.V. did not satisfy the classification criteria, it immediately withdrew the guarantee as well as intimated the complainant that it was doing so (12.8.2010). It is apt to reproduce OP's letter of 12.8.2010 at this stage: "We send herewith a copy of the letter given to the Average Adjusters on the subject. We understand from the Surveyors that the vessel MV Khalijia 3 did not possess classification as required under the Institute classification Clause of the policy. Accordingly, we are constrained to inform you that in terms of the policy conditions, prima-facie, we as insurers would not be liable for loss or expenses in respect of the subject cargo, and hence have been constrained to withdraw the Average Guarantee given to the Adjusters."

26. The above letter clearly reveals that the OPs were surprised when they found, from the surveyor, that M.V. Khalijia 3 did not possess classification as required under the Institute Clause of the policy. Further, in such a situation, they, prima-facie, felt that they would not be liable for the loss and therefore withdrew average guarantee given to the adjusters. This letter answers the question that was put during the arguments by the learned counsel for the complainant: It was mentioned that between issuing letter of guarantee on 10.8.2010 and withdrawal of the guarantee on 12.8.2010, it was not understood what had transpired, leading OPs to deny their insurance liability. The answer lies in the OP's interaction with surveyors of the case. In fact, the OPs were, vide this letter of 12.8.2010, alerting the complainants of the possibility of not being in a position to entertain the claim on account of the loss while immediately withdrawing their guarantee; arguably, not having done so could have led to a further valid argument that the OP did not withdraw the guarantee as soon as it came to know. Indeed, in a contract of utmost good faith, the only proper and defensible course of action is to act as soon as any violation of any kind comes to notice.

27. The principle of utmost good faith, in the instant case, favours the OP strongly. It was the complainant's responsibility, first and foremost, to have kept the OP fully apprised of the classification status of the M.V. as soon as it came to know. As argued by the counsel for the OP, too much cannot be made of the letter of 15.6.2010 which the OP denies having received. Indeed, even if OP had received the letter earlier, it may not have materially had any effect on it's action of endorsement which was carried out in good faith. The letter only mentioned the vessel's name and nothing more. The complainant should have done more than this and apprised the OP about the vessel's seaworthiness. Of course, this could have been done only if the complainant had first made the effort to find out. It failed to do so. It has only itself to blame. It cannot foist it's own negligence on to the OP by arguing that it was not it's responsibility alone. Even if this averment is conceded, it has still to be said that the complainant failed to carry out what was also very much it's own responsibility. By failing to do so, and by then advancing arguments such as have been e.g. not the complainant's responsibility alone, OP cannot deny receipt of letter dated 15.6.2010 , complainant not made aware of the policy condition qua classification properly enough, cannot absolve the complainant. Finally, the underlying factum in the case is that the M.V. was not at all compliant with the policy condition of classification per " Institute Classification Clause with deletion of held cover provision." In the face of this basis, fundamental fact, this consumer complaint cannot sustain.

28. Facts in CC 205/2012 are almost identical, the only difference being in the value of the cargo and the loss claimed.

29. In view of the discussion above, both consumer complaints, CC/206/2012 and CC/205/2012, are dismissed. In the facts of the case, there shall be no order as to costs.
.... ANUP K THAKUR PRESIDING MEMBER

<u>CASE NO.44</u>
FIRST APPEAL NO. 693 OF 2020

(Against the Order dated 05/07/2019 in Complaint No. 303/2018 of the State Commission Uttar Pradesh)
M/S. ABHISHT DEVELOPERS & BUILDERS PVT. LTD. THROUGH ITS AUTHORISED SIGNATORY. ....Appellant(s)

Versus

SUCHITA SINGH W.O SHRI PRADEEP SINGH ....Respondent(s)
BEFORE: HON'BLE MR. DINESH SINGH,PRESIDING MEMBER
For the Appellant : Mr. Rupesh Kr. Sinha, Advocate
For the Respondent :
Dated : 28 Jan 2021

ORDER
Taken up through video conferencing.

1. This appeal relates to a builder-buyer dispute.

2. The award made by the State Commission vide its impugned Order dated 05.07.2019 reads as below: On the basis of abovementioned conclusion, the complaint is partially accepted and opposite party no. 2 M/s Abhisht Developers & Builders Pvt. Ltd is directed to return deposited money Rs. 9,63,589/- of the complainant alongwith interest @ 18 p.a. calculated from the date of deposit to till the date of realisation. Along with this, it shall also pay litigation expenses of Rs. 10,000/- to the complainant.

3. Learned counsel for the appellant builder company submits, on instructions, that the appellant builder company will unconditionally refund the entire amount of Rs.9,63,589/- deposited by the respondent complainant with interest @ 8% per annum from the respective dates of deposit till the actual date(s) of realisation and pay the cost of litigation of Rs. 10,000/- awarded by the State Commission within four weeks from today without fail. He further submits, on instructions, that the appellant builder

company wishes to restrict and confine its appeal before this Commission only to the question of rate of interest over and above 8% on the amount deposited by the complainant. The submissions are recorded. The appellant builder company shall be bound by the submissions made by its learned counsel.

4. It is noted that the subject unit was allotted by the appellant builder company to the respondent complainant on 19.11.2010. The respondent complainant deposited total Rs. 9,63,589/- with the appellant builder company between 29.11.2010 and 16.01.2014. We are now in January 2021. The appellant builder company was not in a position to offer possession of the subject unit to the respondent complainant till the date the State Commission made its award i.e. till 05.07.2019. The appellant builder company is still not in a position to offer possession on the date of arguments on admission before this Commission i.e. on 28.01.2021.

5. Having regard to paras 3 and 4 above, it is deemed lawful, just, equitable and conscionable to summarily dismiss the instant first appeal no. 693 of 2020, with liberty to the appellant builder company to file appeal, afresh, strictly restricted and confined only and only to the question of rate of interest over and above 8% on the amount deposited by the respondent complainant, within thirty days from today.

6. So disposed.

7. The Registry is requested to send a copy each of this Order to the appellant builder company and to the respondent complainant, within three days from today. The stenographer is requested to upload this Order on this Commission's website today positively. .... DINESH SINGH PRESIDING MEMBER

CASE NO.45

REVISION PETITION NO. 1307 OF 2011

(Against the Order dated 03/12/2010 in Appeal No. 151/2009 of the State Commission Gujarat)

MADHUBEN RAMESHCHANDRA SHAH...........Petitioner(s)

Versus

GUJARAT INDUSTRIAL DEVELOPMENT CORPORATION & ORS.

THE REGIONAL MANAGER GIDC

THE DEPUTY ENGINEER GUJARAT ELECTRICITY BOARD

SURAT MUNICIPAL CORPORATION ....Respondent(s)

BEFORE: HON'BLE MR. C. VISWANATH,PRESIDING MEMBER

For the Petitioner : Mr. Varshal Pancholi, Advocate

For the Respondent :

For the Respondents Nos. 1 & 2 : Mr. Chirag M. Shroff, Advocate

For Respondent No.3 : Ms. Jesal Wahi, Advocate

For Respondent No.4 : Ex-parte

Dated : 28 Jan 2021

ORDER

1. The present Revision Petition has been filed by the Petitioner against order dated 03.12.2010 passed by the State Consumer Disputes Redressal Commission, Gujarat (for short "State Commission") in First Appeal No. 151 of 2009 whereby the Appeal filed by the Petitioner was dismissed.

2. Case of the Complainant/Petitioner was that Complainant had applied for allotment of shed pursuant to the advertisement of Opposite Party No.-1.The Complainant made an application dated 05.04.1999 along with an amount of Rs.15,000/- by way of Demand Draft .The Complainant was allotted Shed No. L/278/6 at Pandesara, Surat, vide allotment letter dated 18.09.1999. The Complainant paid an amount of Rs.1,76,000/- towards allotment of the shed as initial payment. The Complainant was informed that he would get electricity connection from the Gujarat Electricity Board in due course.

The transfer of possession of the allotted shed was made, vide letter dated 14.10.1999. Opposite Party No.3 informed the Complainant, vide letter dated 30.06.2000, that the previous allottee of the shed was due Rs.1,26,479/- to the Gujarat Electricity Board towards electricity charges. The Complainant, vide letter dated 17.09.2001, intimated Opposite Party No.-2 that dues were also pending towards municipal tax of Surat Municipal Corporation. The Complainant requested Opposite Party No. 1 to clear both the outstanding dues and issue clear title of the Shed. Since no action was taken by Opposite Party No. 1 and 2, the Complainant filed a Complaint b efore the District Forum with the following Prayer: - "a) The Hon'ble forum by holding the respondent in the present case jointly and severally, get to me the electricity connection immediately and by getting recovered the amount due and payable by the previous party towards electricity consumption bill, municipal tax etc. and the possession of the said shed with clear title may please be given and if the respondent should pay to the complainant an amount of Rs.1,72,000/- and Rs. 4000/- totaling to 1,76,000/- with interest at the date of 18% per annum.Also an order may please be passed that the possession of the said shed afresh from the respondent No.1 to the complainant and also to pass an order to waive the installment of the loan taken from the respondent as business activity could not commence. An order may please be passed that the respondent should pay to the complainant and amount of Rs.75,000/- with interest as the complainant, as stated in the complaint could not commence the business of making cupboard furniture. To award an amount of Rs. 5000/- towards the cost of this complaint application. Taking into the facts of the complaint of the complainant in its entirety any other and specific relief may please be granted."

3. The case was contested by Opposite Party No. 1 & 2 before the District Forum. It was contended that the Consumer Complaint was not maintainable as the Complainant was not a Consumer of the Opposite Parties. On merits, Opposite Parties stated that an Agreement for the said shed was executed between the Parties on 18.09.1999. On receipt of payment of Rs.1,60,000/-, the Opposite Parties handed over possession of the shed to the Complainant. The Complainant, however, did not inform about the dues of electricity bills and Municipal taxes. When the Complainant applied for electricity connection, the Gujarat Electricity Board, Pandesara refused to give connection on the ground that certain dues remained payable. Opposite Parties submitted that they there was no deficiency in service on their part and prayed for dismissal of the Complaint. The District Forum ordered as follows: - OP No.1 and OP No.2 herein jointly and /or severally should pay to the complainant in the present case, with reference to the industrial shed in question the amount of Rs.1,76,000/-(Rupees one lakh seventy-six thousand only) paid to the opponent along with simple interest at the rate of 9% per annum on the said amount from the date of complaint till its realization. The opponent No.1 and 2 herein, jointly and/or severally should pay to the complainant in the present case an amount of Rs.5000/-towards the mental harassment and cost of the complainant. The complainant is not held to be entitled to get the special relief sought for vide para-7 of the complaint. In the present case, the complaint against the OP No.3 and 4 is hereby dismissed. The cost of the Complainant may be borne by the opponent themselves. The opponent should implement and execute this order, within 30 days from the date on which this order is passed. The true copy of this order may be provided to all the parties free of cost. Aggrieved by the order of the District Forum, Respondent No. 1 and 2 filed an Appeal before the State Commission. After hearing the Learned Counsels for the Parties and perusing the record, the State Commission held that the District Forum had not discussed the agreement for sale and set aside the order of the District Forum with the following order: - Appeal of the Appellant Gujarat Industrial Development Corporation is hereby allowed. The judgement delivered by the Consumer Dispute Redressal Forum (Additional), Surat dated 12 January 2009 in Complaint No. 526/2001 hereby set aside No order as to the cost of the appeal is

passed. As per the submission made by the learned advocate of the Appellant an amount of Rupees 50,000 as per the order of the Commission in Consumer Dispute Redressal Forum (Additional) Surat then in that regard after verification, If the amount is deposited then the account payee cheque for the said amount along with whatever interest that accrued on it be given to the learned advocate appearing on behalf of Gujarat Industrial Development Corporation, The Appellant herein.

4. Aggrieved by the order of the State Commission, the Petitioner/Complainant preferred the present Revision Petition before this Commission.

5. Heard the Learned Counsel for both the Parties and carefully perused the record. The Learned Counsel for the Petitioner submitted that the previous allottee of the shed had not paid substantial amount of Electricity Bill as well as Municipal tax. The Petitioner, vide letter dated 17.09.2001, requested the Respondent to clear the dues which they failed to recover from the previous allottee. The Petitioner, therefore, was not able to get the electricity connection for the above mentioned shed. Consequently the Petitioner was not able to pay further amount to Respondent No.-1 due to delay in the commencement of his business.

6. Learned Counsel for Respondent No.-1 and 2 submitted that the answering Respondent No.-1 is a Corporation established under Section-3 of Gujarat Industrial Development Act 1962 and Respondent No.-2 is the Regional Office ofRespondent No.-1, The Petitioner was allotteda shed on the basis of application dated 05.04.1999. The Petitioner was merely an allottee by virtue of allotment letter and had to pay the price of the super structure of the shed and premium of land on which the shed was built. The Petitioner obtained the shed for starting Cup-Board Furniture factory/industry for commercial purpose. The provisions of the Consumer Protection Act, 1986, therefore, would not be applicable in the present case. The Learned Counsel submitted that electricity dues constitute a charge on the premises and applicable rules require such payment to be binding on the purchaser.

7. Admitted facts of the case are that the Petitioner had applied for allotment of shed pursuant to the advertisement of Respondent No.1. Petitioner submitted an application dated 05.04.1999 along with a Demand Draft for Rs.15,000/- and was allotted Shed No.L/278/6 at Pandesara, Surat, vide allotment letter dated 18.09.1999. The Petitioner paid an amount of Rs.1,76,000/- towards allotment of the shed, as an initial payment. The Petitioner was informed that he would be able to get connection from the Gujarat Electricity Board in due course. After the transfer of possession of the allotted shed ,vide letter dated 14.10.1999, the Petitioner came to know, vide letter dated 30.06.2000, from Respondent No.-3 that the previous allottee of the shed had to pay Rs.1,26,479/- to the Gujarat Electricity Board for the shed purchased by him. The Petitioner, vide letter dated 17.09.2001 intimated Respondent No.-2 that dues of previous allottee were also pending towards the municipal tax of Surat Municipal Corporation. The Petitioner requested Respondent No.2 to clear outstanding dues of the previous allottee and to issue clear title of the Shed. Due to failure of Respondent No-1 to pay the requisite dues of the previous allottee, the Petitioner suffered financial loss due to non-commencement of his industry/business, which led to his failure to pay dues on time. Regional Manager, GIDC, as competent officer under the Gujarat Public Premises (Eviction of Unauthorized Occupant) Act, 1972 (referred to as "GPP Act" for short) passed eviction order on 8.02 .2007 under section-4 (i) of GPP Act. Aggrieved by the above, the Petitioner preferred a Complaint before the District Forum alleging deficiency in service.

8. The District forum allowed the Complaint on grounds of deficiency in service by Respondent No. 1 and 2 for not returning the amount of Rs.1,76,000/- paid for the shed allotted by the Opposite Parties. Order of the District Forum was set aside by the State Commission on the ground that the District Forum had not considered the agreement

for the sale. Aggrieved by the order of the State Commission the present Revision Petition has been filed by the Complainant before this Commission.

9. Offer letter No. GIDC/RM/SRT/ALT/3345 dated 27.07.1999 clearly states: - " 9.The allotment will be subject to the terms and conditions of allotment as may be mentioned in the allotment letter and agreement.''

10. I have gone through the allotment letter and the agreement and found that there is no express provision which mentioned that the purchaser of the premises had to pay electricity dues of the previous allottee. The Respondents also have not placed on record any evidence authorizing them to demand arrears of the previous allottee. In the absence of there being any specific statutory provision or clause in the Sale Agreement, the allottee cannot be compelled to clear the dues of the previous allottee. Dues relating to electricity charges cannot be enforced against the next allottee i.e. Petitioner.

11. Hon'ble Supreme Court in Haryana State Electricity Board vs. M/s Hamuman Rice Mills Dhanauri & Ors. in Civil Appeal No. 6817 of 2010 decided on 20.08.2010 held that "electricity arrears do not constitute a charge over the property. Therefore in general law, a transferee of a premises cannot be made liable for the dues of the previous owner/ occupier. Where the statutory rules or terms and conditions of supply which are statutory in character, authorize the supplier of electricity, to demand from the purchaser of a property claiming re-connection or fresh connection of electricity, the arrears due by the previous owner/occupier in regard to supply of electricity to such premises, the supplier can recover the arrears from a purchaser." Hon'ble Supreme Court in Ahmedabad Electricity Co. Ltd. vs. Gujarat Inns. Pvt. Ltd. & Ors. in Civil Appeal No.1691 of 1999 decided on 16.03.2004 held "We are clearly of the opinion that in case of a fresh connection though the premises are the same, the auction purchasers cannot be held liable to clear the arrears incurred by the previous owners in respect of power supply to the premises in the absence of there being a specific statutory provision in that regard."

12. In view of the above, order of the State Commission cannot be sustained and is accordingly set aside and order of the District Forum is upheld . Revision Petition is disposed accordingly with no order as to cost. .... C. VISWANATH PRESIDING MEMBER

CASE NO.46
FIRST APPEAL NO. 186 OF 2020

(Against the Order dated 12/12/2019 in Complaint No. 180/2018 of the State Commission Punjab)

CENTRAL GOVERNMENT EMPLOYEES WELFARE HOUSING ORGANIZATION (CGEWHO), THROUGH ITS DEPUTY DIRECTOR, (ADMINISTRATION), ...Appellant(s)

Versus

SUDHIR MITTAL SON OF SHYAM LAL MITTAL,...........Respondent(s)
BEFORE: HON'BLE MRS. JUSTICE DEEPA SHARMA,PRESIDING MEMBER
For the Appellant : Mr. Apoorv Agarwal, Advocate
For the Respondent : In person
Dated : 29 Jan 2021

ORDER
IA 5384 of 2020 (condonation of delay)

The Respondent/Complainant, who is appearing in person, submits that he has no objection if the delay be condoned subject to costs. In view of this submissions of the Respondent/Complainant and for the reasons given in the application, the delay is condoned subject to payment of costs of 10,000/-. The costs shall be paid by the Appellant to the Respondent/Complainant by way of demand draft within two weeks from today. Issue notice of the Appeal. Notice is accepted by the Respondent/Complainant. Arguments are heard on the present Appeal.

1. The present Appeal, under Section ---51(1) of the Consumer Protection Act, 2019 (for short "the Act") has been filed by the Appellant against the order dated 12.12.2019 of the State Consumer Disputes Redressal Commission, Punjab (for short "the State Commission") in Complaint No.180 of 2018.

2. The Complainant, who is appearing in person, submits that the other allottees of the same scheme had also challenged the action of the Appellant and the matter had been decided in their favour. The Appellant had challenged the order of the State Commission in Appeals and Revision Petitions and those Appeals and Revision Petitions wherein the issue in dispute is the same have already been dismissed. It is submitted that it is a covered case and has relied on the findings of the Bench of Hon'ble Mr.Justice R. K. Aggarwal, President and Mrs. M. Shreesha, Member of this Commission in " Central Government Employees Welfare Housing Organization vs. Subhash Setia, FA No.1472 of 2018" wherein the Appeals of the Appellant qua the said allottees had been dismissed. It is submitted that the order had -3- not been challenged before the superior court and has attained the finality and therefore, this Bench should also follow the same findings and dismiss the Appeal.

3. Learned Counsel for the Appellant has not disputed the fact that several allottees of the same project had filed the Complaints which were decided in their favour and thereafter the Appeals and the Revision Petitions filed by the Appellant qua those orders have also been dismissed. He has not denied the findings of the Bench of this Commission in Subhash Setia's case (supra). Learned Counsel has stated that he is not aware whether any Appeal had been filed against the said orders.

4. I have given thoughtful consideration to the rival contentions of the parties. The present Appeal has been filed by the Appellant against the order dated 12.12.2019 of the State Commission wherein the following directions were issued: 19. In view of our above discussion, this complaint is allowed and following directions are issued to the opposite party:- i) to deliver possession of the flat in question, complete in all respects, to the complainant without payment of any outstanding dues by him within a period of two months. ii) to pay a sum of Rs.1,00,000/- as compensation on account of harassment, mental tension and agony caused to him; iii) to pay a sum of Rs.22,000/- as costs of litigation. In case the opposite parties fail to deliver the possession within two months, as ordered above, then in the alternative i) to refund the amount of Rs.49,60,000/- to the complainant along with interest at the rate of 12% per annum from the different dates of payment of different amounts till the date of payment; ii) to pay Rs.65,000/-, as compensation for the harassment and mental agony suffered by them including cost of litigation."

5. It is an admitted fact that in the execution petition filed by the Respondent/Complainant, the directions have been complied with by the Appellant. All the contentions raised by the Appellant had been the subject matter of discussion in the earlier Revision Petitions/Appeals in other cases. In Subhash Setia's case (supra), this Commission has held as under: "Challenge in this Appeal is to the order dated 29.1.2018 passed by the State Consumer Disputes Redressal Commission, Punjab, Chandigarh (for short "the State Commission") in Consumer Complaint No.761/2017, whereby State Commission has allowed the Complaint directing the Opposite Party, the Appellant herein, to deliver the possession of the flat, complete in all respects to the Complainant without payment of any outstanding dues along with compensation of 1,00,000/- and 22,000/- as cost of litigation within two months failing which shall refund the amount of 34,37,000/- to the Complainant along with interest @ 12% p.a. from the different dates of payment of different amounts till the date of payment and 50,000/- as compensation. Since the issue raised in the present Appeal has already been examined by this Commission in Revision Petition No. 1488 of 2016 (Nasib Singh v.

Central Government Employees Welfare Housing Organization) and other connected Revision Petitions, for the sake of brevity, we deem it unnecessary to narrate the facts, giving rise to the present Appeal and dismiss the Appeal.

6. In view of the above, the Appeal stands dismissed with the direction that in case the costs imposed is not paid by the Appellant, the Complainant shall be at liberty to file the execution for recovery of the same. ....J DEEPA SHARMA PRESIDING MEMBER